Berkeley Walks

Revealing Rambles through America's Most Intriguing City

Robert E. Johnson
and Janet L. Byron

ROARING FORTIES
PRESS

Berkeley, California

Roaring Forties Press
1053 Santa Fe Avenue
Berkeley, CA 94706
www.roaringfortiespress.com

Cover design by Gabriela Vargas; interior design by Nigel Quinney.

Cover photos, top to bottom: mural at La Peña; Thorsen House; the Berkeley Rose Garden. All photos by Robert E. Johnson.

Library of Congress Cataloging in Publication Data is available.

ISBN 978-1938901-39-3 (print)
ISBN 978-1938901-49-2 (pdf)
ISBN 978-1938901-50-8 (Kindle)
ISBN 978-1938901-51-5 (epub)

For all my dear friends who supported and helped me
through this long project
(Bob Johnson)

For my awesome daughter, Julia Wineger
(Janet Byron)

CONTENTS

INTRODUCTION

Berkeley is a 10.5-square-mile city with a population of about 117,000; Oakland is next door and San Francisco is just across the bay. The University of California, known as Cal, founded here in 1868, is the heart of the city—but Berkeley is much more than simply a campus town. Beyond the Cal borders, Berkeley is a regional and national center for theater and the arts, food and culture, religious study, disability rights, and—of course—progressive politics.

And Berkeleyans love to walk!

Walking is in the fabric of Berkeley's culture. When the city was designed in the late 19th and early 20th centuries, planners included a network of about 140 public paths throughout the Berkeley hills, providing pedestrians with routes to retail and commercial areas as well as emergency escape routes. In the early 1970s, Berkeley installed some of the first curb cuts in the nation as part of an effort to make navigating the city easier for people with physical disabilities. In more recent years, pedestrian- and bike-oriented improvements have included upgrades to public paths, the construction of new paths in public rights-of-way, traffic lights just for walkers, "traffic calming" measures to slow down cars (such as mini-roundabouts and speed bumps), and a network of bike boulevards.

Each walk in this book pulls together the many elements that we think make a particular neighborhood so interesting to explore. We are particularly indebted to 41 Berkeley Walking Tours by the Berkeley Architectural Heritage Association. This comprehensive resource is highly recommended for those who want to delve further into the city's historic architectural resources. Go to www.berkeleyheritage.com for more info.

HOW TO USE THIS BOOK

We encourage the use of public transportation to get to the starting points. Check bus and BART schedules at 511.org or Google maps. All starting points are at or within several blocks of a transit stop.

Although almost all the walks are loops, for two of them (Walk 7, Codornices Creek, and Walk 16, Ohlone Greenway), we recommend the use of public transit to return to the starting point.

Each walk begins with an overview of the walk, followed by distance, estimated time to complete it, and elevation gain. Walk times are estimates; your times will vary depending on your walking speed and how long you linger at points of interest. Some walks include side-trips and options to shorten the walk.

Maps for each walk show the routes, and numbers on the maps and in the text identify various points of interest along the way. On most maps, a black dot shows the starting point.

Because much of Berkeley is hilly, some of the walks include significant elevation gains and stairs. Walks that are more accessible to people with disabilities, parents with strollers, and those who prefer a less challenging stroll include Walk 1, Downtown; Walk 4, The South Side of Campus; Walk 6, The Gourmet Ghetto; Walk 11, The Elmwood; Walk 14, Ashby BART Station and the Lorin District; Walk 15, The McGee-Spaulding District; Walk 16, The Ohlone Greenway; Walk 17, Ocean View; and Walk 18, Aquatic Park and the Marina.

Berkeley architecture spans a wide variety of styles. We've included a guide to many of these styles and a glossary of architectural terms.

In California, pedestrians have the right of way in crosswalks; however, be sure to make eye contact with drivers and wait for cars to slow down before you proceed. Take care when crossing both busy and seemingly quiet streets; please don't read and walk at the same time!

LET US KNOW WHAT YOU THINK

Things change, especially in vibrant cities such as Berkeley. We have done our best to ensure that this book is up to date but cannot guarantee that everything listed is the exact same as it was when the book went to press. Please send your notes and updates to info@berkeleywalks.com.

We look forward to hearing how you like the walks, and we welcome comments and suggestions. Please visit our website at www.berkeleywalks.com or write to us at info@berkeleywalks.com.

❊ ❊ ❊

A Map of the Walks

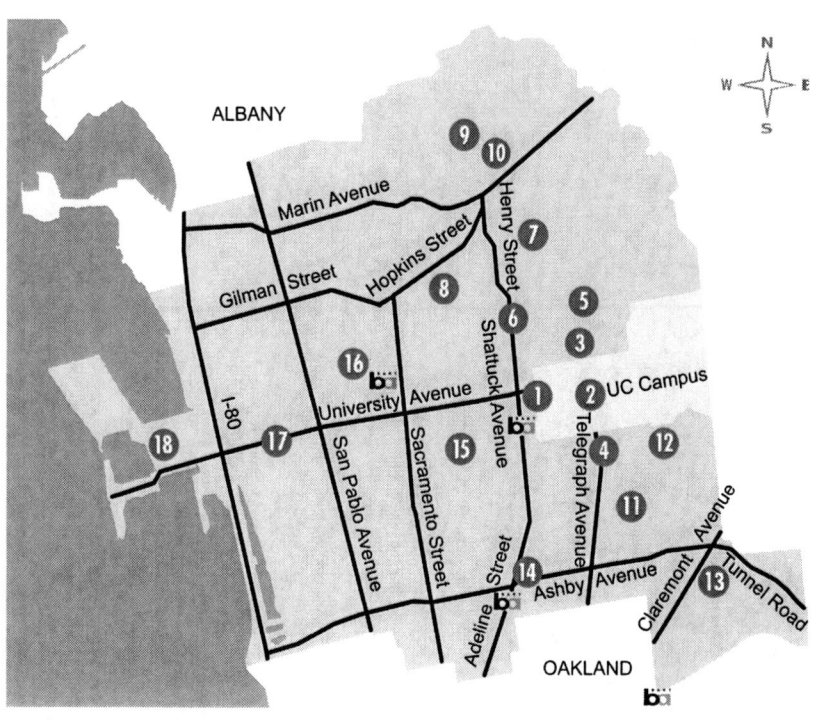

Some Berkeley Bookstores

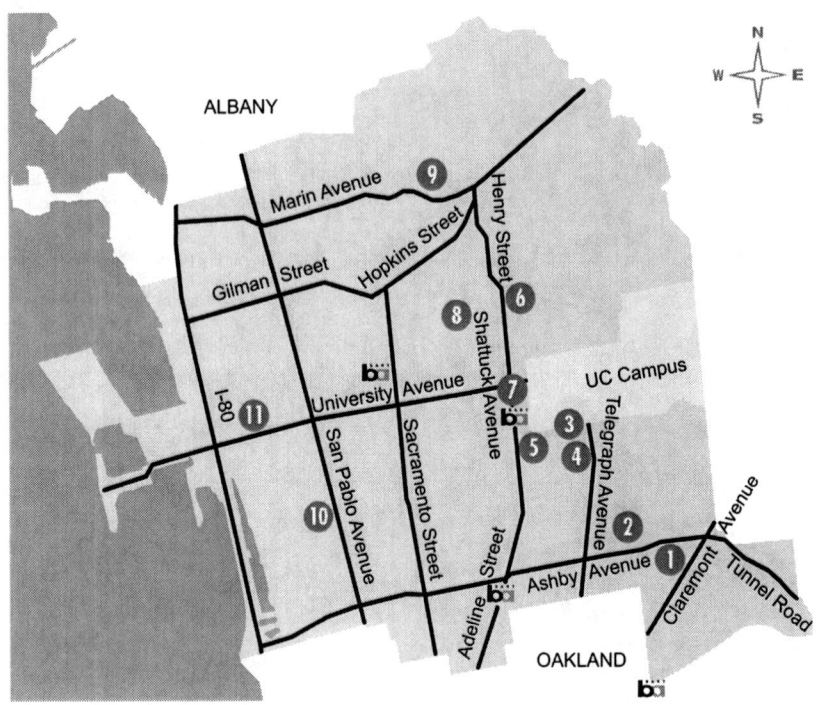

1. Dark Carnival (3086 Claremont; Walk 13, Rockridge to Claremont)
2. Mrs. Dalloway's (2904 College; Walk 11, The Elmwood)
3. University Press (2435 Bancroft, Walk 4, The South Side of Campus); and Cal Student Store (Sproul Plaza; Walk 2, The UC Campus)
4. Moe's Books (2476 Telegraph; Walk 4, The South Side of Campus;)
5. Pegasus (2439 Shattuck)
6. Books Inc. (1491 Shattuck; Walk 6, The Gourmet Ghetto)
7. Half Price Books (2036 Shattuck; Walk 1, Downtown), Berkeley City College (2050 Center; Walk 1, Downtown)
8. Mr. Mopps' Books and Toys (1417A MLK Way; Walk 8, Hopkins and Monterey Market)
9. Pegasus (1855 Solano)
10. Black Oak Books (2618 San Pablo)
11. Builders Booksource (1817 4th Street, Walk 17, Ocean View)

Part I
Central Berkeley

WALK 1
DOWNTOWN

Overview: This level walk explores the commercial side of Berkeley's downtown, its civic center, the arts district, and the area around the high school, as well as lesser-known treats such as the Gourmet Gulch. Downtown is vibrant with restaurants, art venues, and modern residences. Architecture ranges from 100-year-old buildings to brand-new edifices.

Highlights:
- Historic commercial and civic architecture
- Thriving arts district
- Eateries for all tastes and budgets

Distance: 2.5 miles
Time: 2 hours
Elevation gain: 50 feet

Start at the main entrance of the Downtown Berkeley BART station, at the corner of Center Street and Shattuck Avenue, in front of Chase Bank. Cross Center, heading north on Shattuck (with the hills to your right). In front of Wells Fargo Bank, a plaque on the ground at the corner marks the first sidewalk curb cut in the nation; the lobby of the bank has large murals of Bay Area scenes.

As you wander around downtown, keep an eye out for attractive and amusing street-side utility boxes. Earth Island Institute's Streets Alive! project pairs local artists with the formerly gray boxes; the artists paint the boxes directly or make designs that are transferred to large polymer stickers.

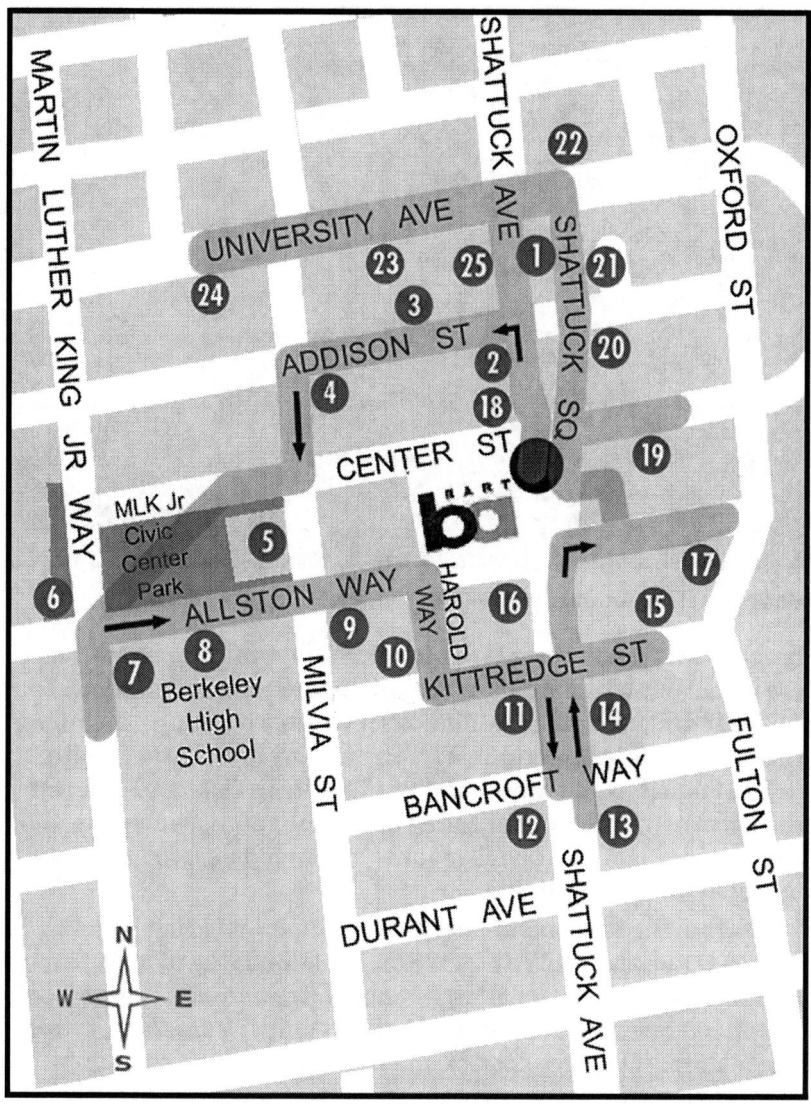

At Addison Street, look across Shattuck. The area in between the divided section of Shattuck was once called Stanford Place. The rail terminus for the steam train line from Oakland was originally here. The block to the left (north) was originally a freight yard and subsequently a park; it was developed with buildings in 1926. Timothy L. Pflueger, a San Francisco architect, designed three

One of the three Art Deco buildings by Timothy Pflueger.

flamboyant ❶ **Art Deco/Spanish Colonial buildings** here that are varied but harmonious, with cast-concrete ornamentation. Pflueger designed many well-known Bay Area buildings, including the Pacific Telephone and Telegraph Building and Castro Theatre in San Francisco and the Paramount Theatre in Oakland. Contrast this block with the less-appealing one to the south, which was developed in a hodge-podge manner at a later date, after the train terminal was removed.

Across the street on the northwest corner (now Half Price Books) is the beautiful Art Deco S. H. Kress Building of 1932. Samuel H. Kress, president of a national chain of five-and-dime stores, took a keen interest in the architecture of his company's buildings; this one features light-brown brick and polychrome terra-cotta ornaments in a style known as zig-zag modern. The curved windows on the Shattuck-side first-floor retail area were recently restored. On the Addison side, the California Jazz Conservatory, or Jazzschool, founded in 1997 and part of the Berkeley Arts District, is located in the basement, as is a cafe.

The ❷ **Francis K. Shattuck Building** (currently housing Revival restaurant), on the southwest corner of Shattuck and Addison, was completed in 1901 and was the first masonry building on Shattuck. Francis Kittredge Shattuck was an Oakland mayor, a

California assemblyman, and an Alameda County supervisor. In the 1860s, along with three partners, he bought 160 acres in what is now downtown Berkeley. Shattuck played a key role in bringing the steam train to Berkeley in 1876, which in turn fueled early downtown development. This building, a city landmark, now houses a restaurant, retail shops, and offices. Ill-conceived modernization in the 1950s removed many historic features, including a turret, but in 1999 architect Jim Novosel did a restoration that brought back the turret and a handsome storefront while adding a fourth story under a mansard roof.

Addison between Shattuck and Milvia Street is the designated Berkeley Arts District. As you walk through it, notice metal plaques embedded on both sides of the sidewalk. The 55-pound plaques, which feature 123 poems by diverse writers, add up to 3 tons of poetry. Robert L. Hass, UC professor and former US poet laureate, chose the poems; all the writers have a connection to Berkeley. Pavers on the southwest corner of Shattuck and Addison and at Milvia and Addison mark events in Berkeley history such as the arrest of Janis Joplin and the planting of nonnative eucalyptus trees in the hills.

Turn left on Addison, noting the red-brick, 1905 Golden Sheaf Bakery building across the street at 2071 Addison, which now houses the Aurora Theater and Nevo Education Center. Next to it is the Tony Award–winning ❸ **Berkeley Repertory Theatre**, which has two stages (thrust and proscenium). Founded in 1968, this regional theater has a national reputation and a School of Theatre.

On the south side of Addison, the Freight & Salvage Coffeehouse—a.k.a. the Berkeley Society for the Preservation of Traditional Music—is a nonprofit community arts organization that has been dedicated to promoting public awareness and understanding of traditional music since 1968 and has been in this downtown location since 2009. It hosts performances almost every night.

A wall mosaic on the ARTech building.

The city parking garage just beyond Freight & Salvage has changing art displays in its street-facing windows. On the southeast corner of Addison and Milvia, the ❹ **ARTech building**, developed by Panoramic Interests, is a mixed-use structure with 21 residential units, 4 of which are for very-low-income tenants. It has rooftop gardens, mosaics, and an attractive sculpted-metal garage portcullis, but perhaps most interesting is the high corner-wall sculpture of a salamander.

Cross Milvia, turn left, and walk to Center. The building across the street on the southwest corner is Berkeley's ❺ **Martin Luther King, Jr., Civic Center**, formerly the Federal Land Bank. Constructed in 1938, this New Deal project was designed in Moderne style by James Plachek, whose firm also designed the main Berkeley Public Library, the Claremont and North Berkeley branch libraries, and other notable buildings around town. Originally a regional bank supporting agriculture, the King Civic Center now serves as Berkeley's city hall.

Cross Center and turn right on the sidewalk adjacent to city hall, which leads to a park. On Saturdays, Center Street is closed for the Berkeley Farmers' Market, one of three run by the Ecology Center throughout Berkeley.

What is now called Martin Luther King, Jr., Civic Center Park, behind city hall, was built between 1938 and 1942, with a design team that included architects Henry Gutterson, Bernard Maybeck, and Julia Morgan. Although it was completed long after planning commenced, it was an expression of the early 20th-century City Beautiful movement for public spaces. The currently nonworking fountain was likely inspired by one at the Golden Gate International Exposition on Treasure Island in 1939–40. The park is a venue for numerous events and festivals throughout the year, and is well used by Berkeley High School students, skateboarders, and others.

Cross diagonally through the park on the path heading to the corner at Martin Luther King, Jr., Way (MLK Way) and Allston Way. Across the street to the west is the ❻ **old Berkeley City Hall** (2134 MLK Way), dating to 1909, an elegant building in French classical style that was designed by the same architects who designed San Francisco's Civic Center. The Berkeley Unified School District occupied the building from 1975 to 2012; now it is vacant and deemed seismically unsafe (although the city council still meets there), and a lack of funds for a $30 million retrofit threatens its future.

Cross Allston and continue walking south along MLK Way to see **❼ Berkeley High School.** Each building on campus is assigned a letter; the Science Building (H), close to Allston, was built in 1940. Designed by Henry Gutterson and William H. Corlett, it combines elements of both Art Deco and Streamline Moderne styles. Bas-reliefs and carvings depict wisdom and academic subjects with the names of great scientists, explorers, engineers, and inventors, as well as images of St. George slaying the dragon and, farther on, of the goddess Cybele. Jacques Schnier and Robert Boardman Howard were the sculptors.

Farther along, the Art Deco Shop building (G), also known as the Mechanic Arts building, was built in 1939 and also was designed by Gutterson and Corlett. It has bas-reliefs by California sculptor Lulu Braghetta depicting the tools of industrial arts, and it features the names of inventors such as Wright, Edison, Bell, and Marconi at the far end of the building. The New Deal Works Progress Administration provided financial assistance for Buildings G and H. Building G also is home to Berkeley Community Media, which helps citizens learn how to produce and share media and provides community TV channels.

Return back to Allston, turn right, and walk up the street past the high school's theatre complex. The Florence Schwimley Little Theater (also by Gutterson and Corlett) was completed in 1950 and dedicated in 1953. The rounded **❽ Berkeley Community Theatre**

A bas-relief herald on the Berkeley Community Theatre.

(with its entrance inside the high school compound) seats 3,500. The large bas-relief on the high wall represents sculpture, painting, music, dance, poetry, and drama, with male and female heralds on the right and left flanking walls; the sculptures are by Robert Boardman Howard, son of famous architect John Galen Howard. With the onset of war in 1941, construction here came to a halt; only a steel framework had been completed, and construction did not resume until 1949, giving the building the nickname the "bird cage."

Take a look at the street on Allston Way between MLK Way and Milvia. This is Berkeley's first street segment with permeable pavement, completed in 2014. The environmentally friendly pavers filter water into the ground, rather than redirecting it to storm drains, and absorb less heat than traditional pavement. These pavers also reduce greenhouse gas emissions and save money because they require less maintenance than asphalt.

When school is not in session and the gate just past the theatre is open, you can enter the campus. The Community Theatre lobby is lined with "hall of fame" plaques of well-known Berkeley High graduates.

Back on the street, continue to the corner of Allston and Milvia. Two newer buildings on campus, D and E, extend from the southwest corner along Milvia; these were designed in a simple style in keeping with the campus's Streamline Moderne structures.

Look catty-corner at the red-brick building on the northeast corner (2001 Allston): it is the YMCA, founded in 1903 and moved to this site in 1910. The building was designed by Benjamin McDougall in a neo-Georgian style of red brick with light trim and ornamentation. Two additions from 1960 and 1994 are to the east of this busy and popular YMCA; the more recent one (farthest right) better complements the original.

Cross Milvia and continue up Allston. On the right is Berkeley's imposing main ❾ **US Post Office** building of 1914, designed by Oscar Wenderoth. With its Tuscan columns and arches, the building is an adaptation of Filippo Brunelleschi's Renaissance-era Foundling Hospital in Florence, Italy. If it's open, step inside the lobby. At the far right, in the arch, is a mural of figures from the Spanish and pioneer period in Berkeley's history, painted in 1936 and 1937 by Suzanne Scheuer for the Treasury Relief Art Project, another New Deal program. As you exit, notice the WPA sculpture by David Slivka of postal workers on the wall to the far right of the colonnade. In 2012, the US Postal Service announced plans to sell the building and move operations to other facilities in Berkeley, stirring public opposition. Berkeley's landmark designation protects the building's exterior but not the interior, and this venerable building's fate is uncertain.

Continue up Allston and turn right on Harold Way. On the southwest corner is the colorful Elks Club building, designed by Walter Ratcliff, Jr., and completed in 1913 in Beaux-Arts style. Since 2008, the building has housed the Mangalam Research Center for Buddhist Languages, which restored and repainted the landmarked building. The associated Tibetan Nyingma Meditation Center also renovated the formerly dull one-story building midblock with ornamental detail and restored the ⑩ **Spanish Colonial Revival building** at the other end of Harold Way. Originally Armstrong College, a private school for more than 70 years, the current edifice is the home of Dharma College; it was also designed by Ratcliff. A high-rise residential project is proposed for across the street and would replace the current nondescript structures. This would be the tallest building in downtown Berkeley, with retail shops along Harold Way.

Walk to the end of Harold, which is lined with graceful Chinese elm trees, cross Kittredge Street, and turn left. Ahead on the right is the Art Deco (also called zig-zag modern) ⑪ **Berkeley Public Library**, opened in 1930. Designed by James Plachek, the building is on the National Register of Historic Places. Notice the Mayan-inspired details high up on the pilaster on each side of the old main doors and the friezes by Simeon Pelenc of Egyptian-like figures in book production on the exterior walls, with designs resembling printed circuit boards. These were done by creating layers of plaster in different colors and incising the top layer to reveal the color underneath.

Berkeley residents passed a $30 million bond in 1996 that, supplemented by $4 million in private donations, allowed the library to double its space. The west wing, dedicated in April 2002, complements the older exterior and enhances the library's useful-ness. If the library is open, go in to view the impressive main reading room with its high, decorated ceiling, one floor up and to the left; there are also public restrooms on this floor. This well-regarded and landmarked structure replaced an older historic Carnegie Library on the same spot.

Continue to Shattuck, turn right, and walk to Bancroft Way. On the southwest corner, the CVS pharmacy is part of the ⓬ **Corder Building**, another Berkeley landmark with fine-looking pilasters and cornices; Plachek designed it in 1922.

Cross Bancroft, then turn left and cross Shattuck. Walk right toward the former Fidelity Guaranty Building and Loan Association, now Namaste Madras Cuisine at ⓭ **2323 Shattuck**. Ratcliff, who was part owner of the bank, designed the building. Inside, the beautiful high ceiling with words incised on the beams about the virtues of saving has been preserved; the arches on the facade are highly ornamented. Adjoining it on the left is a five-story residential building with ground-floor retail, added in 2014.

Turn around and walk back (north) on Shattuck. At the northeast corner of Bancroft and Shattuck is the Classical Revival–style Masonic Temple, with an entrance at 2105 Bancroft; note the stained glass above the entry and on upper floors. The architect was William Wharff, a trained carpenter who came to San Francisco from Maine in 1875 at the age of 39 and moved to Berkeley in 1899. Wharff was a Civil War veteran (Union) who lived to be 100; he continued practicing architecture until age 75 and attended Civil War reunions well into his nineties. He designed more than 100 buildings in San Francisco that were lost in the 1906 earthquake and fire; four of his Berkeley designs are city landmarks.

Continue north on Shattuck to ⓮ **2277 Shattuck**. Hezlett's Silk Store, now the Used Computer Store, was designed by Charles F. Masten and Lester W. Hurd in 1925 in a Mediterranean Revival style. Note the terrazzo tile on the entranceway floor and the colorful upper-story ceramic tile, which was added in 1931 and made by Rigney Tile of Oakland (tile was once a major California industry). For decades, this was the home of Tupper & Reed, Berkeley's leading purveyor of musical instruments and sheet music, founded by partners John Tupper and Lawrence Reed in 1907. The walk-through display windows with the island are unique to Berkeley, though not well utilized today.

Next to this is a storybook edifice by William R. Yelland, local master of the genre (see Chapter 3, North Side of Campus). Dating from 1925, this Berkeley landmark (2271 Shattuck) was an earlier home of Tupper & Reed that included small rooms upstairs for music lessons and a tea shop. In recent years, restaurants and pubs have been based here. Note the recessed entryway, sculpture on the

Spotlight: James Plachek (1885–1948)

Over his 35-year career, James Plachek was best known for impressive civic buildings as well as elegant private residences. Typical of leading Berkeley architects, Plachek had an eclectic style that included:

- Arts and Crafts: Grace North Church (2138 Cedar St.), "Berkeley's bungalow church," his first commission in private practice
- Art Deco and Streamline Moderne: The current Civic Center Building on Milvia Street (built as the Farm Credit Administration building) and the Berkeley Public Library main branch (2090 Kittredge St.)
- Neoclassical: Odd Fellows Temple building (2288 Fulton St.)
- English half-timbered: John Muir Elementary School (2955 Claremont Ave.)

Born in Chicago to parents who emigrated from Prague, Plachek became an apprentice architect at 15 and subsequently studied engineering and attended the Art Institute of Chicago. He was sent to San Francisco by the mayor of Chicago to study the effects of the 1906 earthquake and fire, and ended up settling in the Bay Area. Plachek worked for the city of Berkeley and architect William H. Weeks in San Francisco before setting up his own office in Berkeley in 1912.

The small, two-story Heywood Building (2014–18 Shattuck Ave.) downtown, with a magnificent terra-cotta facade, which Plachek designed, is where he had his architectural office. Plachek also designed one of the most imposing commercial buildings in downtown Berkeley, the Corder Building on Shattuck between Bancroft and Durant.

Plachek designed many handsome residences in various styles throughout Berkeley. Outside of Berkeley, he had major commissions such as Glide Memorial Church in San Francisco, and he codesigned the Alameda County courthouse in Oakland with four other architects, including William H. Corlett. ❄❄

upper wall, and the stair and balcony on the right. Recently, it has again been named Tupper & Reed, but it is now a cocktail bar.

Continue on Shattuck and turn right on Kittredge to see the red-brick building at 2138 Kittridge. Walk a few steps down the driveway on the far (east) side of the building for a view of the Colonial Revival house (from 1904, by William Wharff), to which the red-brick structure was added in 1935. Across Kittredge, notice a similar phenomenon, where **⓵ Razan's Organic Kitchen** and another restaurant are each located in a commercial addition to a historic house. The restaurant on the left side uses the interior of the former home as part of the dining area. Such shop fronts were a popular way to augment the use of residences when commercial areas expanded in the early 20th century.

Return to Shattuck, passing the Art Deco California Theatre; turn right and walk to the corner of Allston. Look across the wide street to the **⓵ Hotel Shattuck Plaza** (entrance on Allston). This 1909 Mediterranean-style building is a Berkeley landmark, one of the signature buildings that help define downtown. The five- and six-story building—expanded to the south in 1913 and 1926—has remained an operating hotel through several ownership changes. The building runs an entire city block north to south. The J. F. Hink and Son department store (known as Hink's) occupied the lower southern portion from 1913 to 1985. A cinema complex—one of three in downtown Berkeley—occupies the ground floor, although a proposed plan to build residential towers on the west side of the block could temporarily close the complex.

At this point, Shattuck Avenue is a true boulevard, with separate slow lanes for parking. This layout provides a buffer for pedestrians from fast traffic; moreover, the wide sidewalks, street trees, and shop fronts built up to the sidewalk create a comfortable pedestrian ambiance despite the street's width and traffic.

Turn right on Allston and continue to the seven-story Gaia Building at 2116 Allston, with a red-and-blue tile facade, completed in 2001 by architects Kirk E. Peterson & Associates and developer Patrick Kennedy. Although the Gaia Building was controversial when it was proposed because of its height, many citizens feel that it fits well into Berkeley's downtown environment and its architecture reflects the Mediterranean style of the nearby Hotel Shattuck Plaza. For the 91 units, there are 42 parking spaces in the building (in a space-conserving, three-tiered stacking system partially visible through the grilled driveway gate on the right), but most of the tenants do not own cars. By providing housing near the campus, downtown Berkeley, BART, and other public transit, the city hopes to encourage residents to forgo cars altogether. For short trips, several electric vehicles are provided free of charge to tenants, and a pod of City CarShare vehicles resides in the garage. A performance space, the Marsh Berkeley Arts Center, is on the ground floor.

Just beyond the Gaia Building at 2134 Allston is Cancun Taqueria in a small, Spanish-style commercial building from 1930, somewhat dwarfed by its neighbors but retaining charm.

Next to it, the ⓱ **David Brower Center** was completed in 2009, replacing a parking lot. The building was named for the famed environmentalist, a Berkeley native who was executive director of the Sierra Club and who founded the Earth Island Institute. The structure has LEED platinum certification (it meets the highest standards for environmental design and green features) and a 68-kilowatt solar-cell array on the roof to meet about 35 percent of the building's electricity demand. The center has a free photo gallery in the lobby and is home to nonprofit organizations focusing on environmental issues. On the ground floor at Oxford Street, Gather restaurant emphasizes organic and sustainably sourced foods and beverages.

Cross Allston at the Oxford crosswalk and return back down Allston on the other side to see Allston Place (2121 Allston), which replaced a surface parking lot with 60 rental units and 13 parking spaces. The developer preserved the mature, beautiful oak in front and provided a public arcade between the ground-level retail spaces. However, this street does not seem to generate enough foot traffic to make the arcade a successful retail space.

Continue back down Allston toward Shattuck. Next door to Allston Place is the Magnes Collection of Jewish Art and Life in a building that originally was a printing plant. The museum also has a library and archives for research on the global Jewish diaspora and western Jewish Americana. The collection was formerly housed in a large, private home on Russell Street in the Elmwood neighborhood; it moved to this downtown location in 2012 to be closer to transit and other amenities.

Just past the museum, turn right into Trumpetvine Court if it is open (if it is not, continue on to Shattuck and turn right) and wind past Cafe Panini into the trellised courtyard of Jupiter, a popular outdoor dining and drinking spot. Continue along the walkway between the tables and exit left through the open corridor. Located in one of downtown Berkeley's oldest buildings (a livery stable from the 1890s), Jupiter's interior features a staircase to the mezzanine and stamped-metal walls.

Back on the sidewalk, walk right toward the corner of Center and Shattuck. Berkeley's first skyscraper, the ⓲ **Wells Fargo Building** (originally the Berkeley Chamber of Commerce building) is catty-corner across the intersection. Built in 1925 during the economic boom, the 12-story building is in Classical Revival style; the first-floor arches were added in 1927. In 1970, the Great Western Building, in an undistinguished modern style, was added on the southwest corner.

Across Center Street on the northeast corner is the one-story Bank of America building, which looks strangely suburban for downtown Berkeley; a historic six-story office building was demolished in the 1970s with plans for a skyscraper, but a weak economy left the city with this alternative. UC Berkeley proposed building a hotel/condo/conference center on the site, but the economic downturn of the late 2000s shelved the plan. In early 2015, developers proposed a mixed-use high-rise project with retail, condominiums, a conference center, and an extended-stay hotel for the site.

Turn right and walk up Center toward the University of California campus. This main route to campus from BART and bus stops is a lively widened sidewalk with street trees and outdoor dining; contrast this south side of the street with the north side, which lacks vitality. This may change when the Berkeley Art Museum and Pacific Film Archive, under construction farther up the street, opens in 2016. It will use part of the historic UC Printing Plant building, where the United Nations Charter was printed.

The 1902 ⓳ **Mikkelsen and Berry Building**, at 2124–26 Center, in a picturesque Mission Revival style, is one of the few small, wood-frame buildings left downtown. Next to it, 2128–30 Center was originally Ennor's Restaurant, designed by Plachek and completed in 1923; in 1970, an unattractive tile was added to the first-floor facade when it became the popular Act I and Act II Cinema, which showed independent and foreign films until it closed in 2006. The building has been restored and it is now home to Japanese restaurant Ippuku and other businesses. Just beyond this are Sliver Pizzeria and other eateries in a long building designed by Wharff.

Return to Shattuck and turn right, crossing Center Street, and walk to Addison Street. On the southeast corner, at ⓴ **2010 Shattuck**, is another building by Ratcliff, now a furniture store but originally the 1928 home office of Mason-McDuffie. The premier real estate development company created Berkeley's Northbrae and

Claremont neighborhoods, laying out neighborhoods in harmony with the natural surroundings. This Mediterranean-style building is notable for its high, pilastered windows. (Duncan McDuffie was not only a canny developer but also an avid conservationist, acting as Sierra Club president and helping to found the East Bay Regional Park District and California state park system.)

Directly across Addison on the northeast corner is the ㉑ **Studio Building** of 1905 (2045 Shattuck), with rounded bay windows and tiled mansard roof; initially, the top floor was artists' studios. It was briefly the original home of the California College of Arts and Crafts (now the California College of the Arts in Oakland), then a hotel, and eventually offices in the 1970s.

Continue along Shattuck to University Avenue. Across the street, at 2119 University, is the ㉒ **Bachenheimer Building**, with elements of Italian Renaissance style. Built in 2004 by developer Patrick Kennedy and architect Kirk E. Peterson & Associates, it is one of the most attractive new mixed-use buildings in Berkeley, providing a focal point for Shattuck Avenue (which jogs left and

then right here). Look right, up University, to see the popular Pedro's Brazil Cafe, a shack in the parking lot of Mike's Bikes. Development plans for new buildings to the right and left of the Bachenheimer building include the retention of some historic facades.

Cross Shattuck to the left and continue west on University past Citibank.

Stop in front of the ㉓ **UC Theatre** at 2036 University. Another Plachek design, the theater opened

The Italianate Bachenheimer Building.

in 1917 to showcase first-run movies. In the 1970s, new owners presented classic domestic and foreign films, including double and triple features, and the theater hosted 22 consecutive years of midnight screenings of *The Rocky Horror Picture Show*. In dire need of an expensive seismic retrofit, the UC closed in 2001. In 2014, a nonprofit consortium, the Berkeley Music Group, initiated a major renovation; when it opens, the revamped theater will offer a full schedule of live concerts, movies, and educational programs.

Continue to ㉔ **1952–66 University**. This landmarked compound, with six small shops separated by a driveway, includes commercial fronts added in the 1920s onto historic residences. A courtyard in the back provides outdoor seating surrounded by historic buildings. Several of the original buildings were developed by French immigrants Alexandre and Marie Bertin, who had a dry cleaning and laundry business here as well as a flower nursery. John Gordon renovated the historic buildings around 2007–2008. The proprietor of innovative Chocolatier Blue encouraged other food-oriented enterprises to rent space here, earning the area the nick-name Gourmet Gulch (as opposed to the more-famous Gourmet Ghetto on North Shattuck, which includes Chez Panisse). At this writing, the other shops included a branch of Pedro's Brazil Cafe, the A Dora Pie bakery, and a saxophone shop. Return up University, passing the six-story Koerber Building at 2054 University, just beyond the UC Theatre, with its terra-cotta ornamentation. Turn right on Shattuck.

At 2014–18 Shattuck, the ㉕ **Heywood Building** of 1917 features an exuberant, cream-colored, terra-cotta facade with Gothic arches over the windows and a rope-framing design, also designed by Plachek. The first-floor storefront has been restored to something closer to its original design, and currently is home to Belli Osteria, which serves tasty Italian fusion food. Across the street is a better view of the three landmarked buildings designed by Pflueger, including the Roos Brothers Building, which is framed by two large bears. Continue walking to Center Street and the starting point.

❋ ❋ ❋

WALK 2
THE UC CAMPUS

Overview: Although UC Berkeley continues to squeeze in buildings, it is a pleasant campus conveniently located adjacent to downtown Berkeley. This walk includes the options of touring publicly accessible buildings and going to the top of Sather Tower. It is moderately uphill, with a short, steep climb at the east end of the main campus.

Highlights:
- John Galen Howard's lasting legacy
- Verdant campus with historic and modern buildings
- Strawberry Creek, Sather Tower, Sproul Plaza

Distance: 3 miles

Time: 2–3 hours

Elevation gain: 225 feet

Start at Center Street and Shattuck Avenue, near the Downtown Berkeley BART station and accessible via numerous AC Transit lines. UC construction projects and special events can close off parts of the route; use the map to stay on track and check the Cal football schedule to avoid home football game days.

Walk up Center toward the campus of the University of California, Berkeley (known locally as "Cal," "UC Berkeley," and simply "UC") on the right (south) side of the street. The sidewalk was widened in the 1990s, when the city planted more street trees and encouraged outdoor dining. As the main route from BART and buses to the campus, one side of Center has become a lively corridor. The other side was completely moribund for decades;

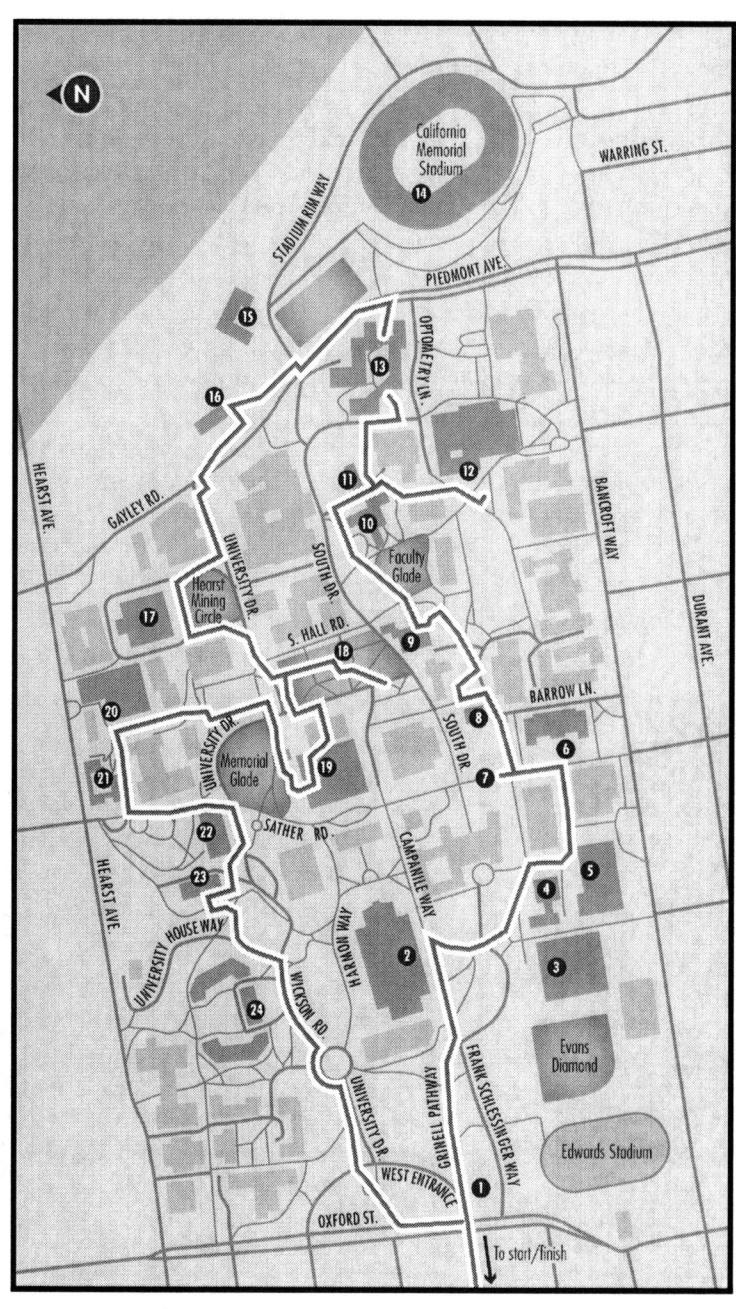

however, the new Berkeley Art Museum and Pacific Film Archive, scheduled to open in 2016, is likely to instill vitality.

Cross Oxford Street and head up the sidewalk along the campus entry drive, noting the fascinating spherical sculpture. *Rotante dal Foro Centrale*—roughly translated as *Revolving from the Central Forum*—is by Italian sculptor Arnaldo Pomodoro. As you walk through the campus, keep your eyes open for sculptures along the way.

Take a few steps to the right of the sculpture to the banks of ❶ **Strawberry Creek**; a historic marker is nearby. The creek enters a culvert here and does not emerge until the other side of Sacramento Street, about a mile away, although it originally flowed through downtown. The presence of the creek and its fresh water was a major factor in the selection of this site for a university campus. Watching out for cyclists on campus walkways, continue past the sculpture and take the curving path to the right onto the footbridge for a nice view of the creek.

The private College of California was founded in 1855 in Oakland, but purchased 30 acres on this site in Berkeley in 1860.

The sculpture by Arnaldo Pomodoro that stands at the campus entrance.

In 1868, the college merged with the newly chartered public land grant, the University of California. This was the first campus in the UC system, and it continues to be the flagship of the now 10-campus-strong system. The name Berkeley was chosen in honor of philosopher Bishop (George) Berkeley, who came from Ireland to the United States to establish colleges; he was the author of a poem that includes the line, "Westward the course of empire takes its way." UC Berkeley now has more than 25,000 undergraduate and 10,000 graduate students. Famous for its Nobel laureates, UC Berkeley is one of the most prestigious universities in the world.

Just past the bridge, if you meander off the path to the left, you will see eucalyptus woods at the confluence of two forks of Strawberry Creek. Planted in 1882 as a windbreak for a track, UC Berkeley claims that the eucalyptus grove—trees native to Australia—is the tallest stand of hardwood in North America. In calm areas of the creek, you might notice aquatic life such as water striders, stickleback fish, and crayfish. There are also native live oaks, bay laurels, and buckeyes along the creek. You will cross Strawberry Creek numerous times during the course of this walk.

Return to the paved path and continue toward the hills. At the second bridge (with Stars of David in the iron railings), note the human-made cascade on the right. After crossing, continue straight (rather than bearing right) toward Campanile Way (with a view of Sather Tower, also known as the "Campanile").

On the left is the huge **②** **Valley Life Sciences Building**, designed by George W. Kelham in Art Deco style with neoclassical elements and Egyptian motifs. Bas-reliefs of animals are below the windows, and the names of college disciplines are declared below the cornice. The sculptures are attributed to Robert Boardman Howard, son of campus architect John Galen Howard. The interior was completely modernized in the early 1990s; partial funding by Wayne and Gladys Valley now gives this impressive building its name. This was the largest concrete building west of the Mississippi when it was built in 1930, and it is still the largest on campus, with 400,000 square feet of space. The University of California Museum of Paleontology and the University and Jepson Herbaria (with huge collections in their fields) are on the first floor; the Museum of Vertebrate Zoology is on the third floor.

Some exhibits are free and open to the public (when the building is unlocked). Enter using the stairs at the middle of the

The Valley Life Sciences Building.

building. Once inside, walk up the steps and along a corridor, noticing the skeletons of a saber-toothed tiger, primates, and other animals. In the central atrium, there are skeletons of a pterodactyl and a menacing Tyrannosaurus rex.

Exit the building where you entered and walk straight onto the pathway that leads away from the building, passing a parking area to your left; you will also pass two deciduous conifers, a tall and straight bald cypress on the right and a dawn redwood on the left; the latter was known only through fossils until it was rediscovered in China in 1944 and seeds were brought to UC. Cross the street and the wooden footbridge; the ❸ **Haas Pavilion** is straight ahead to the right. This sports arena was built in 1933 and renovated in 1999.

Take the path to the left along Strawberry Creek, with a view of an attractive stone bridge upstream. To the right, the 1953 ❹ **Alumni House** has large windows looking out on trees. This modern building, which hosts numerous receptions, is harmonious with its surroundings. To the left, across the creek, Dwinelle Annex—designed by Howard—is a rustic 1920 building with unpainted wood siding that houses UC Berkeley's Department of Theater, Dance, and Performance Studies. As supervising architect (appointed in 1901) and director of UC Berkeley's architecture program for more than 20 years, Howard exerted a profound influence on the look and feel of the campus.

At the stone bridge, turn right between Alumni House and the 1960 César E. Chávez Student Center, the modern building with projecting roof elements. Take the wooden walkway and turn left up the stairs into the plaza in front of ❺ **Zellerbach Hall**, with its large, glass-fronted lobby. Zellerbach Hall is the venue for Cal Performances, which presents dance, music, and drama performed by well-known national and international troupes and performers. Zellerbach Playhouse, a more intimate theater, is in the rear. Designed by UC Berkeley architecture professor Vernon DeMars, Zellerbach was completed in 1968. A major renovation of lower Sproul Plaza—voted on by students in 2010—is expected to finish in late 2015. The revamp includes the replacement of Eshleman Hall near Bancroft Way and the renovation of other buildings.

Walk away from the front of Zellerbach Hall, across the plaza, and up the big staircase to the left of the Martin Luther King, Jr., Student Union building to ❻ **Upper Sproul Plaza**, with its fountain and the classical-looking 1940 Sproul Hall administration building, designed by Arthur Brown, Jr. This plaza was the site of major demonstrations during the Free Speech Movement in 1964–65, during which students insisted that the university administration lift the ban on political activities held on campus. Numerous protests and sit-ins have taken place here in the years since, including protests by the Occupy movement in 2012.

A metal plaque on the steps to Sproul Hall, placed in 1997, marks them as the Mario Savio Steps; Savio, a leader of the Free Speech Movement, made his most famous speech here ("There's a time when the operation of the machine becomes so odious . . ."). To see the plaque, go up four steps to the first landing; the plaque is centered with the building's front doors. For the 25th anniversary of the Free Speech Movement, a six-inch hole, ringed by a six-foot granite circle, was placed in the center of Sproul Plaza; text around the circle declares that the soil and space above it is not part of any nation.

Sproul Plaza features pollarded plane trees. When classes are in session, the plaza is busy with student groups recruiting new members and candidates campaigning for student elections. (The UC Berkeley scene in the movie *The Graduate* was not filmed here, but at the University of Southern California in Los Angeles.)

Walk through ➐ **Sather Gate** north of the plaza and look over the bridge on either side to see Strawberry Creek. The gate was built in 1910, dedicated to Peder Sather and designed by Howard to be strong but light and airy. The nude, bas-relief, Classical-style sculptures on the piers (males on the bridge side and females on the other) were removed shortly after the gate was built, but restored in 1977. An inscription on one pier below a nude says, "Erected by Jane K. Sather"; the donor, wife of Peder, was not happy about that. Until the 1940s, Sather Gate was the edge of campus, with private homes and businesses extending where Sproul Plaza is now and toward Bancroft Avenue; the university expanded southward during the 1940s.

Return to the Sproul Plaza side of the bridge and walk left (east) up the paved path next to the parking area. When passing the brick building on the left, cross toward it in the crosswalk and walk around to the ➑ **Old Art Building**'s front.

This was the campus's first steam powerhouse, built in 1904 and designed by Howard. Helen Bruton and Florence Alston Swift created the impressive mosaic murals depicting (in a quasi-Byzantine style) music and painting in 1936–37, as part of the Depression-era Works Progress Administration Federal Art Project. The building was an art gallery from 1934 to 1970 and has been occupied by various other facilities since.

Sather Gate, by John Galen Howard.

The Pelican Building, by Joseph Esherick.

Turn around to see the adjacent Pelican Building, now known as Anthony Hall. This building was a legacy of Earle C. Anthony, a UC Berkeley graduate who set up the first radio station in Los Angeles, one of that city's first TV stations, a bus company that became part of Greyhound Lines, and a service station chain that became Chevron. He also had the distributorship for Packard autos in California as well as three grand auto showrooms, one of which still survives on Van Ness Avenue in San Francisco.

While at UC, Anthony started the *California Pelican* humor magazine, which survived until about 1980. As a wealthy alumnus in the late 1950s, he convinced UC to let him build a structure specifically for the student-run magazine (note the pelican statue in front). Anthony wanted Bernard Maybeck to design the building, but Maybeck declined due to his advanced age, and the job went to Joseph Esherick, a talented Bay Area architect known for the Monterey Bay Aquarium and a host of sensitively designed residences. Esherick paid tribute to Maybeck in the traditional design, which mixes styles, although he added modern touches such as concrete columns called sonotubes. Some time after the demise of the *Pelican*, the Graduate Assembly took over the building.

Turn left (north), walking between these two buildings toward a bridge. Notice the terrace and pergola behind the Pelican Building.

Cross the bridge and immediately turn right on the narrow asphalt path following the stream; native plants line the banks. Turn right again and back over another bridge, passing around the Pelican Building, then left when you get to the small street. Stay on the path, noting mundane, modern Barrows Hall to the right. UC Berkeley's campus is attractive, with the trees and creek, and has many handsome classical and modern buildings, but it is also a hodgepodge, with many modern buildings declaring themselves and the architect's ego without any attempt to fit in with the rest of the campus. All campus designers face the issue of how to accommodate new buildings without losing the natural environment that has always enhanced the campus.

When you come to a bridge on the left, take the path just to its right, going uphill and then curving to the left. Bear left at the fork to pass through a grove of redwoods; turn left again after passing the corner of ❾ **Stephens Hall** (on the left), a 1923 Tudor Gothic building by Howard that houses the Townsend Center for the Humanities and other departments. Just for fun, make a little loop in front of the building by turning left down the steps and over the first bridge, right alongside the front of the building, and then right again to cross back over another bridge.

On the right is a statue of Lynn Osbert "Pappy" Waldorf, legendary Cal Golden Bears football coach from 1947 to 1956. Another bridge is on the left just past a giant sequoia; take the paved path angling to the left but not over the bridge.

Continue northeast on the path, with the grassy hillside to the right and Strawberry Creek to the left. Off to the left is a partly hidden nude statue called *The Last Dryad*. Up ahead on the left side is an ancient California buckeye tree, planted in 1885. It lost its main trunk many years ago, and the lower trunk is hollowed out and only partially there, but the tree carries on impressively, producing spikes of white flowers in April and May.

Continue on the path toward the ❿ **Faculty Club** (originally the men's faculty club); Bernard Maybeck designed the original building in 1902–3, with additions by Howard, Warren Charles Perry, and George Downs. It is a lovely building in a Mediterranean/Craftsman style. The splendid Great Hall is used as the main dining room; the hall's windows can be seen on the building section that extends to the right. The building fits well in its wooded creekside location at Faculty Glade.

Turn left and then right, parallel to the creek, just before a concrete, stepped bridge. After passing the Faculty Club and crossing a wooden bridge, take the path to the right, and walk over another wooden bridge through a redwood grove. Cross in front of the redwood log cabin called **⓫ Senior Hall**. This rather surprising campus structure was designed by Howard and completed in 1906, funded by the Order of the Golden Bear as a "symbol of senior control of campus." It must have been a diverting project for classicist Howard.

Turn left and ascend the steps or the driveway, then make a sharp right to pass between the back of the Faculty Club and a concrete building, the Minor Hall Addition. After about 25 steps, turn left to pass along the side of the Alfred Hertz Memorial Hall of Music (Hertz Hall), with its pale orange stucco. Emerge into a grassy plaza and bear right on the path to the center. You are now in front of Hertz Hall and the large concrete Wurster Hall (east side), with a tall tower. Built in 1964 for the College of Environmental Design, **⓬ Wurster Hall** is unpopular with many for its Brutalist concrete facade. Designed by a group of architects including Joseph Esherick, it is praised, however, as a functional building for students and teachers.

Hertz Hall is a 678-seat space with excellent acoustics, where UC Berkeley Department of Music students and professional groups perform. Built in 1958 and designed by architect Gardner A. Dailey, it features paintings by Gottardo Piazzoni in the lobby. Piazzoni was a Swiss-Italian immigrant who came to the United States as a teenager in 1887; as a painter, he is regarded as a Tonalist, a group that includes George Inness and James Abbott McNeill Whistler. He was particularly interested in lighting effects at different times of day and night. Several of his fine, muted landscape paintings are in the building.

Turn around and follow the same route back between Hertz Hall on the left and Wurster Hall, and then the Minor Hall Addition (University Eye Center) on the right. At the Faculty Club, bear right past the club along the driveway, with the log cabin on the left, and pass the tall hedge to see the 1923 Women's Faculty Club. Howard designed this building in a simple classical style with unpainted wood shingles.

Continue on the driveway and turn right on the sidewalk at the road, and bear left to cross in the crosswalk, then turn right on the opposite sidewalk and left up the wide steps of the ⓭ **Haas School of Business**.

Walk up through the Doris and Donald Fisher Gate into the courtyard. This 1995 building by Charles Moore—which replaced the former campus medical clinic—returns to a more traditional mode of design, while not adopting any particular style. A notable feature is the concrete exterior that mimics wooden boards. The structure spills down the hillside with angled buildings, varied levels, and archways that create an interesting spatial feeling and make this one of the most appealing new campus buildings in recent decades. However, some students complain it is a confusing maze inside. Renovated in 2013, the plaza has tables and shade trees and is a popular hangout. Walk up the steps or ramp on the opposite side to pass through the William F. and Janet Cronk Gate.

Walk out to Gayley Road. Across the street from the business school is ⓮ **California Memorial Stadium**. Built in 1923, it was one of Howard's last projects as campus architect. Howard objected to the location of the stadium—as did the neighbors—because it is atop the Hayward Fault and Strawberry Creek and it displaced a bird and wildlife sanctuary; he felt the stadium should be situated closer to downtown. After this disagreement, Howard left his position as campus architect in 1924.

Additional controversy came in 2007 and 2008, when UC Berkeley decided to place the Simpson Center for Student-Athlete High Performance in front of the stadium, which is a Classical-style bowl. The Simpson Center is built low into the hill so as not to interfere with the stadium facade, but a number of mature trees, particularly California oaks, had to be cut down to make room for it. This led to a 21-month period of protest in the form of tree sitting, which lasted until police removed the protesters and construction moved forward. Some mature redwoods and oaks do remain. As part of a seismic retrofit, the interior of the stadium was gutted and replaced (only the exterior wall is original), and a press box and seating for major donors were placed on top. Some people feel the structure mars the classic design, although it was done with a fairly light touch. Walk left along the sidewalk on Gayley, noting the tall parking garage with an athletic field on the roof.

Just before the stop sign for Stadium Rim Way, look uphill to the right for a glimpse of the castle-like building on the hill. Built in 1929, ⓯ **Bowles Hall**—the first university-owned residence hall—was designed by George W. Kelham (who designed the Valley Life Sciences Building and International House) in Collegiate Gothic style; it is on the National Register of Historic Places. Bowles Hall is all male and has many traditions such as self-governance and an emphasis on fellowship.

Cross the small street opposite Stadium Rim, then cross Gayley to the right. Walk up Stadium Rim a few steps and then turn left up the walkway (or parking lot) to the side of the 1903 **16 William Randolph Hearst Greek Theatre**; you can get a partial view inside by peeking through the gate. This was Howard's first completed structure on campus. Financed by Hearst (who founded a publishing empire that included the *San Francisco Chronicle*; built Hearst Castle at San Simeon; and was the model for the title character in the Orson Welles movie *Citizen Kane*), the theatre was built in classical Greek amphitheater style (based on the one at Epidaurus) and is the site of numerous public and private events. Julia Morgan, just back from studying in Paris, assisted Howard. In May 1903, President Theodore Roosevelt delivered a commencement address at the newly constructed theater.

Return back to Gayley by turning right, around the corner of the theater complex, then left down the steps, then right on a walkway that descends parallel to the street on the theater's west side (through redolent eucalyptus trees) to arrive at a small plaza. Recross Gayley in the crosswalk, turn right across University Drive in the crosswalk, and turn left to proceed downhill on the sidewalk along University Drive. A severe, modern building is on the left (Latimer Hall) and beyond that another modern concrete building (Tan Hall), which has a tile roof and massing (the shape of the exterior) somewhat like the traditional campus halls. Follow the sidewalk as it curves right in front of Stanley Hall, built in 2007 for various science disciplines.

Continue around the circle to the **17 Hearst Memorial Mining Building** of 1907, a gift of Phoebe Apperson Hearst in memory of her husband George Hearst, who made a fortune in mining. (William Randolph Hearst was their son.) Howard broke from a Beaux-Arts Classical style to harmoniously meld Spanish Mission, Craftsman, and neoclassical elements in this building; this and the Charles Franklin Doe Memorial Library are his campus masterpieces. Note the huge wooden brackets supporting the eaves, with sculptural corbels underneath; the arched openings with columns

Spotlight: John Galen Howard (1864–1931)

As supervising architect for UC Berkeley during the first quarter of the 20th century—a time of tremendous growth and expansion—John Galen Howard did more to define the current look and feel of the campus than any other architect. He designed many of Cal's signature structures, including Doe Library, Sather Tower, Sather Gate and Bridge, and California Memorial Stadium.

Working primarily in the neoclassical style favored by East Coast and European architects at the end of the 19th century, Howard incorporated design touches from other styles and produced a varied but harmonious set of campus buildings. The Hearst Memorial Mining Building is perhaps his most admired, combining neoclassical with regional Spanish Mission and Craftsman elements. Elsewhere on campus, he employed simple, brown-shingle style for the Naval Architecture Building and North Gate Hall, and designed a log cabin for Senior Hall.

Born in Massachusetts, Howard attended MIT and then the École des Beaux-Arts in Paris. He was an apprentice with prominent architect Henry Hobson Richardson and worked in New York, Boston (with McKim, Mead, and White), and Los Angeles. In 1901, he moved to the Bay Area to execute the Hearst master plan for the University of California. While serving as supervising architect, Howard founded the university architecture program and was its director from 1903 to 1926. In addition to Classical-style commercial buildings throughout the Bay Area, Howard designed rustic Craftsman residences and made significant contributions to the look and feel of Berkeley neighborhoods surrounding UC.

Despite strong objections to the location (over Strawberry Creek and the Hayward Fault, and far from downtown Berkeley), he reluctantly completed the design for the California Memorial Stadium in 1923 at its current site. This was a major factor contributing to Howard's subsequent departure in 1924.

Howard was also a poet. In 1917, he took a sabbatical to write poetry; after leaving UC, he wrote and published his own verse. ❋ ❋

and sculpted metal; the wooden front doors; and other decorative and structural elements. If the front door is unlocked, go inside to see the impressive lobby, which rises up three floors, with metal lattice railings around the galleries, a beautiful Catalan vaulted

The Hearst Memorial Mining Building.

ceiling, and three glass-dome skylights (try peeking in the window if the door is locked). Julia Morgan assisted Howard in the design. The building was nicely restored in 1999–2002 and given a seismic retrofit.

Walk back down the steps; turn right and continue around the circle counterclockwise past the nondescript modern Evans Hall. Look across the plaza for a better view of Stanley Hall; it has some varied surfaces and colors, but the massing is a jumble of shapes that lack unity. Take the sidewalk that angles down the hill to the right, and cross the street in the second crosswalk to the left toward a stairway.

Ascend the steps to enter the ⑱ **Sather Tower** esplanade, with its pollarded plane trees. During Sather Tower's open hours, it is well worth paying a few dollars to take the elevator and then 38 steps up to the observation platform for terrific views. At 307 feet, this is the third-tallest bell and clock tower in the world. Named for donor Jane K. Sather and designed by Howard in 1914, it is called the Campanile due to its resemblance to the famous clock tower in Venice's Piazza San Marco. Three times daily, the 61-bell, 40-ton carillon plays music performed by Department of Music students, and a bell chimes for each hour. According to UC, the four clocks are the largest in California. The tower has steel-frame, reinforced concrete walls and is clad in granite, and the bells were cast in

England and France. The building also stores 50 tons of dinosaur, human, and other bones from the Department of Integrative Biology's collection, mainly from the La Brea Tar Pits in Los Angeles; its cool, dry interior is suited for their preservation (it is not open to the public).

Walk to the terrace on the tower's west side (to the right, facing downtown Berkeley, the bay, and the Golden Gate Bridge) for a view to the left of the oldest building on campus, South Hall, in red brick and stone. Completed in 1873, South Hall is all that remains of original campus structures; a twin called North Hall once stood where the Bancroft Library is now. Originally housing UC Berkeley's College of Agriculture, the building is a reminder of the university's land-grant roots, designated by the federal government in 1866 to establish an agricultural and technical college. David Farquharson, a Scotsman, designed South Hall and North Hall in the Second Empire style, which is rare in the Bay Area. It does not look like anything else on campus; bas-reliefs display California crops, and devil's head gargoyles glare down from each corner. It is on the National Register of Historic Places and is a city landmark. Behind Sather Tower is a grove of Canary Island pine trees.

Head north, back through the esplanade, away from the Campanile, with LeConte Hall on the right, and take the same stairway you ascended. Walk left to the intersection for a view of the main library complex. Straight ahead is the Classical-style **⑲ Doe Memorial Library** with its enormous arched window, designed by Howard and completed in stages from 1911 to 1917. Cross the street and turn left to enter the Bancroft Library's east entrance (on the right). Designed by Arthur Brown, Jr., the Bancroft houses a world-class archive of historic books, periodicals, letters, documents, and special collections, including the Mark Twain Papers and Project.

(If the Bancroft is closed, you can often enter the Doe Library by walking back on the sidewalk past the big window and a stairway, turning left on the asphalt path at Memorial Glade and going up the circular steps. If both libraries are closed, skip ahead one paragraph.)

If the libraries are open, go straight through the two-story rotunda of the Bancroft and then down a corridor with historical wall displays to the Roger W. Heyns (East) Reading Room, with ornate, carved, high ceiling, the names of famous writers high on the walls, and a large painting of George Washington in battle. Exit through the big portal on the right and turn left and then right to enter the impressive North Reading Room, one of the largest in the nation at 210 feet long, with a high, barrel-vaulted ceiling and large windows and skylights. Exit, passing through the anteroom, and pass through double doors to go down the long stairway to the lower level, then turn left just before the building exit to enter the Morrison Memorial Library, with its beautiful plaster ceiling, wood paneling, and upper-level cozy nooks. Outside this room, a statue of Mark Twain sits on a bench. Exit the Doe Library building to the left.

Reflecting Berkeley's desire to be the Athens of the West, a bronze bust of the Greek goddess Athena is above the Doe Library entrance. A major library renovation in 1995 added four stories under the grass of the Memorial Glade, just ahead, rather than ruin campus open space or mar views of the main building.

Go down the circular steps and walk to the right, following the paved path along the side of the library buildings back to the street that runs between the libraries and Sather Tower. Cross the small street. A few steps from the curb, walk left (north) on the sidewalk parallel to the road. Bear right at each of the two path intersections and take the wide brick stairway up to the left. Continue north up the concrete ramp and past sculptures of reclining bears on the left and Brutalist-style Davis Hall on the right.

The next building on the right is ⓴ **Sutardja Dai Hall**, a combination of modern and traditional styles. Completed in 2009, the hall houses CITRIS (the Center for Information Technology Research in the Interest of Society), an interdisciplinary research program. The color and texture of the concrete feels much warmer here than in Davis Hall, and there are ample windows. Directly ahead is much older Blum Hall, home of the Blum Center for Developing Economies, a campus hub for antipoverty innovation; it's named for investment banker Richard C. Blum, husband of US Senator Dianne Feinstein. The building—a Berkeley city landmark that is on the National Register of Historic Places—was once known as the Drawing Building (an annex to the School of Architecture) and later housed the Department of Naval Architecture. A 2010 addition to the left, with unpainted wooden siding and a peaked roof, is harmonious with the original shingled building despite the large, modern glass windows.

Turn left past Blum Hall and walk downhill along the small street. Walk to the right and up a curving ramp to North Gate Hall, a 1906 Howard design that initially housed the School of Architecture (until 1964) and was called the Ark, but is now the Graduate School of Journalism. The structure, with its brown shingles, ample windows, intimate courtyard, and wisteria vines, is an embodiment of regional architecture.

Return to the road and walk farther downhill. On the right is the ㉑ **North Gate**, with tree-lined Euclid Avenue beyond. The north side of campus is considerably quieter than the south side, but the first block of Euclid has numerous cafes, eateries, shops, and some attractive historic buildings (see Walk 3, The North Side of Campus).

Turn left to walk away from the North Gate and Euclid Avenue, passing a circular green plaza on the right and a grove of mature California live oaks. After starting downhill, take the paved walk on the right, which leads to an elevated walkway connected to the second floor of the 2008 ㉒ **C. V. Starr East Asian Library**, which contains the Chang-Lin Tien Center for East Asian Studies. If it's open, go in and look around. Reading rooms on the second and the third floors look out on the wooded hillside to the north. Note the angled ceiling with partially hidden skylights and the atrium effect of the open stair areas. The library has almost one million volumes, mainly in Chinese, Japanese, and Korean, and claims the most valuable collection of historic Japanese maps outside Japan, as well as a huge collection of materials on China.

Exit the building where you came in, walk across the small bridge at the end of the elevated walkway, descend the stairs, go around to the left, and walk down wide steps toward the small road (University Drive). At the road, turn right on the paved walkway, which goes down through a landscaped area. Notice the intricate metal grill–like pattern over the library's south-facing windows; on the left are views of the main library and Sather Tower.

Follow the sidewalk and turn right when you reach the end of the Starr Library, then go left then right around to the front of ㉓ **Haviland Hall**, another Howard design from 1924. Walk down the steps to the left, heading away from the entrance, take the paved path to the left, bear right on the unpaved path, and cross the bridge to the right over the north fork of Strawberry Creek, pausing to see if there is anything interesting in the water. Angle slightly left on a path to the paved drive and turn left, passing a large ginkgo tree with fan-shaped leaves that turn golden yellow around November. At University Drive, cross and turn right to take the sidewalk, noting a majestic deodar cedar on the left with big branches that swing down and then arch up again.

Across to the right is a composition of **three Beaux-Arts classical-style buildings**, designed in similar style, but each a bit different. Together they form a ring around a large interior courtyard, now used mostly for parking. The center building with the circular entry area is Wellman Hall, designed by Howard and completed in 1912. The left building is Hilgard Hall, also designed by Howard and completed in 1917. The right building is Giannini Hall, honoring the San Francisco founder of the Bank of Italy, which became Bank of America. Completed in 1930 with a design by William Charles Hays, Giannini Hall fits in well with the other two. The huge olive tree with spreading above-ground roots was planted on the grassy slope in the 1880s or 1890s as part of a grove for the agriculture school.

Continue to the traffic circle, cross to the right, and follow the circle counterclockwise to stay on University Drive, heading west toward downtown. At The Crescent, look right to see the Li Ka Shing Center for Biomedical and Health Sciences, completed in 2012 with a major gift from the Hong Kong business tycoon. It replaced a 1950s-era building that had seismic problems. Cross The Crescent in the crosswalk, enter the small shaded plaza, and walk down the steps toward Oxford Street. Turn left at Oxford and right on Center to return to the starting point.

❋ ❋ ❋

WALK 3
THE NORTH SIDE OF CAMPUS

✻ ✻ ✻

Overview: This hilly walk explores late 19th- and early 20th-century mansions and cottages as well as later UC buildings, the Graduate Theological Union, apartment buildings in diverse styles, and the fairy-tale Normandy Village. A 1923 fire destroyed more than 600 homes in this area but spared UC Berkeley and downtown; post-1923 buildings dominate farther north of campus.

Highlights:
- Seminaries and schools of Holy Hill
- Maybeck's first commissioned work
- Normandy Village, a hidden gem

Distance: 1.2–2 miles
Time: 1.5–2.5 hours
Elevation gain: 250–415 feet

✻ ✻ ✻

Start at the northwest corner of Euclid and Hearst avenues, near the North Gate entrance to UC. The starting point is about a half-mile walk from the Downtown Berkeley BART station and is on AC Transit bus routes 65 and 52.

The north side is the UC campus's quiet side. Walk north up Euclid away from the UC campus. On the right corner, at  **1865 Euclid**, is a landmarked apartment block by John Galen Howard from 1912; the handsome columned balconies add a cosmopolitan European look. The commercial area on the first block of Euclid and

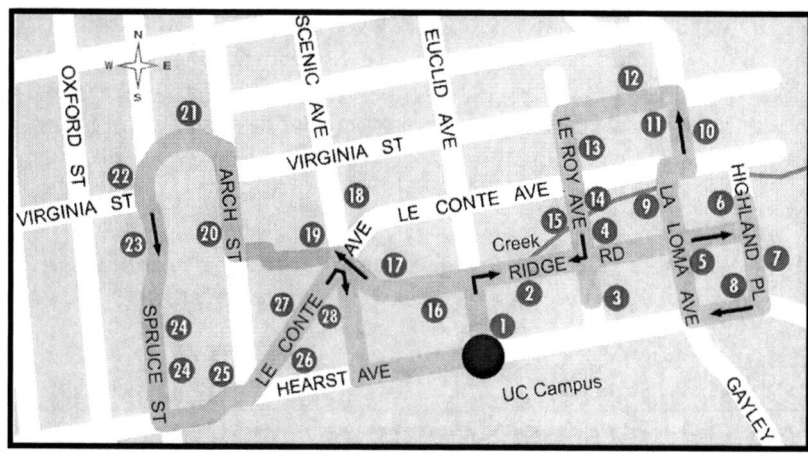

parts of the north side of Hearst serve the neighborhood and UC, with coffee shops and eateries as well as a small grocery store, travel agency, and retail shops. The tree-lined street is pedestrian friendly and intimate.

The commercial area was built after a major fire in 1923 that destroyed a large swath of this area. The first Cody's Books was located here; it became an institution after it moved to Telegraph Avenue. At midblock (1828–34 Euclid), the Spanish-style building has an archway leading to a pleasant courtyard with graceful Chinese elm trees and tables for dining at several different eateries.

At the stop sign, cross and turn right up Ridge Road, noting the Spanish-style Garden Court apartment building on the northeast corner at 1799 Euclid. Midblock on the right is the back of the hulking ❷ **Etcheverry Hall** (mechanical, nuclear, and industrial engineering). Just opposite are the Treehaven Apartments at 2523 Ridge, built in 1909 with an intriguing double-balcony design and bay windows.

Just beyond Etcheverry Hall, going uphill, is Jacobs Hall, home to the Jacobs Institute for Design Innovation. Between Etcheverry Hall and Jacobs Hall, a walkway lined with columns has a large wood and steel trellis overhead. Although it does not provide full protection from the sun or rain, it does create a pleasant ambience.

Turn right at Le Roy Avenue. On the right (west) side is Soda Hall (computer science), with a wall surface of various green-tinted tiles; it is architecturally more attractive than neighboring Etcheverry Hall. Viewed from the building's side, floors step down to the back, windows look out on landscaped terraces, and large arches grace the second floor. On the east side of Le Roy, the ❸ **Goldman School of Public Policy** has a traditional residential architectural look, more in keeping with the historic neighborhood than many off-campus UC buildings. A fine 1893 English Tudor–style home by Ernest Coxhead was demolished on this site to make room for the new building.

Return to Ridge and cross catty-corner to admire buildings on both sides of Ridge. On the northeast corner at ❹ **2601–15 Ridge**— behind the ivy-covered brick retaining wall—is the Allenoke Manor, or Freeman House. Ernest Coxhead designed this clinker-brick 1903 mansion, which is a cross between Georgian and Dutch Colonial styles, with a high-peaked gable and gambrel dormers. The gardens at Allenoke Manor are beautiful, with formal boxwood landscaping and trellises. The house was built for Allen Freeman, a businessman who made his fortune in fruit packing. However, for almost 50 years it was the home of Robert Sibley, a UC professor of mechanical engineering and executive manager of the Cal Alumni Association. Sibley helped found the East Bay Regional Parks District, and Sibley Volcanic Regional Preserve in the Oakland hills is named for him.

Opposite Allenoke Manor at 2600 Ridge is Cloyne Court. Designed by John Galen Howard in 1904, this simple brown-shingle, three-story structure has shallow balconies facing the street and a three-sided courtyard in back. It was an apartment hotel until 1946, when it became university cooperative housing.

Ridge Road is lined with sweetgum trees that put on a long and colorful leaf display in autumn and early winter. Keep going up Ridge past La Loma Avenue to see ❺ **Foothill student housing** on the right. Although the building dates only to 1990, the height and shingled siding puts it in character with neighborhood buildings such as Cloyne Court.

Going up the steep block, look up the wide driveway on the left side between 2705 Ridge and 2709–15 Ridge to see the back of a red house. When you get to the end of Ridge, turn left on Highland Place (marked "Not a Through Street"); the red house on the left, ❻ **1770–90 Highland**, is Bernard Maybeck's first commission and thus gets serious attention from architecture aficionados.

The 1895 house was designed for Charles Keeler, an author, poet, naturalist, and advocate for the arts. In *The Simple Home*, Keeler laid out his ideas for architecture in harmony with nature;

the book was a bible for the Hillside Club, of which Keeler and Maybeck were members. The house eschews unnecessary ornamentation but can hardly be called simple, with a proliferation of gables and various window designs (also oddly shaped interior doors) that give it a charming storybook appearance. The house escaped the great 1923 conflagration and was stuccoed soon after to make it more fire-resistant. Just uphill, 1736 Highland is the Charles Keeler studio from 1902, another Maybeck design. The steeply roofed brown-shingle cottage is relatively unaltered.

This street does not go through, so return to Ridge and continue south on Highland toward campus. On the left, where Ridge comes into Highland, was the longtime home—now gone—of Jackson Stitt Wilson, Berkeley's first socialist mayor. Wilson served from 1911 to 1913 but did not seek re-election due to his frustration with the conservative city council. Midblock on the left (uphill) is the imposing ❼ **Psi Upsilon House** of 1912 by Benjamin McDougall. It is now the Nyingma Institute of Tibetan studies. The color scheme and prayer flags give it an exotic look, belying its original Classical Revival style.

Walk down Highland and turn right at Hearst to see another chapter house, ❽ **Phi Delta Theta** at 2717 Hearst, designed in 1914 by John Reid, Jr., a member of the fraternity and the city architect for San Francisco. The columned veranda of this Italian Renaissance design is grand, and recently the building got a much-needed refurbishing.

A left turn on Hearst up the hill will take you to the gated entrance of the Lawrence Berkeley National Laboratory, a US Department of Energy laboratory with close ties to the university. The lab, which boasts 13 Nobel laureates, was founded in 1931 and employs about 4,200 scientists, staff members, and students. Unfortunately, the 200-acre lab grounds are not open to the public.

Heading down Hearst, you'll pass more of Foothill student housing on both sides, with a foot bridge joining the two sections over Hearst and a large courtyard that you can see through the corner entryway on the right at La Loma. Turn right at the signal onto La Loma footbridge and continue to Ridge. Just after crossing Ridge, look left toward the northwest corner (2627 Ridge/1770 La Loma) at a building that is now apartments but was built as the Phi Kappa Psi Chapter House in 1901 in a shingle style by the fraternity's founder. Although altered over the years, it retains original features such as the triple-peaked third-floor dormer on the La Loma side. Continuing north on La Loma, the next house on the downhill side is a large, white, three-story house, now called **❾ Kingman Hall**, which was a fraternity house from 1914 to 1964, then a virtual hippie commune, and then the Living Love Center. Since 1977, it has been student co-op housing.

At the corner, walk across Le Conte Avenue in the crosswalk. Turn right and immediately left on the next section of La Loma, which is now a one-way street. Walk up the sidewalk on the left side, passing a 1908 house at 2695 Le Conte, somewhat obscured by foliage on the northwest corner, that Julia Morgan designed with Ira Wilson Hoover. When you see the stairs and concrete posts with the number "1715" on the opposite side of La Loma, cross the street and walk up the steps to the sidewalk.

You are now in front of the **❿ Lilian Bridgman House**, 1715 La Loma. Bridgman came from Kansas, earned a master's degree in science at UC in 1893, and then became interested in architecture. She designed this house for herself in 1899 in collaboration with William Knowles and with advice from Maybeck, who was a mentor to many local architects. She re-enrolled at UC to study architecture and in 1915 became one of the first registered female architects in California, designing a number of homes and other buildings in the Bay Area and in Kansas. This house has many elements of the First Bay Tradition style, with a lack of ornamentation, emphasis on natural light, barn shingles, and an interior with redwood paneling. The outward flare of the roof eave and the bargeboard at the bottom of the roofline are notable features in the simple facade.

Continue left up La Loma to Virginia Street. When you reach the stairs, the house to the right (2700 Virginia/1705 La Loma) is the 1905 William Rees House, a First Bay Tradition version of a Swiss chalet with balconies, shutters, and dummy log-ends projecting from the corners. According to some sources, E. A. Hargreaves, an architect who worked for several years in Maybeck's office, designed the house; it is not clear if Maybeck played a role. The house just missed being burned in the 1923 fire.

Take the steps down to the left, cross La Loma, and head downhill on the left side of Virginia. William Knowles designed the house on the corner, **⓫ 1700 La Loma**, in 1900; the first owner was botanist Joseph Burtt Davy, renowned for his work in California, South

Africa, and his native England. Fittingly for the former home of a botanist, the house is mostly hidden by foliage.

As you descend on Virginia, you can catch views of Marin County across the bay when there is no fog. On the right, **⑫ 2661 Virginia** is a Tudor-style house in brick, stucco, and half-timbering. Spanish-style residences are at 2627 Virginia (Alpha Chi Sigma, a co-ed house of mainly chemistry majors) and 2623–21 Virginia. At the end of the long block, cross Le Roy and turn left. The **⑬ Jesuit School of Theology** is on the opposite side at 1735 Le Roy. Around 2004, a large, Colonial Revival–style house and a kooky modern apartment building to the north were extensively remodeled to create the school. This is one of many theology and divinity schools in this area.

Continue on Le Roy and cross Le Conte. The large Spanish-style house at 1756 Le Conte (southwest corner) is part of the Jesuit school. On the left (southeast corner), **⑭ Weltevreden**, at 1755 Le Roy, is also known as Moody House and Tellefsen Hall. A. C. Schweinfurth designed the house as a clinker-brick Dutch Colonial with a stepped gable in 1896. A talented architect, Schweinfurth died of typhoid in 1900 at the age of 36. In 1957, UC

The William Rees House, in Swiss chalet style.

architect Michael Goodman destroyed and remodeled the upper portion; only the exterior wall of the ground floor and the bridge are original. For a time, this was the home of pictorialist photographer Oscar Maurer and his wife Margaret Robinson Maurer, one of the founders of the Hillside Club. A fraternity house in the 1920s, the building is now a residence for members of the UC marching band.

A little farther along on the right, just beyond where the sidewalk temporarily ends for a narrow bridge, is the 1907 **15 Oscar Maurer Studio** at 1772 Le Roy. Maybeck designed this eclectic building as a photographic studio, with a side elevation that rambles down above the north fork of Strawberry Creek. A row of bright flags hangs above the stream.

The skinny live oak tree in the middle of Le Roy would have been on the much larger grounds of Allenoke Manor, between the mansion and the carriage house. Maybeck's wife Annie saved the original large live oak tree from pavers; when that tree died, it was replaced by a young oak. When you are about in line with the tree, look to the west, or downhill, between two residences to glimpse— behind several buildings—the original red-brick carriage house of the large Allenoke estate (now subdivided and bisected by Le Roy).

Turn right at the next intersection to walk down Ridge, passing the old wrought-iron Allenoke carriage house gate at 2533–35 Ridge, now in front of an apartment building. (To shorten the walk and return to the starting point, turn left on Euclid.)

Cross Euclid and walk west uphill on the right (north) side of Ridge. On the opposite side, the goofy modern **16 Berkeley Student Cooperative** is at 2424 Ridge; next to it, at 2422 Ridge, is Casa Zimbabwe, another student housing cooperative. The older stucco and half-timbered part of the building on the right was originally a home designed by John Galen Howard. The south side of the street is lined with tall Mexican Washingtonia fan palm trees, lending Berkeley a tropical feeling on warm days.

This area features seminaries and theological schools that are part of the Graduate Theological Union. Founded in 1963, the union is the largest such partnership, with nine member schools and 11 multifaith or interdisciplinary centers. Although some are located farther afield in Berkeley or the Bay Area, the main concentration is in this area—hence, some locals refer to this area as Holy Hill.

The Church Divinity School of the Pacific's **17 Gibbs Hall and All Saints Chapel** are at 2449 Ridge. Walter Ratcliff, Jr., designed this charming 1929 brick Gothic Revival hall and 1937 chapel, which are connected by a short, Gothic-arched, covered walkway. Across the street is the colorful Graduate Theological Union Library, designed by modernist architect Louis Kahn in 1974; it has landscaped terraces and an attractive interior atrium (viewable by the public if the library is open). The Dominican School of Philosophy and Theology, in Tudor Revival style, is at 2401 Ridge; it was designed by Stafford Jory in 1923 and rebuilt in the original style in 2006.

Cross Scenic and then Le Conte catty-corner toward the Pacific School of Religion campus, part of the Graduate Theological Union. Before entering, turn around to look across and to the left (north) down Scenic at the **⑱ University Christian Church**. Ratcliff also designed this 1931 brick English-parish Gothic church with an imposing squarish tower. The largest redwood beams in Berkeley support the roof of the nave. It is now home to Zaytuna College, the first Muslim liberal arts college in the United States.

Enter the campus at 1798 Scenic. On the right is **⑲ Holbrook Hall**. Also designed by Ratcliff and serving as a library and administration building, the 1925 English-collegiate Gothic design has rusticated stonewalls with buttresses and ornate finials on top.

Holbrook Hall, in Collegiate Gothic style, at the Pacific School of Religion.

Inside the library wing (which projects forward on the right) are a huge chandelier, massive roof beams, and a large Tudor fireplace.

Walk across the campus, past buildings with Tudor elements (such as half-timbering) on the left and a 1980 modernist gray building by Charles Stickney. Descend the steps at the end, taking the fork to the right; when you get to the paved driveway, cross and go down another set of steps to Arch Street. Cross and go right. The Spanish-style house at ㉚ **1750 Arch** has Moorish-arched windows; wide, sloping corbels on the main floor; and Islamic-style glazed tile on the second and ground floors on the left side of the facade (partly hidden by a tree).

Proceed right and downhill, turning left on Virginia. Across the street, the one-story house at 2275 Virginia was for many years the ㉑ **home of Josephine Miles**, a poet and literary critic. The first tenured woman in the UC English department, she founded the *Berkeley Poetry Review* and was a champion of the Beat poets, helping Allen Ginsberg publish "Howl." 2274 Virginia is a charming stucco house with some Spanish features and an unusual entryway.

Turn left on Spruce Street. Across the street at 1650 Spruce is the ㉒ **William Acheson House**, one of a pair of side-by-side 1923 Prairie School designs by James Plachek, who also designed Berkeley's main library.

Continue on Spruce past Virginia. At 1730 Spruce, the 1914 ㉓ **Loring House** was designed by John Hudson Thomas and is one of the best examples of Prairie School architecture in the Bay Area. The design is clearly influenced by Frank Lloyd Wright's published prototype plans, although Thomas added his own touches. Details include a low sloping roof with wide eaves, a horizontal emphasis, bands of windows with delicate muntins, and some decorative vertical elements. Farther along on the left are two older multi-unit developments: a Colonial Revival at 1739–59 Spruce with five townhouse-style, two-story residences; and a Spanish style at 1761–77 Spruce with nine detached cottages. Both are built around landscaped entry courtyards, a civilized approach to dense residential design.

㉔ **Normandy Village** is at 1781–1813 and 1817–49 Spruce. This whimsical collection of apartment houses in a Hansel and Gretel style was designed by a master of the genre, William R. Yelland, as well as the developer Jack Thornburg. Yelland designed the initial and most striking part of the complex at 1835–49 Spruce in 1926,

A detail of Loring House, in Prairie style.

and Thornburg designed subsequent sections from 1927 to 1928 in a similar style. Thornburg designed and developed many storybook houses in Berkeley (he later became a decorated wartime pilot). The crazily exaggerated gables, curving stairways, frescoes, interesting brick and stone work, spiral chimneys, and humorously carved gargoyles on beam ends may seem Disneyesque, but the village has superb craftsmanship; historically authentic construction materials were used to achieve the Norman style.

Built in the 1950s, the middle section, 1815 Spruce, was designed by a less-talented hand than the surrounding buildings. The Yelland structures beyond this are impressive, giving the feeling of an ancient village, with each unit unique. Yelland also designed Tupper & Reed's original music store, now a cocktail bar, in a similar style at 2271 Shattuck Avenue. This is a private residential complex, so please view it from the Spruce sidewalk.

At Hearst, turn left and walk uphill toward the signal, passing nondescript, modern campus buildings on the right and an attractive **㉕ Tudor-style apartment building** at the corner of Arch and Hearst (1890 Arch), with brick, stucco, wood window framing, and fine-looking bay windows. Cross Arch and Le Conte at the signal to

Normandy Village, a storybook-style wonderland.

see the 1936 ㉖ **Streamline Moderne residence** at 2300 LeConte. This triangular building between Hearst and Le Conte has curved rooms that make it seem like a ship; it was the long-time home of Ernest Callenbach, a writer, social thinker, and film critic probably best known for his books on sustainable living, including *Ecotopia* and *Ecotopia Emerging*.

Walk up steep Le Conte. A lovely ㉗ **Maybeck house** with a red tile roof is on the left at 2357 Le Conte, set back from the street amid the trees. The house was built in 1924 for the dean of the UC law school on the site of a Maybeck design that was lost in the 1923 fire.

The 1902 Colonial Revival house by Ernest Coxhead at 2368 Le Conte was briefly the **㉘ home of Phoebe Apperson Hearst**, a philanthropist, feminist, and suffragist who married George Hearst in 1862. He made a fortune in mining and became a US Senator. Their son, William Randolph Hearst, built a newspaper empire as well as Hearst Castle at San Simeon; he was the model for Citizen Kane in the Orson Welles film of the same name. Phoebe Hearst was a generous donor to UC Berkeley, as well as to causes such as the Baha'i Faith. She founded the Phoebe A. Hearst Museum of Anthropology on the UC Berkeley campus and donated more than 60,000 objects, many from her own expeditions. She was the first female regent of the university, serving from 1897 until her death in 1919.

Turn right on Scenic, which is lined on the west side with tall palms. At 1816 Scenic, a reception hall designed in 1902 by Ernest Coxhead is linked to the Phoebe Apperson Hearst home you just passed. William Charles Hays, a long-time UC professor of architecture, designed a second floor and other alterations in 1910. It is now part of the New Bridge Foundation, a drug and alcohol treatment center. The original entryway—with a large lantern—remains.

At 1820 Scenic, another part of the New Bridge Foundation is housed in a Berkeley brown-shingle designed in 1900 by Edgar A. Matthews for Benjamin Ide Wheeler, UC president from 1899 to 1919. The house, which has a handsome glassed-in porch, was significantly altered in 1911, according to the Berkeley Architectural Heritage Association.

Continue down Scenic and turn left at Hearst to return to the starting point at Euclid. Alternatively, to go to the Downtown Berkeley BART station, turn right and walk down Hearst for several blocks, then turn left on Shattuck.

❋ ❋ ❋

WALK 4

THE SOUTH SIDE OF CAMPUS

Overview: The walk includes student dorms and apartments, commercial buildings, historic homes, People's Park, and architectural masterpieces such as Bernard Maybeck's First Church of Christ, Scientist. It is easy, with minimal elevation gain and moderate traffic on some streets.

Highlights:
- UC student area
- Historic Telegraph Avenue and People's Park
- Mishmash of old and new, including architectural gems by Maybeck and Morgan

Distance: 1.1–2.8 miles
Time: 1–2 hours
Elevation gain: 100–200 feet

Start at 2301 Telegraph Avenue at the southeast corner of Bancroft Way, opposite the bustling entrance to the UC Berkeley campus. The starting point is just over a half-mile from the Downtown Berkeley BART station and near several AC Transit bus lines, including the 1 and the 51B.

On this corner is ❶ **El Granada Building**, built in 1905 in Mission Revival style; its characteristic curving gables were restored in 1995 with sculptural ornamentation. This historic apartment building across from the UC campus was part of an upscale development that advertised quality two- to four-bedroom apartments

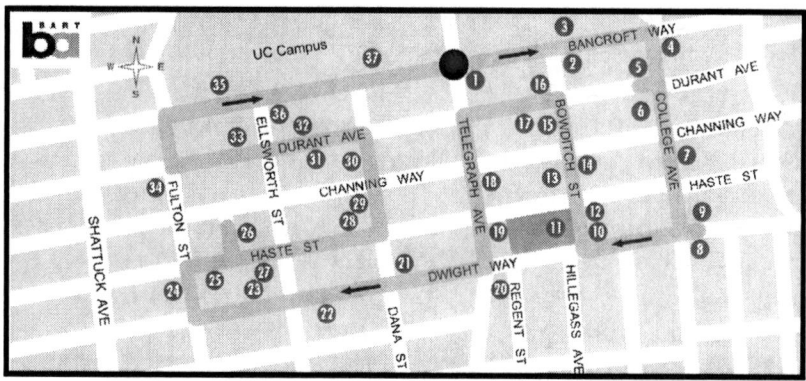

renting for $13 to $30 a month when it opened in the early 20th century. It anchors this corner well.

Walk east up Bancroft toward the hills. Julia Morgan—probably best known for designing Hearst Castle in San Simeon—designed the 1940 Fred Turner Building at 2546–54 Bancroft. The building once had an open courtyard, and it still has attractive features, including large, multipaned windows. The south side of Bancroft here is lined with Chinese elms, a semideciduous tree with tiny leaves, graceful curving trunks and branches, and scaly bark in grays and tans.

Continue up Bancroft. At the southeast corner of Bowditch Street is the ❷ **University YWCA**, designed by Joseph Esherick in 1958. The simple but elegant design includes exposed beams and "stick work" on the walls and balcony, beautiful window detailing, large trellises, a side courtyard, and another courtyard inside.

Maybeck and Morgan—Berkeley's two most famous architects—designed the building across the street, the 1927 ❸ **Phoebe Apperson Hearst Memorial Gymnasium for Women**. William Randolph Hearst donated funds to build the gym in memory of his mother, a major university benefactor. In addition to sporting facilities, the complex includes places to eat and rest such as terraces and courtyards. The design includes elements of Classical architecture, but in the eclectic style so common to these two architects (who both studied at the École des Beaux-Arts in Paris). The unique marble north pool features classical statuary and is a nonstandard 33 1/3 yards long; one theory for why it was not built to the more common lengths of 25 yards or 50 meters (the latter is Olympic size) is that the odd size discouraged men from using the elegant and beautiful facility. Lion-faced urns surround the building. (More of the building is visible as you walk up Bancroft.)

On the right, the Berkeley Art Museum, completed in 1970 and designed by Mario Ciampi, is a prime example of Brutalist-style design and construction in steel and concrete. Brutalist architecture was popular in the 1950s–70s, mainly for government and university buildings. It features massive, fortress-like construction, usually with exposed concrete to express strength and functionality. Many critics find it cold, and it often weathers poorly.

The collection began in 1963 with a donation of 47 paintings and $250,000 from painter/teacher Hans Hofmann. It currently encompasses more than 14,000 art objects, from early American to abstract expressionism and other modern trends, as well as an important Asian section. Seismically unsound, the Berkeley Art Museum is being replaced by a new museum, slated for completion in 2016, at Oxford and Center streets in downtown Berkeley; the museum on Bancroft closed in December 2014, and the building's future is uncertain.

Farther up, at 2680 Bancroft, is the landmarked College Women's Club, now the boutique bed-and-breakfast Bancroft Hotel. The 1928 Mediterranean-style building has innovative design details by Walter T. Steilberg, including geometric stained-glass windows and columns that are rounded but not precisely circular.

On the corner of Bancroft at College Avenue is Caffe Strada, a popular restaurant with outdoor seating, trees, hedges, wooden railings, and planter boxes. Just across College is the English Tudor-style ❹ **Westminster House**. Walter Ratcliff, Jr., designed this building, originally the Presbyterian campus ministry, in 1926. It is a delightful structure with a colorful shingle roof, half-timbering, tall windows, a Gothic entrance, and complex massing (the shape of the exterior). An addition behind is deferential to the historic structure. The complex is now used for undergraduate housing and is known as The Berk.

Turn right on College. At Durant Avenue, turn right and walk a bit to see the impressive 1916 Tudor-style Delta Deuteron chapter of the ❺ **Theta Delta Chi fraternity** at 2647 Durant on the corner, with half-timbering and a two-story bay window. Next to it at 2639 Durant is the Theta Xi fraternity, in a dark-shingled 1897 Colonial Revival home originally built for UC English professor and early environmentalist Cornelius Beach Bradley.

Return to College, cross Durant (to the right), and continue walking south into an area of high-density student housing. On the block between Durant and Channing Way, look across the street to 2333 College. Michael Pyatok designed the Ida Louise Jackson Graduate House. One of the more attractive recent buildings in the area, it incorporates traditional Craftsman elements and has an attractive corner tower.

On this side of the block is the first of four older university residence halls (the whole block is known as **6** **Unit 1**); they are typical mid-20th century towers built in modern International style in 1958 and designed by Warnecke and Warnecke. Architects who designed in this style, which started in the 1920s and became widespread after World War II, disdained ornamentation. However, the designs became so boring that architects often added large elements such as open screens of geometric concrete to hide mostly blank walls. In the case of these buildings, the screens were removed during a seismic retrofit, making the buildings even less attractive. The horizontal piece around the roofline seems only to serve the purpose of ornamentation.

Cross Channing and look down the street to see newer dormitories between the older towers, done in an edgy modern style with metal, cement, and panels of other materials that relate to the pedestrian-oriented streets. The dorms were designed by EHDD, a San Francisco–based architecture firm founded by Joe Esherick and Associates. There's a row of extremely tall California Washingtonia fan palms on Channing on the right.

Past Channing, Underhill Field, on the right, was built over a parking garage—an example of the efficient use of land to alleviate population growth. Across the street at 2409 College is the landmarked 1913 **7** **Channing Apartments**. Designed by Walter Ratcliff, Jr., the building mixes Craftsman (exposed wooden rafters and brackets), Mediterranean (tile roof), and Classical design elements (impressive arched entranceway).

Continue along College past Haste Street, which has more university residence halls on the right (Unit 2) in the same 1958 design as Unit 1, two blocks back. On the southeast corner of College and Dwight Way is **8** **Newman Hall**, in the Brutalist style. Ciampi designed this building in raw concrete for the university's Roman Catholic community in 1966.

Cross College and walk up Dwight on the left side to 2709 Dwight, the ❾ **Bishop Berkeley Apartments**. Designed by William H. Weeks in 1928, the brick apartments have impressive ornamentation over the Gothic entranceway and decorative wrought iron near the base of the large first-floor windows.

Return to College, cross the street, and continue down Dwight. At the corner of Dwight and Bowditch Street is ❿ **First Church of Christ, Scientist**, considered by many to be Bernard Maybeck's masterpiece. Called "one of the three finest uniquely American churches in the United States" by the American Institute of Architects, the 1910 church is a National Historic Landmark. Maybeck used industrial siding materials and window framing to save money, yet the elegant building mixes Gothic, Mediterranean, Japanese, Renaissance, and Byzantine styles in a way that only Maybeck could pull off. The trellises and wisteria (blooming in spring) further soften the look. The interior is stunning and can be seen the first Sunday of each month when Friends of First Church offer tours at 12:15 pm (www.friendsoffirstchurch.org). Henry Gutterson designed the Sunday school and office (completed in 1927) along Dwight to the right of the sanctuary in a manner that complements the church.

The First Church of Christ, Scientist, by Bernard Maybeck.

Look across Dwight to see the American Baptist Seminary of the West (formerly the Berkeley Baptist Divinity School). The 1919 Hobart Hall, at the corner of Dwight and Hillegass, was designed by Julia Morgan. The brick Tudor features ornamented bay windows, red-trimmed window frames, and fine Gothic details. Ratcliff and his son, Robert Ratcliff, added the other buildings from 1949 to 1964 to create a complex similar to a medieval cloister.

Turn right on Bowditch to pass the side of the First Church of Christ, Scientist; ⓫ **People's Park** is across the street. In 1968, the university demolished structures on this block to build dormitories, but community members wanted to create a park instead. UC tried to close off the area with a fence, but a park became a cause célèbre, with marches and demonstrations to support the effort. In May 1969, one of the demonstrations turned into a riot, and a student named James Rector was fatally shot. UC eventually gave up, and the land became a de facto park; homeless people primarily utilize it now. Over the years, the university has made several attempts to develop the property, but community opposition (which has included marches and riots) has prevented substantial changes.

Continue north on Bowditch. On the southeast corner of Bowditch and Haste is the 1939 ⓬ **Vedanta Society temple**, designed by Henry Gutterson. The Vedanta Society was founded in the United States in 1894 by a visiting swami. It follows one of the six orthodox schools of Indian Hindu philosophy; more recently, it has been spiritually affiliated with the Indian Ramakrishna order. When the temple was first proposed, conservative Christian residents strongly opposed the building. In the end, this simple and attractive Mediterranean-style building with a Romanesque entry and lotus window was built—it does not seem too menacing!

Across Haste at the northeast corner, an older apartment building, the Spanish-style Casa Bonita from 1928, was the home of Josephine Miles in the early 1940s. A well-known poet and literary critic, Miles was the first woman tenured professor in the UC English department, founded the Berkeley *Poetry Review*, and helped Allen Ginsberg get his most famous poem, "Howl," published.

Continue on Bowditch. Just after crossing Haste, ⓭ **2420 Bowditch,** on the left, is a large complex of brown-shingle buildings by Soule Edgar Fisher, completed in 1892, with additional buildings by Ratcliff built between 1911 and 1927. Originally the

Anna Head School, the main building is believed to be the first brown-shingle building in Berkeley, a style that was enthusiastically adopted for residences throughout the city. Anna Head founded a private school for girls in 1887; the school continued here under subsequent owners until 1964. Tennis stars Helen Wills Moody and Helen Hull Jacobs, artist Claire Falkenstein, and actress Jane Connell were graduates. UC acquired the property by eminent domain and the school moved to the Oakland hills in 1964, merging with Royce, its affiliated boys school; in 1979, it became the Head-Royce School.

These superb Arts and Crafts–style buildings could use some TLC. They are utilized by the Institute for the Study of Societal Issues and by the UC Miller Institute for Basic Research in Science, named after Adolph C. Miller, a UC alumni, professor, and high-ranking government official who set up a trust to establish the institute after his death in 1953; former fellows include Carl Sagan. New residence halls were built on the west side of the property in 2012. On the southwest corner of Bowditch and Channing, the tall trees are a unique type of eucalyptus with dark bark and red flowers, unfortunately prone to falling over.

On the right at 2415 Bowditch is UC Berkeley's **⓮ Crossroads dining facility**, the first certified-organic kitchen on a college campus and Cal's first green-certified building. The 2001 building by Dworsky Associates uses metal, frosted glass, and stone; the curving roofline, as well as surrounding redwoods and other trees, further enhance the design.

Catty-corner from Crossroads at Bowditch and Channing (2547 Channing), is a large, shingled 1899 Colonial Revival house with a round, sizable bay and turret as well as unique small windows. William Mooser, who designed the house, also did most of the Ghirardelli chocolate factory in San Francisco. Continue across Channing; on the left, 2350 Bowditch, a charming 1930 **⓯ storybook cottage**, has a stone and brick chimney. The university moved the landmarked house here from Channing Way in 2001 to make way for a redevelopment project. The cottage, designed by Carl Fox, is called Rose Bertaux Cottage or Fox Cottage. Fox was a UC mining engineering graduate who, with his brothers, designed and built numerous charming homes in Berkeley, including the city landmarks Fox Common and Fox Court on University Avenue, also in storybook style.

Continue to the corner of Durant and Bowditch. The Durant Hotel, with its front entrance on Durant, has Spanish-style design elements and claimed to be the city's only luxury hotel when built in 1928. The hotel received unwanted renown in 1990 when a deranged gunman killed 1 man, wounded 7 people, and held 33 hostages in the corner pub for seven hours, until police shot him and rescued the hostages.

Look across the street to the northeast corner of Durant and Bowditch; the 1933 Christian Science Organization designed by Henry Gutterson has diamond-paned windows and other Gothic features. Turn left and walk downhill. Across the street with a large cross in front, a small but unique 1974 church and seminary, **16 St. Joseph of Arimathea Chapel**, designed by William Dutcher, has an orange stucco facade and barrel-vault roof. As you walk past, peek around the left side to see where the modern building is attached to an 1881 cottage behind.

17 Top Dog at 2534 Durant, a Berkeley institution since 1966, serves a variety of sausages. At 2520 Durant, the 1911 neoclassical Beau (Blue) Sky Hotel—originally a women's boarding house called the Brasfield—is reminiscent of an antebellum Southern mansion, with colonnaded verandas. On the corner at 2500 Durant, is the five-story, red-brick Cambridge Apartments, designed by Ratcliff in 1914 in Italian Renaissance style.

Continue to Telegraph Avenue. Originally the main route linking Oakland to Berkeley, Telegraph has been the scene of numerous demonstrations and protest marches over the years. Despite its scruffy image, the four- to five-block stretch extending south from Sproul Plaza on the UC campus is a destination for student eating and shopping (famous for book and music stores), with sidewalk vendors selling jewelry, clothing, T-shirts, and crafts.

Turn left and walk south on Telegraph. On the southeast corner with Channing, the 1923 building at 2409 Telegraph, with its pilasters, colorful signage, and terra-cotta ornamentation, houses **18 Rasputin Music** on the ground floor. Stop at the next corner, Haste. The vacant lot on the left is all that remains after fires in 1986 and 1990 destroyed the Berkeley Inn, though there are plans for a new building here. Across Telegraph, another fire in 2011 gutted a large mixed-use building that included busy Raleigh's Bar and Grill and Cafe Intermezzo. The building was promptly demolished; construction began for a new mixed-use structure in 2014.

The *People's History of Telegraph Avenue* mural on Haste at Telegraph.

Catty-corner on the southwest corner at 2454 Telegraph is the former Cody's Books building, home to the beloved bookshop for more than four decades; it closed in 2008. In 2015, the building was renovated and turned into a food and entertainment venue called the Mad Monk Center for Anachronistic Media.

⑲ Amoeba Music, which claims to be the world's largest independent record store, is on the southeast corner at 2455 Telegraph, with a mural on the Haste side wall. Designed by Osha Neumann and painted by three artists in 1976, the mural commemorates the Free Speech Movement and turbulent times at nearby People's Park. Continuing on Telegraph, three-story Moe's Books—founded in 1959 and selling new, used, and rare books—is across the street at 2476 Telegraph. Moe was a fixture at the front desk with his ever-present cigar until his death in 1997; the business is still family-owned and operated.

This is a good stopping place if you would like to explore the shops on Telegraph, return to the starting point, and pick up the tour's second half on another day.

If you decide to continue the walk, cross Telegraph to the right and view from the corner of Telegraph and Dwight the assemblage of ㉔ **historic commercial buildings** catty-corner on the left (east) side of Telegraph just south of Dwight; three of the first four buildings are city landmarks. A. Dodge Coplin designed the well-preserved 1901 Colonial Revival commercial building with round corner bay windows at 2501 Telegraph (2502 Dwight). Next door at 2509–13 Telegraph, is the three-story Soda Water Works Building, (later the Telegraph Repertory Theater), built in 1888 and expanded in 1905. On May 15, 1969 ("Bloody Thursday"), James Rector was shot and killed by Alameda County deputy sheriffs while innocently watching People's Park demonstrations from the roof of this building.

The building at 2517 Telegraph is a modern hodgepodge, and 2525 Telegraph is one of the three city landmarks. Completed in 1907 with Mission Revival elements, it became an important location for Berkeley's Japanese-American community. From 1939 to 1941, it housed the studio and art supply store of Chiura Obata, who taught at UC and promoted the appreciation of nature and blending of Japanese and Western art traditions in both his art and his teaching; his wife Haruko was a respected teacher of Japanese ikebana flower arranging. He closed the studio and store after Pearl Harbor was attacked in 1941 and a gunshot was fired into the store; the Obatas were subsequently sent to an internment camp, they returned to Berkeley after the war, and Chiura resumed teaching at Cal.

Walk right (west) to 2437 Dwight on the right; the restaurant (Joshu-ya Brasserie) is an Italianate building, circa 1869, one of the oldest in the city; the front is an addition. Continue down this noisy stretch of Dwight. On the right, just before Dana Street (2401 Dwight), is Maybeck's ㉑ **Town and Gown Club**, built in 1899. Exposed structural elements of the brown-shingle building serve as ornamentation, such as the outriggers supporting the roof. Founded by Emmanuel Marie Paget, the women's club has been in existence here for more than 100 years.

Continue on Dwight; past Dana, look across the street to 2338 Dwight and its neighbor 2336 Dwight, two cute Victorian cottages between drab 1960s apartment buildings. At 2314 Dwight, the ㉒ **Judge Benjamin Ferris House**—built circa 1867—reveals its antiquity despite alterations in various styles; a few rounded-top Italianate windows remain from the original edifice. This was the first location of Alta Bates Hospital, an eight-bed sanitarium for women founded by nurse Alta Alice Miner Bates in 1905 that grew to become Berkeley's main hospital (now located on Ashby Avenue).

Walk on to Ellsworth Street. On the corner, the 1920s Picardo Arms Apartments, 2491 Ellsworth, has six floors, quite tall for that period in this neighborhood. With Spanish-style design elements in the stucco ornamentation and four-story window bays, it holds up well against the 1960s-era apartment buildings in the area.

Cross Ellsworth to see the 1895 Colonial Revival with red shingles on the northwest corner at 2247 Dwight. Across the street at 2248 Dwight, a slightly altered 1878 Italianate house can be seen behind a small storefront that was added later. At 2239 Dwight, the 1892 **㉓ Victorian house** by George Embry has quirky windows in the octagonal turret; the style is more Stick than Queen Anne, despite the home's completion date. At 2226–28 Dwight, cottages were built facing a driveway, reminiscent of early highway motor courts.

Turn right on Fulton Street. The housing across the street on the northwest corner from 2002 fits in with the historic style and scale of the neighborhood much better than the 1960s apartments in the 2300 block of Dwight. Continuing on Fulton, several 1880s' **㉔ Victorian cottages** on the left at 2430, 2426, and 2424 Fulton are well maintained and good examples of restoration and reuse. All have either added an in-law cottage or been raised up to accommodate additional residential units. The latter two are city landmarks; 2430 Dwight is a Queen Anne with lots of spindle work and a wrought-iron fence.

Cross Haste and turn right (east). Across the street, the big gray 1914 **㉕ Colonial Revival mansion** at 2214 Haste has a wealth of fine detail and a variety of window designs; it was nicely fixed up and painted in 2013.

Take a short diversion left on Atherton Street to view several Colonial Revival houses on the left (west) side that are surprisingly intact for this area. The grounds of the **㉖ Harold E. Jones Child Study Center** are opposite at 2425 Atherton. The center was founded in 1927 by the Institute of Child Welfare to provide a quality nursery school for children while giving scholars and students access to a young population for observation and research. Now affiliated with the UC Berkeley Institute of Human Development, the center moved here in 1960. The buildings were designed by Joseph Esherick in cooperation with UC Berkeley psychology professor Catherine Landreth and Harold E. Jones, the center's first director of research. In 2013, it was landmarked for its historic and architectural importance.

Toward the end of the block was the home—now gone— of William Keith, an artist renowned for watercolors and oils, primarily landscapes. In the late 19th century, the house he lived in with his wife May McHenry Keith was a gathering place for artists and writers of bohemian Berkeley. A street in the Berkeley hills is named for Keith.

Return to Haste, turn left, and continue a short distance to 2232 Haste, once the **㉗ compound of the Brower family**. David Brower grew up here and went on to become a pioneering environmental leader and conservationist; as a young man, he helped develop modern rock-climbing techniques and planted the redwood tree that towers over the front yard. Later he was executive director of the Sierra Club and founded the Earth Island Institute. In 2014, the buildings were renovated for use as apartments.

Continue up Haste past Ellsworth, noting the diverse older apartment building facades at 2320 and 2322 Haste. Continue past the tennis courts—built over a parking lot on the left—to 2339 Haste, the **㉘ Haste Street Child Development Center**. This modern building has wood siding and numerous windows, including pop-up dormers that bring in lots of light.

At the southwest corner of Haste and Dana Street is the First Baptist Church of Berkeley, with an impressive 1914 Beaux-Arts–style entrance and windows on the Dana Street side. Cross Haste and turn left (north) on Dana. On the southwest corner of Dana and Channing, 2400 Dana is a **㉙ Queen Anne Victorian** by George Embry from 1892—altered but still recognizable with lots of ornamentation. The house was featured in interior scenes in the 1967 movie *The Graduate*.

At Channing, look right to see numerous sweetgum trees lining the street; they turn brilliant red in late autumn. Continue past Channing to the **㉚ First Congregational Church of Berkeley**, on the left. Designed by Horace G. Simpson, the 1925 red-brick complex could have been transplanted from New England. Also notice the large clock/bell tower. The elegant sanctuary has excellent acoustics for musical performances.

Turn left on Durant; across the street is the 1928 Trinity United Methodist Church in Gothic Revival style, with a large tower. The

The McCreary-Greer House, in Colonial Revival style.

abundance of churches around campus is a reminder that Berkeley has one of the highest concentrations of churches in the Bay Area.

The 1901 **31** **McCreary-Greer House** at 2318 Durant is a superb Colonial Revival mansion featuring a beautiful old ornamented wood door with oval beveled windows, a third-floor dormer, Ionian columns, and a striking Palladian window with stained glass. It even has the original carriage house in back. The house is now home to the Berkeley Architectural Heritage Association.

Across the street at 2315 Durant is the **32** **Berkeley City Club**. Originally the Berkeley Women's City Club and financed entirely by Berkeley women, this Julia Morgan design from 1929 is on the National Register of Historic Places. Gothic and Romanesque styles are mixed in handsome fashion; the style is sometimes called Italian Renaissance. Morgan was masterful at creating unique buildings using elements of various traditions. The interior has a number of beautiful features, including a restaurant, short- and long-term lodgings, a spectacular indoor pool, and two courtyards. The restaurant is open to the public (reservations needed) and free public tours are held the fourth Sunday of every month from 1 to 3:30 p.m., except in December. Events can be arranged, but otherwise it is a private club and hotel. Toward the end of the block, three large camphor trees line the street on the left; the bright green or red leaves are fragrant when crushed.

Continue walking on Durant past Ellsworth. Several historic buildings are on the left, including the simple and elegant 1914 Colonna Apartments at 2236 Durant, also designed by Julia Morgan, with rounded window frames. Across the street on the right, the ㉝ **University Health Services Tang Center**, a 1991 building by Anshen + Allen, features Craftsman elements in a modern design that blends old and new with striking aqua details.

Julia Morgan's Berkeley City Club.

At the southwest corner of Durant and Fulton, the ㉞ **former Howard Automobile Company Buick showroom** was housed in a 1930 Art Deco building. Charles Howard made a fortune as a Buick dealer, but his biggest claim to fame was as owner of the legendary racehorse Seabiscuit, about which books have been written and movies have been made. Restored and added onto in 2006, the building now houses the Buddhist Churches of America's Jodo Shinshu Center, a member of the Graduate Theological Union.

Turn right on Fulton and then right on Bancroft one block later. UC's ㉟ **Edwards Stadium and Goldman Field**, on the north side of Bancroft, opened in 1932 as the only exclusively track field in the United States. Numerous records have been established here.

Spotlight: Joseph Esherick (1914–1998)

Joseph Esherick taught at UC Berkeley for 33 years beginning in 1952, eventually becoming chair of the architecture school (1976–1982). He received the prestigious Gold Medal of the American Institute of Architects in 1989. Esherick's designs and teaching were tremendously influential in contemporary architecture and architectural education.

Perhaps most admired for his residential architecture, Esherick was sensitive to site, climate, and client needs while avoiding preconceived ideologies; he was also a mentor to a generation of architects. His inspiration was his uncle Wharton Esherick, a sculptor and woodworker whose legacy to his nephew was an appreciation for the nature of materials and the wisdom of vernacular architecture, which is architecture based on local needs, materials, and traditions.

Born in Philadelphia, Esherick studied the University of Pennsylvania's rigorous Beaux-Arts architecture curriculum. Arriving to the Bay Area in 1937, he initially worked with Gardner A. Dailey, an innovative architect.

Along with William Wurster, Vernon DeMars, and others, Esherick helped transform the architecture school into the trend-setting College of Environmental Design (CED) in 1959; the CED integrated the architecture, landscape architecture, city planning, and environmental planning disciplines into a single, self-contained college. He was part of a team that designed the Brutalist but well-loved Wurster Hall as the home for the CED (1964).

In 1963, Esherick formed Joseph Esherick and Associates, a partnership with George Homsey, Peter Dodge, and Charles Davis; in 1972, the firm became EHDD (Esherick, Homsey, Dodge, and Davis). EHDD is still going strong and is well known for projects such as the Monterey Bay Aquarium and the Cannery in San Francisco.

A 2007 book on Esherick's residential design by CED faculty member E. Marc Treib is aptly titled *Appropriate*. Esherick designed some of the original trend-setting houses at Sea Ranch along the Sonoma Coast (including some with living roofs). In Berkeley, his work is part of the Second Bay Tradition (a classification he did not apply to himself), building on the legacy of earlier Bay Area architects with modern design elements and increased emphasis on building in harmony with locale.

Berkeley residential designs include Lyon House on Hillcrest Road, Hewlett House at 2727 Marin Avenue, and Ackerman House at 3 Greenwood Common. He also designed the Pelican Building on the UC campus, the University YWCA at 2600 Bancroft Way, and the Harold E. Jones Child Study Center at 2425 Atherton St. All three are city landmarks. ✷✷

In 1999, the Art Deco stadium also became home of UC men's and women's soccer.

Walk up Bancroft to Ellsworth (with the stadium and UC Recreational Sports Facility on the left). **36** **St. Mark's Episcopal Church** on the southeast corner is a splendid Mission Revival building by William Curlett, completed in 1901 (it's interesting that Episcopalians would commission their church in a style identified so closely with Spanish Catholics). It has twin bell towers and beautiful Tiffany stained-glass windows.

Farther along, at 2334–38 Bancroft, are the nicely restored Bancroft House apartments. In front of 2362 Bancroft is a row of Japanese cherry blossom trees that bloom in March. On the corner with Dana at 2398 Bancroft, Wesley House student housing features traditional design elements that complement the historic Trinity United Methodist Church on Dana.

Across the street on the UC campus, after you pass Dana, is the 1898 **37** **First Unitarian Church**, with brown shingles, a long roofline, a huge circular window, and redwood columns with bark still on them. The talented architect, A. C. Schweinfurth, died at a young age from typhoid.

University Press Books, at 2430 Bancroft, is in a building on the right next to a parking lot with a mural showing an idealized Bay Area nature scene. Continue on up Bancroft one block to the starting point.

WALK 5
MAYBECK COUNTRY

✳ ✳ ✳

Overview: This walk starts in the Berkeley flats, then moves uphill (with a few short, steep stretches) to Bernard Maybeck's home ground. On the way, you will explore the Berkeley Rose Garden and unique residential communities such as Rose Walk and Greenwood Common.

Highlights:
- Variety of Maybeck creations
- Diverse historic architecture
- Rose Walk, Berkeley Rose Garden

Distance: 2.7–3.0 miles
Time: 2–3 hours
Elevation gain: 560–660 feet

✳ ✳ ✳

Start at the northwest corner of Cedar and Oxford streets, accessible from AC Transit (including lines 18 and 52) or about a 10-minute walk from the Downtown Berkeley BART station. Street parking is available, but be mindful of two-hour time limits on most days.

Walk north (with the hills to your right) on the left side of Oxford to 1536 Oxford, the 1889 **❶ Captain (Charles C.) Boudrow House**. A city landmark and on the National Register of Historic Places, this imposing Queen Anne Victorian was built by a retired sea captain from Nova Scotia who made his fortune in the Bay Area by salvaging obsolete steamboats and sailing ships. This elegant residence includes a four-story tower, a balustraded front stairway, extensive wood ornamentation, and a stained-glass window (depicting Boudrow's flagship in small inset to left) set into a carved

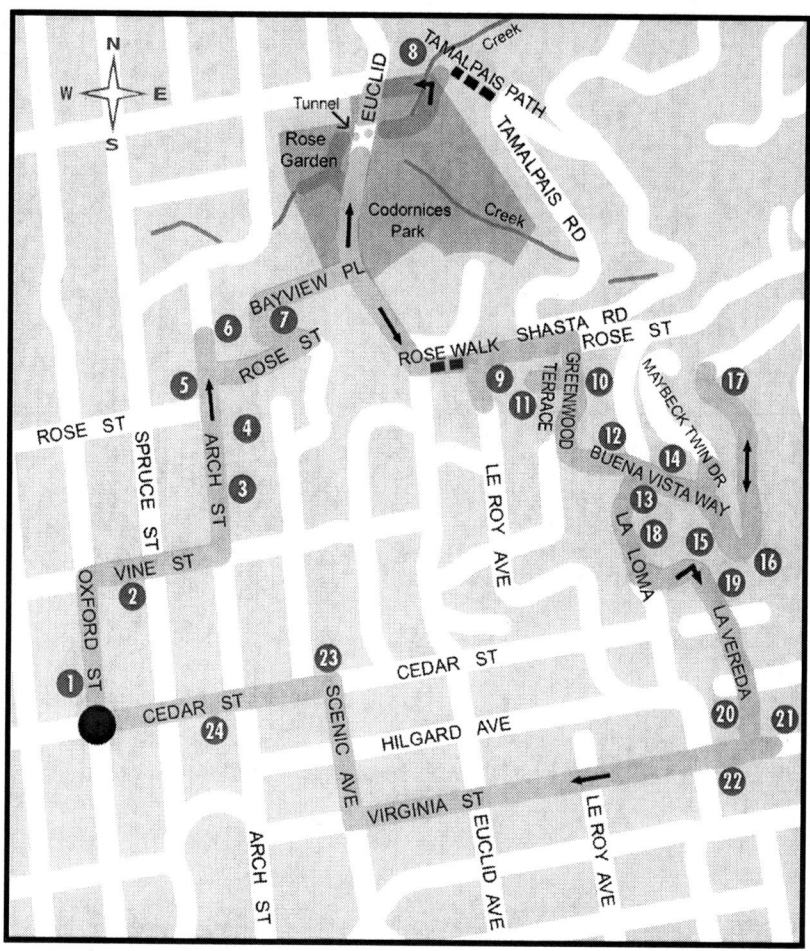

redwood door. Now divided into apartments, the house has been repainted to accentuate the detail. The cast-iron fence railings continue intermittently on Cedar and Walnut streets, marking the boundaries of the original Boudrow property.

Continue north on Oxford, noting the two matching Victorians at 1510 and 1506-08, the Captain (William) McCleave houses. Designed by George Embry, these two Queen Anne Victorians were built speculatively in 1891 as rentals for McCleave, captain of the first California cavalry during the Civil War.

Cross Vine Street at the signal, cross Oxford to the right, and walk up Vine toward the hills. On the left, 2213 Vine is a large Queen

The Queen Anne–style Captain Boudrow House on Oxford Street.

Anne Victorian circa 1890 with a three-story turret. The enclosed, lattice-windowed sun porch was probably added later. Along Vine, the eastern red oaks turn their namesake color in autumn, much more vivid than native oak species.

At the corner of Vine and Spruce Street, look across the street to 1500 Spruce, the 1910 Colonial Revival ❷ **Captain (William Harrington) Marston house**, with an unusual and lovely angled porch with glass windows. Marston brought the first load of Hawaiian sugar to the United States via San Francisco in 1876; he served as president of the Berkeley town board of trustees from 1899 to 1903. The city has installed a swale at this corner to filter rain and runoff.

On the next block, the red-shingle house at 2277 Vine was remodeled and expanded from an 1898 barn. At the northeast corner of Vine and Arch Street, the Dominican School of Philosophy and Theology—in stucco and brown shingles—was formerly Congregation Beth El, a Reform Jewish congregation that is now located on Oxford near Rose Street. It was built in 1950 and expanded in 1958, replacing an 1899 mansion.

After crossing the street, turn left (north) on Arch and continue to 1431 Arch. The ❸ **Donovan House**, a Queen Anne Victorian, has an unusual hexagonal tower integrated into the building's L shape. Attributed by one source to Ira Boynton, a Victorian-era architect, this is the oldest recorded house on Arch (circa 1886) and the sole survivor of a group of 1880s "view homes" (positioned slightly uphill with a view of the bay) built after Henry Berryman—a local businessman and developer—persuaded Union Pacific to extend the steam railway to Oxford and Rose Street. (The house is sadly in need of repair at this writing.)

Continue to 1415 Arch, built in 1897. The house embodies the transition from Victorian to Colonial Revival, with a square instead of round turret, classical ornamentation such as pilasters, and sculptural relief in the pediment. The modest ❹ **cottages** behind 1409 Arch (look down the driveway to the left of the house) date to 1896. Originally workers' cottages and later summer homes for San Franciscans, they more recently have served as rental units.

At the northwest corner with Rose, the 1905 ❺ **Wallace-Suaer House** at 1340 Arch is an example of the First Bay Tradition style popularized by Bernard Maybeck, Ernest Coxhead, and others. The style features a link to nature, locally sourced materials such as redwood, and an emphasis on craftsmanship. This house blends elements of the Swiss chalet style with balconies, huge brackets, and green shutters. John White, Maybeck's brother-in-law and a prominent architect in his own right, designed the house. The original owner was Frederick William Wallace, a manufacturer's purchasing agent; later owners were geographer Carl Ortwin Sauer and writer Amy Wallace.

Continue past Rose to 1325 Arch. Maybeck designed the 1907 ❻ **Schneider-Kroeber House** in Swiss chalet style. Note the cross-sawn wood balconies and extending eaves with large brackets. Professor Alfred L. Kroeber, who occupied the house for many of its early years, was a founder of the UC Berkeley Department of Anthropology and served as director of the Museum of Anthropology; UC Berkeley's Kroeber Hall is named in his honor. His wife Theodora later chronicled their experiences with Ishi, a member of the Yahi tribe who was believed to be the last native Californian to live a traditional lifestyle. Their daughter Ursula K. Le Guin (neé Kroeber), a Berkeley High graduate, is a writer of novels, children's books, short stories, and screenplays but is best known for fantasy and science fiction.

Directly across the street, at 1320 and 1324 Arch, are two restrained brown-shingle houses by Julia Morgan, built in 1906 and 1910, respectively. Morgan was often commissioned to do pairs of homes in different styles, situated harmoniously, although in this case they were commissioned separately. In the early 20th century, 1324 Arch was the home of Laura Adams Armer, a photographer who created artistic portraits of high-society people. She later pursued art, photography, and writing about Native Americans; in 1928, she produced *The Mountain Chant*, a silent film of a Navajo ceremony, which in its early showings was accompanied by live Navajo chanters. Her husband Sidney Armer was a successful commercial illustrator.

Walk back down Arch to Rose, cross the street, turn left, and walk uphill on Rose. Near the top of the block on the left (northwest) corner of Rose and Bay View Place, at 2333 Rose, note a house with a turret, half-timbering, and stonework in French Norman style.

Cross over to the left and continue walking uphill on Bay View. The next house on the left, 1336 Bay View, is a 1915 Tudor with variations that give it a Germanic look. It was designed by James Plachek, architect of the Berkeley Public Library's main branch in downtown Berkeley.

The 1907 **7 Senger House**, opposite at 1321 Bay View, was built by Maybeck for a UC professor of German. In typical fashion, Maybeck artfully blended Tudor, Craftsman, and Japanese elements. A purely ceremonial entrance faces west with the real front door opening onto the sidewalk on the north. The main house forms an L shape around the garden with a large carriage house in back.

As you round the curve, on the left side at 1322 Bay View is another charming Swiss chalet–style house, this one built by Henry Gutterson in 1924 with folk-style stenciled patterns under the second-floor windows. As you go up Bay View from the curve, the street is lined with plum and then ginkgo trees, providing flowering color in February and leaf color in autumn. At 1310 Bay View you may see some pet ducks in the fenced front yard.

Turn left when you reach Euclid Avenue and walk to the paved overlook to enjoy the view from the top of the Berkeley Rose Garden. This city landmark is situated in a deep ravine formed where three forks of Codornices Creek (*codornices* means "quail" in Spanish) come together. An early water supply site for Berkeley, this area was originally somewhat swampy. Streetcars passed over

The Berkeley Rose Garden.

on a trestle before the embankment for Euclid was built. In 1913, a group of neighbors established a park and playground here. Then, in 1933, the Works Progress Administration (WPA) began a four-year Depression-era relief project to build the Rose Garden, which was jointly designed with the city. The amphitheater has wide stone terraces and a semicircular redwood pergola. The East Bay Counties Rose Society planted 2,500 rose bushes in a color spectrum.

Whether you explore the lower part of the rose garden or not, descend to the right to the area between the tennis court and the public restrooms. Just beyond the restrooms, walk through the tunnel on the right, which leads to Codornices Park on the other side of Euclid. The park is named for Codornices Creek, Berkeley's least-culverted creek, which winds through parks and backyards before entering the bay in Albany (see Walk 7, Codornices Creek). Codornices Park and the Rose Garden are popular sites for picnics, recreation, and wedding receptions.

Walk past the basketball court. At the playground, look straight ahead to see the park's unusual cement slide. Go left past the playground, and walk up the cement steps that ascend the slope to the right between the playground and the stream. Take the path to the left until you reach a private bridge across Codornices Creek (passing first the park bridge on the left that goes back toward Euclid; do not go up the spiral part of Tamalpais Steps).

On the far hillside above the bridge, the ❽ **John White/ Dorothea Lange House**, a large, brown-shingled house well up the hill, was the home and studio of documentary photographer Dorothea Lange and her husband, UC Berkeley professor Paul Taylor, for the last 25 years of her life (1940–65). Lange is best known for her iconic 1930s photographs of poverty-stricken migrant farm workers during the Depression. Architect John White designed the main house as his own home in 1911. The original section of the house just across the bridge was Lange's studio.

Turn around and walk across the park bridge over the creek and continue on the paved path toward Euclid. Cross Euclid in the crosswalk at the stop sign and turn left, passing the Rose Garden, and then the East Bay Municipal Utility District reservoir (on the opposite or left side). About 200 yards past Bay View, take the crosswalk across Euclid to a double-stairway with pink-tinted concrete walls—Rose Walk.

Walk up to the top of the stairway. Rose Walk has been called Berkeley's perfectly planned environment compressed into one block. Maybeck designed the walk, with its concrete retaining walls, in 1913, and it was built with neighborhood contributions. Frank and Florence Dickens Gray later acquired the land. After the disastrous 1923 Berkeley fire, which destroyed hundreds of houses in this area north of the UC campus, the Grays hired architect Henry Gutterson to design one- and two-family houses on the north side. Designed in consultation with Maybeck, the houses are ingeniously sited to provide private spaces and the air of gracious living on a small scale. The south-side houses were built in 1928; the final house on Rose Walk at the top of the stairs was built in 1936.

Despite the 1923 fire, the north side of campus remains architecturally rich. It was the home of architects Maybeck, Ernest Coxhead, and John Galen Howard, mainly active from 1900 to 1930. These architects were known for the freshness of their designs and the use of natural materials. They were members of the Hillside Club, which offered programs on aesthetics and literary topics, and they gave design advice to members. Following in the tradition of William Morris of the British Arts and Crafts movement and Berkeley's Charles Keeler (who wrote *The Simple Home*), they emphasized craftsmanship and simplicity rather than ostentation. Streets following the contours of the hills also became a feature of the area. The north side is still popular with academics and writers such as Michael Lewis, the American financial journalist who wrote *Liar's Poker*, *Moneyball*, *The Big Short*, and other books, and his wife Tabitha Soren, a photographer and former MTV news reporter.

Walk up Rose Walk between the houses, up another set of steps, turn right at the top onto Le Roy Avenue (a hedge blocks your view of the street) and continue to the Davidson House, at 1404 Le Roy, a large brown-shingle Craftsman designed in 1923 by Lilian Bridgman. Along with Julia Morgan, Bridgman was one of the earliest women to become registered architects in California, although she was initially a scientist.

Turn around and walk past Rose Walk on Le Roy. On the opposite side, where Le Roy curves, 1401 Le Roy is a 1912 **❾ house designed by John Galen Howard**. Although his buildings on the UC campus were often classical in design, Howard's residences were more informal. This house was built for Warren Gregory, an attorney and UC faculty member, but Howard leased it and lived here for a number of years. In 1927, Julia Morgan added a library wing toward the back that blends in with the original. The house was badly damaged by fire on the second floor in 1998, but has since been restored.

Proceed uphill on Rose Street; at the intersection with Tamalpais Road, carefully cross the street and continue straight uphill on Rose. Turn right on Greenwood Terrace.

Past 1437 Greenwood Terrace, 1459 Greenwood Terrace is uphill amid trees and behind 1437. This is the **❿ Warren Gregory House**, originally designed as a country retreat for San Franciscans (like many homes in the East Bay hills) and then moved and expanded after the 1906 earthquake. For more than 20 years, it was the home of William Wurster, Bay Area architect and a founder and dean of the UC Berkeley College of Environmental Design. Wurster subdivided the property on the flat meadowland opposite the house into 10 sites around a grassy common, formed an investment group, and helped potential owners establish development principles for the site. The architects of the **⓫ Greenwood Common** houses (eight were built) did not necessarily design in the same style, but they were able to provide a harmonious grouping by following common guidelines.

A view of the bay from Greenwood Common.

You are allowed to go through the gate and walk up the path to see the houses and enjoy the spectacular bay view, but no dogs are permitted. The setting by landscape architect Lawrence Halprin—who designed Levi Plaza, Sea Ranch, and Sproul Plaza—fits well with the houses. The simple, low-maintenance gardens are a public amenity. The rows of old flowering plum trees were replaced recently with similar young trees to preserve the initial appealing design. Halprin also did original landscaping for some of the homes.

The house addresses (lot numbers) on Greenwood Common, construction dates, and their prominent mid-20th century architects are (lots 5 and 6 were never built):

1: 1955, Donald Olsen
2: 1957, Robert Klemmedson
3: 1954, Joseph Esherick (architect of the Cannery in San Francisco, Monterey Bay Aquarium, and numerous homes)
4: 1954, Harwell Hamilton Harris
7: Original 1920s, architect unknown, remodeled subsequently by Rudolph M. Schindler, William Wurster, and Henry Hill

8: 1953, Howard Moise

9: 1954, Henry Hill

10: 1953, John Funk

The original plan was for all the houses to face the common, but most owners built fences; only two now openly face the common. No. 10 is notable for its butterfly roofline and glass windows facing an inner courtyard garden.

Back on Greenwood Terrace, continue right a few steps to 1471 Greenwood, a 1954 house with a pattern of exposed bolts, built by W. S. Wellington, as well as an open center at ground level with a deck above. Two contrasting houses are on the right: 1476 Greenwood from 1907 with a long, sloping rear roof was designed by Maybeck, while 1486 Greenwood, next door, with brown shingles and decorative sun porch, is a 1912 Howard house that looks more like a typical Maybeck.

Cross Buena Vista Way and turn left to take the sidewalk uphill. On the left at **⓬ 2683 Buena Vista** is the Maybeck-designed home where composer and UC Berkeley music professor Charles Seeger lived from 1915 to 1919; the round brown-shingle outbuilding was his music studio. Renowned as a pioneer of modern music theory and musicology, Charles will more likely be remembered as the father of folk singer and activist Pete Seeger. Charles was forced to resign from UC due to his outspoken World War I pacifism; his son Pete was born in 1919 in New York. Charles's pacifism may have been an inspiration for Pete to coauthor *Where Have All the Flowers Gone*. For many years, the house was also the home of Nobel laureate biochemist Melvin Calvin, who did ground-breaking work on photosynthesis.

Continue up Buena Vista to the stop sign at La Loma Avenue. It is now time to enter Maybeck country, where the architect lived and helped develop a style that combined craftsmanship, natural and new materials, and the harmonious mixing of disparate architectural styles (see sidebar). Maybeck was a mentor for an entire generation of California architects, including Julia Morgan and William Wurster. In 1951, he was awarded the Gold Medal of the American Institute of Architects.

Many of Maybeck's early homes were destroyed in the Berkeley fire of 1923, which swept through this area; he built with more fire-resistant materials afterward. Look across the street. 2704 Buena Vista, is the 1915 **⓭ Mathewson, or "Studio," House** where Maybeck used wood craftsmanship in large, extending eaves. The

Spotlight: Bernard Maybeck (1862–1957)

Berkeley's most influential architect, Bernard Maybeck is known for his innovative use of building materials and creative and eclectic style. Comfortable mixing styles from Tudor to Swiss chalet to Japanese, Maybeck somehow made them work together. Craftsmanship was important to him; he liked to be involved in the construction of his buildings, especially the chimneys. His structures were carefully integrated into the landscape, a notion embraced by members of Berkeley's influential Hillside Club.

Maybeck was born in New York City. His father, a German immigrant woodcarver, encouraged him to study furniture making in Paris; instead, he studied architecture at the École des Beaux-Arts. After working in an architectural office in New York, he migrated to Kansas City, where he met his wife, Annie White. In 1890, he and his family arrived in California, where he joined the UC faculty in 1894 as a drawing teacher in civil engineering. In 1898, he was appointed the university's first professor of architecture.

In 1903, Maybeck left UC to establish an architecture office in San Francisco, designing mostly homes, churches, and club buildings. Although most of his work was built in the Bay Area, Maybeck also designed buildings at Principia College near St. Louis, Missouri; a large home and Packard dealership in Los Angeles; and the town plan for Brookings, Oregon.

In San Francisco, Maybeck's Romanesque Palace of Fine Arts pavilion, built for the 1915 Panama-Pacific International Exposition, was so popular that it was the only structure rebuilt in permanent form (a development that Maybeck was not happy about). In Berkeley, the First Church of Christ, Scientist, at Dwight Way and Bowditch Street, is considered his masterpiece; it is recognized by the American Institute of Architects as one of the finest original American church designs. The church features an incredible but harmonious blend of Byzantine, Romanesque, Gothic, and Japanese influences, as well as materials ranging from concrete to carved wood to industrial sash windows.

In his adopted hometown of Berkeley, Maybeck designed the Town and Gown Club (2401 Dwight Way), the Faculty Club at UC Berkeley, and the Phoebe Apperson Hearst Memorial Gymnasium for Women (with Julia Morgan), also on campus. Maybeck also designed varied and influential residences such as a Romanesque villa for geologist Andrew Lawson (1515 La Loma Ave.), one of the first prestressed concrete buildings in the state; and a wood-sided Swiss chalet for Professor Alfred L. Kroeber (1325 Arch St.). For one of his own homes, at 2711 Buena Vista Way, he dipped burlap bags in cement to create a fire-resistant wall.

Throughout his long and varied career, Maybeck mentored a generation of important Bay Area architects, including Julia Morgan, William Wurster, and Lilian Bridgman. The American Institute of Architects awarded Maybeck its prestigious Gold Medal in 1951. ❋❋

north-facing windows rise up through the roof, giving the studio its nickname. It survived the 1923 fire.

Cross La Loma and head up Buena Vista, passing the north side of the studio house. The sidewalk ends farther up; proceed with caution. The second house on the left side of the street, 2711 Buena Vista, is the 1924 ⑭ **Maybeck Studio or "Sack" House**, Maybeck's own residence for many years. His innovative "bubblestone" siding was created by dipping gunny sacks in concrete to make fire-resistant walls.

Make the first left onto Maybeck Twin Drive. The first house on the right (2751 Buena Vista) was designed by Maybeck in 1933 for his son Wallen; it includes a mix of modern and traditional materials and design. After a house fire, Maybeck restored it, sanding away charred surfaces to reuse much of the wood; several renovations and additions followed. Opposite is 2733 Buena Vista, with its brick wall and stencil-patterned garage, though the rest of this Maybeck design is virtually impossible to see due to the dense jungle of plants. This street is a dead end, so return to Buena Vista and walk uphill again to the left.

The 1914 house at 2753 Buena Vista on the left was designed by William Charles Hays. With its upper loggia, it is like a small palace in Florence, but in Berkeley brown-shingle. The right side is a fairly faithful later addition.

Maybeck designed the shingled ⑮ **First Bay Tradition house** at 2780 Buena Vista. A plaque to the right of the pebbled entryway says that the house was built for him and his wife in 1933; another to the right on a fence declares that the other plaque is incorrect and the house was built for Maybeck's daughter Kerna. In any case, it includes one of Maybeck's signature poured-concrete chimneys; he loved to work on interior and construction details, especially chimneys.

The 1914 ⑯ **Boynton House**, or Temple of Wings, is at 2800 Buena Vista, where the road angles left. Designed by several people, the light and airy residence was destroyed in the 1923 fire and rebuilt in a heavier style (the columns survived). Berkeley fashioned itself as the Athens of the West, and the classical structure was a stage set for dance. The original owner, Florence Treadwell Boynton, was a friend of Isadora Duncan, a founder of modern dance; Boynton passed on Duncan's theories to her own dance students here. There is a partial view toward campus and the bay from just before the entrance. More of the house can be seen uphill from the mailbox.

If you are game for another steep climb, more points of interest and views are uphill. (If you are not, skip ahead two paragraphs.) Up the road but set on a steep slope on the left, 2851 Buena Vista was the home of Jaime de Angulo in the 1920s and early 1930s. De Angulo was a linguist, novelist, cross-dresser, and ethnomusicologist who was born in Paris of Spanish parents but came to the United States in 1905 to be a cowboy, medical doctor, and psychologist. Based in Berkeley, he studied Native American languages and music by immersing himself in their cultures. His book *Indian Tales* was a bestseller, and he was a friend to famous writers and scholars, including Alfred L. Kroeber.

A little farther uphill, where the road turns to the left and then to the right, are the high concrete and stone walls—glimpsed initially through the trees—of Hume Cloister, popularly called **17 Hume Castle**. The home of Samuel J. and Portia Bell Hume was designed by John Hudson Thomas in 1927. Rather than a castle, it is based on an Augustinian monastery in Toulouse, France, complete with Gothic cloister. The interior details are reported to be fascinating, but it is not open to the public. Samuel Hume was an assistant professor of theater at UC; as innovative director of the Greek Theatre from 1918 to 1924, he staged major dramatic and musical

The Lawson House, in Roman villa style.

productions as well as plays in Wheeler Hall. He also set up a small museum on Shattuck Avenue and a rare books store, and was the author of *Twentieth Century Stage Design*, used as a text for decades. His wife Portia, the daughter of a US congressman, was a psychiatrist who was considered a pioneer in the field.

Return downhill to La Loma, cross the street, and turn left. Next to the Maybeck Studio house is 1509 La Loma, a Tudor-style house by Charles F. Masten and Lester W. Hurd from 1930, with modern touches. 1512 La Loma is a compound of 1924 concrete-block buildings with slate roofs by John K. Ballantine; the structures are reminiscent of English rural cottages.

Up the hillside on the left is the striking **18 Lawson House** at 1515 La Loma. View the house from the side before getting a full view from farther down the sidewalk. Maybeck designed this house in Roman villa style, with arched openings on the side loggia and the projecting sides of the rear balcony. An urn is in the balcony opening, and there are bands of color-impregnated stucco and decorative incised patterns. This was one of the first two prestressed concrete houses built in the state; Maybeck's client, Professor Andrew Lawson, was a geologist who mapped and named part of the San Andreas Fault, and he wanted an earthquake-proof residence. The 1907 house survived the 1923 fire.

At the next intersection, cross La Loma in the crosswalk and turn up La Vereda Road; this narrow street also has no sidewalks. On the right, plum trees flower in February and Japanese cherry blossoms cover two trees with ephemeral beauty in March. The house at 1553 La Vereda has exposed concrete and large tile blocks. Lawson helped build this for himself in the 1930s, when he was 85. In front of 1585 La Vereda, a brick **19 Colonial Revival cottage**, two lovely pink dogwoods bloom in March.

At the corner of Hilgard Avenue at 1650 La Vereda is a landmarked **20 early modernist house** from 1937 by Wurster in a basic-box design. The 1895 Peterson House at 1631 La Vereda was built by George P. Jensen, a Danish carpenter and interior decorator. He designed this with a full facade porch for his brother-in-law, Theodore C. W. Petersen, who specialized in painting friezes—including the ones in UC's California Hall.

At the end of La Vereda, up the steep slope to the left, 1731 La Vereda is a brown-shingled, steeply gabled house, circa 1890–1900, built for a German immigrant dairy farmer who provided milk for much of the UC campus; though remodeled in 2014, the basic historic form remains. Opposite, at 1730 La Vereda, is the **㉑ Lezinsky House** of 1894, with Dutch Colonial features such as its large gambrel roof.

Walk back downhill. Past the driveway for 1700 La Vereda, take the stairway at the bottom of the curve; the stairs immediately turn left and later right. At the curving street, turn left and continue to 2708 Virginia at the next curve. Take the steps and sidewalk on the left side of the street (near 2708), going downhill.

You are now on Virginia Street. On the left, 2700 Virginia (also 1705 La Loma) is the large 1905 **㉒ William Rees House**, a First Bay Tradition version of a Swiss chalet, with balconies and dummy log-ends projecting from the corners. According to some sources, E. A. Hargreaves, an architect who worked for several years in Maybeck's office, designed the house; it is not clear if Maybeck played a role. It just missed being burned in the 1923 fire.

Take the steps to the left just past 2700 Virginia; the steps soon twist to the right. At the bottom, cross La Loma to continue downhill several blocks on Virginia. Between Euclid and Scenic, the street is lined with large London plane (sycamore) trees.

Turn right on Scenic and walk two blocks to Cedar. Cross Cedar carefully (there is no crosswalk) and go left to **㉓ 2375 Cedar** at the corner with Scenic, which jogs a bit. The house has a quirky collection of sculptures and artwork, particularly along the Scenic side, including pieces by the couple who live here (both scientists), sculptures by Bay Area artist Mark Bulwinkle, and an elephant sculpture by a college student friend of the owners. Continue downhill on Cedar.

At 2286 Cedar is the **㉔ Hillside Club**, founded in the late 19th century to promote good design practices in the Berkeley hills. Today it is a community-based membership organization supporting the arts and culture. The original Maybeck-designed building was lost in the 1923 fire. Maybeck's brother-in-law, John White, designed the current Arts and Crafts structure—with its handsome meeting room—just afterward.

Continue down Cedar to the starting point at Oxford.

❄ ❄ ❄

Part II
North Berkeley

WALK 6
THE GOURMET GHETTO

✳ ✳ ✳

Overview: Featuring Victorian and historic buildings as well as modern infill, this walk explores how design determines if change is compatible or incompatible with an area. Mostly level, it includes a lively commercial district and quiet neighborhoods.

Highlights:
- The birthplace of California Cuisine
- Lively mix of historic and contemporary architecture
- One of the earliest city parks, graced by a creek

Distance: 2.7–3 miles
Time: 2–2.5 hours
Elevation gain: 120–140 feet

✳ ✳ ✳

Start at the northeast corner of Shattuck and Hearst avenues in front of ❶ **Bistro Liaison** at 1849 Shattuck, four blocks north of the Downtown Berkeley BART station. This building, the Shattuck Lofts, was developed by Patrick Kennedy of Panoramic Interests and completed in 1995. A plaque along the Shattuck side says it was the first mixed-use project downtown in 30 years when it was built. "Mixed use" is a traditional form of commercial-area design combining retail and residential, office, educational, and other uses. Shattuck Lofts has 24 residential apartments and the first-floor restaurant. Kennedy argued for less parking than city regulations called for due to the

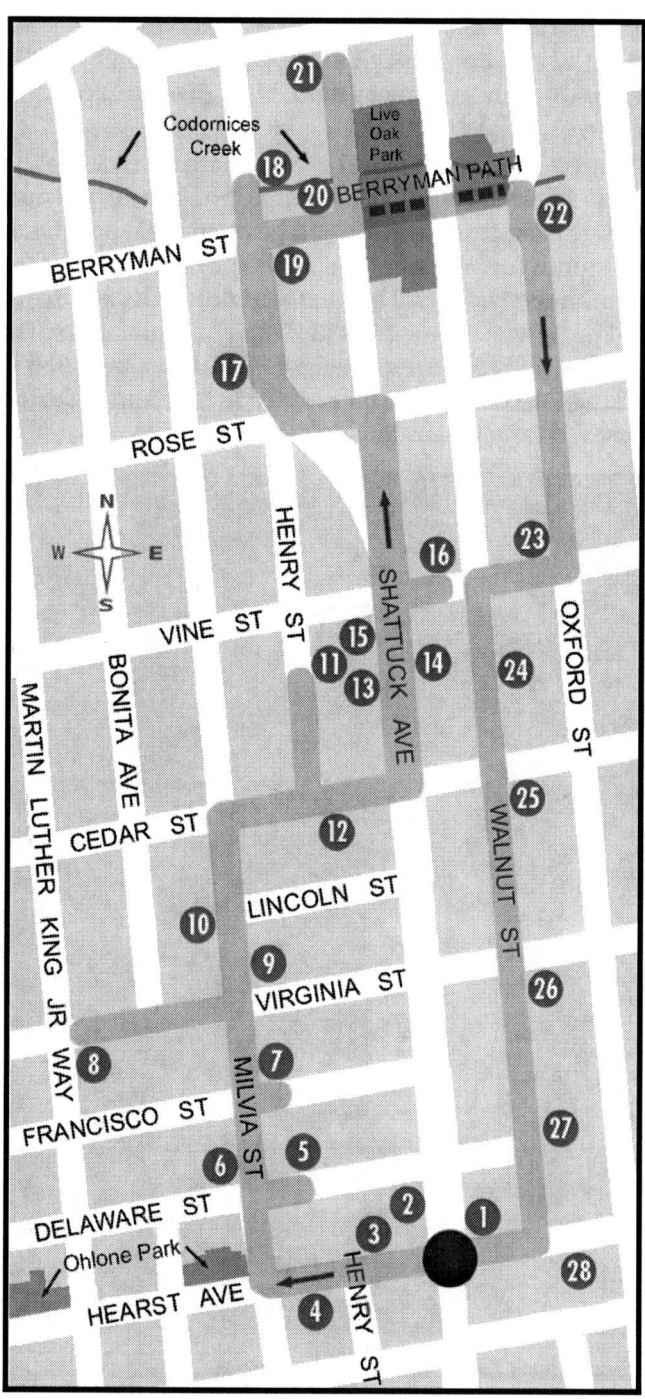

building's proximity to downtown and transit. Walk along the Shattuck side of the building to peek in the garage; Kennedy installed an innovative European parking system, with cars stacked on electric lifts that move up and down.

Look north on Shattuck, just beyond Shattuck Lofts on the same side, to the Hillside Village Apartments. The farther one, 1797 Shattuck, was completed in 2005 and has 72 rental apartments, gardens, a community lounge, and a hillside terrace on the fourth floor for building residents. The nearer building, at 1801 Shattuck, completed in 2008, has 22 significantly larger rental units. These three mixed-use buildings replaced a gas station, a fast-food outlet, and a parking lot, which were far less productive and pedestrian-friendly uses of valuable urban land.

A late Victorian cottage, circa 1890s, at 2019 Hearst.

Hillside Village and Shattuck Lofts hark back to a traditional pattern of mixed-use development, with first-floor retail and residences above looking down on the street, providing greater security. By comparison, look across the street to the ❷ **Amistad House** at 2050 Delaware Street, independent-living apartments for seniors and disabled adults built in 1981. The development is softened somewhat by weathered shingles, usable balconies, and landscaping, but the metal fence, utility box at the corner, and absence of interface with the Shattuck sidewalk counteract urban street vitality.

Cross Shattuck and walk west on Hearst (away from the hills). Along Hearst are numerous ginkgo trees, with fan-shaped leaves that turn brilliant yellow around November. On the right side of the block, note the ❸ **six late-Victorian cottages** at 2035, 2033, 2029, 2027, 2019 (the least altered), and 2009 Hearst. These feature a mixture of Stick and Queen Anne Victorian as well as later Colonial Revival details. Pleasing remnants of 1890s Berkeley, the cottages are surprisingly close to downtown, despite development pressure to replace historic structures in such areas. Most of these cottages have been raised up or added on to, but they are still recognizable as historic homes.

On the opposite side, at 2010–14 Hearst, the multiunit ❹ **Hearst Commons** was developed by Laurie Capitelli, designed by James Novosel of the Bay Architects, and completed in 1993 after a four-year battle between the developer and members of the community. This development includes a shared garden space, and parking is placed mainly under the west unit. With its warm brown shingles, landscaping, and village-like grouping of units, the development is an improvement over the concrete-block apartment buildings hastily built in this and other areas of Berkeley between the 1950s and the early 1970s, helping to turn many citizens against development. (Capitelli was later elected to the Berkeley city council.)

Walk to the corner of Milvia. A 1960s plan to widen Hearst to four lanes to take pressure off University Avenue was cancelled due to community opposition after the first two blocks west of Shattuck were completed (now this part of Hearst has two wide traffic lanes with ample parking lanes). The rest of Hearst remained narrow, preserving pedestrian ambience. Ohlone Park, which begins along Hearst just beyond Martin Luther King, Jr., Way (MLK Way), is a community amenity (see Walk 16, The Ohlone Greenway). Ohlone

Greenway—a bicycle and pedestrian trail—starts in the park and threads through Berkeley, Albany, El Cerrito, and Richmond.

Turn right on Milvia, cross Delaware Street, and turn right again. Note the innovative modern-home complex in red stucco at ❺ **2015 Delaware**. Two homes share a garden space, with one residence built over the garage in front and the other residence in the garden behind. Even though the 1997 modernist design is different from that of nearby historic homes, the scale is appropriate for the neighborhood. Return to Milvia and turn right. Opposite, the ❻ **Colonial Revival house** at 1746 Milvia (northwest corner with Delaware) has ornate porch columns, a projecting second floor, and an angled corner bay.

Walk to about midblock and notice the speed bumps, "bulb-outs," and planting areas that create a curving street along six blocks of Milvia. The goal of this "slow street" project, completed in 1989 with $100,000 in development-mitigation funds, was to slow down traffic and improve safety for pedestrians and cyclists.

Continue north on Milvia to Francisco Street. The Colonial Revival at 1729 Milvia, on the corner, was built around 1898. It has a high peak and a curved, overhanging bay window along the Francisco side, with a small Palladian window above, a large second-floor bay on the front, fine narrow clapboarding, and some leaded windows. Moved to this location from Addison Street near Shat-

tuck circa 1906, it retains historic features (but could use a paint job as of this writing).

Walk right (east) on Francisco to the lot behind this Colonial Revival house to see the narrow, brown-shingle, modern house at 2008 Francisco. It rises vertically to maximize its floor space on a small lot, an interesting urban design solution. Return to Milvia.

At the northeast corner of Milvia, 2000 Francisco is a superb example of a ❼ **Stick-Eastlake villa** with a three-story turret. It was built around 1889 by English ship carpenter John Paul Moran

A Victorian villa at 2000 Francisco.

for Jonathan C. Wright, owner of the Golden Sheaf Bakery (whose building still stands on Addison in downtown Berkeley). The home was leased to UC professor Isaac Flagg, and later Wright lived here. The Colonial Revival porch was probably added during the early 1900s. Continue on Milvia (noting the blue bottles in the windows, which likely influenced the current house color); at the rear of the house, look up to see Moran's signature—twin sets of carved anchors—below each corner of the rear-gable bargeboard. The bargeboards under the eaves feature unusual beveling along the bottom.

Continue north on Milvia to Virginia Street. Around the southeast corner to the right, note a couple of duplex buildings at 2000 and 2002 Virginia and 2004 and 2006 Virginia. Duplexes combine two residences, saving on land and construction costs and making homes more affordable. There are many scattered about Berkeley, often with appealing designs.

For a two-block diversion, turn left and walk down Virginia toward MLK Way. The red ❽ **Italian Renaissance–style building** on the southeast corner at 1701–05 Virginia, best viewed from the northeast corner, is an excellent example of historic mixed use. The first floor is the studio of David Lance Goines, a graphic artist and calligrapher known for his posters (including graphic works for Chez Panisse), writing (including a nonfiction account of Berkeley's Free Speech Movement), and publishing company, Saint Hieronymus Press. There are six residences on the upper floors. On the Virginia side of the building, an exterior staircase leads to a decorative metal gate and a charming upper courtyard. Goines owns the 1920s building.

Return to Milvia and turn left. Between Virginia and Lincoln streets is the ❾ **Berkeley Arts Magnet (BAM) at Whittier School**, in a landmarked Streamline Moderne–style building. Built as the University Elementary Demonstration School in 1939, it offered up-to-date educational facilities and a "hall of health" with lots of natural light and fresh air. The Allen Ginsberg Memorial Poetry Garden on the Milvia side commemorates the author of "Howl," who wrote parts of the poem when he lived across the street in a cottage behind 1624 Milvia (the cottage is gone now, though Ginsberg's poem, "A Strange New Cottage in Berkeley," which he wrote while living there, remains).

On the west side, opposite the poetry garden, is a jarring row of cinder block and stucco two- and three-story ❿ **apartment houses** built between the 1950s and the early 1970s. In response to such structures being plopped down willy-nilly in neighborhoods throughout Berkeley, the citizens' Neighborhood Preservation Ordinance was passed in 1973, followed by the city council's Landmarks Preservation Ordinance in 1974. Most such apartments in the city do not fit in with their neighborhoods, and a survey found that most people living in them felt that the buildings never should have been built due to poor sound insulation, shoddy construction, and other factors. Likewise, the "soft" first-story parking is dangerous in an earthquake. Although these types of apartments were built when the American economy was booming, paradoxically, homes from earlier eras hold up much better. For example, note the well-maintained 1893 Queen Anne Victorian at 2001 Lincoln on the northeast corner of Milvia and Lincoln.

Continue on Milvia, crossing Cedar Street at the stop sign. Turn right on Cedar and then left again after crossing Henry Street and walk to 1509–19 Henry, the 1990 Patrick Kennedy development called ⓫ **Henry Court**. Designed by Kirk E. Peterson, the six townhouses were built on two former single-home lots. Originally, Kennedy planned one long building on one lot, but opposition caused him to alter the plans, and he settled on three separate units, one behind the other. Later, the adjacent site became available, and he built three more and integrated them with a common walkway. The city's onerous parking requirements made it necessary to include parking next to the sidewalk. However, the trellises and permeable paving are a pleasing alternative to the dreary parking areas standard in many earlier apartment buildings (e.g., the one across the street at 1516 Henry).

Return to Cedar and look across the street at 2022–28 Cedar, a ⓬ **Colonial Revival apartment building** from 1900 with a Doric-columned portico (porch) and frieze and cornice line above each bay. This four-unit building is one of the earliest apartment houses in Berkeley and fits well in the neighborhood of single-family homes; less congenial is the newer apartment block next door, although the redwood and pine trees hide most of it.

Walk left up Cedar. As you approach the corner, note 1600 Shattuck on the right, a colorful mixed-use development that combines office and retail space. Neither big nor blocky, this building relates well to the pedestrian realm and includes outdoor dining. The

Sidewalk dining in the Gourmet Ghetto.

site was originally a mortuary; it was subsequently a strip mall in the 1980s (fittingly called the "dead center"). Urban Development + Partners and Kava Massih Architects created this much livelier development in 1999.

Turn left at Shattuck and walk north toward the ⓭ **French Hotel** (1538 Shattuck), with its busy, table-laden sidewalk. Note the pedestrian-friendly elements from here looking north: buildings next to the sidewalk with large windows and doors, parked cars providing a buffer zone, trees and planters, and sidewalk seating. Contrast these elements with the sidewalk-facing parking lot that you just passed at Andronico's Community Market, although the hedges and sweetgums soften the effect. More sweetgums and ginkgos add brilliant autumn color along the next several blocks.

This area, called the Gourmet Ghetto, is central to Berkeley's food movement, an outgrowth of the political activism of the 1960s and 1970s. Founded in 1971 by Alice Waters, ⓮ **Chez Panisse**, across the street at 1517 Shattuck, emphasizes fresh, local ingredients and is credited with inventing California cuisine. Waters was active in the Free Speech Movement and shifted from her emphasis on political change to promoting a change in the way Americans grow and eat food. The restaurant suffered a major fire in 2013, but it was quickly rebuilt and reopened several months later. Also on this block are César (1515 Shattuck), the Cheese Board Collective and pizza shop (1512 Shattuck), a produce market, and Epicurious Garden (1509–13 Shattuck), a gourmet take-out emporium located in a remodeled former appliance store. In front of the Cheese Board Collective is the city's first "parklet"; parking spaces were removed in 2014 to provide outdoor seating for the customers of the Cheese Board's busy pizza shop as well as the non-pizza-eating public.

The Cheese Board Collective and its popular pizzeria are examples of a Berkeley phenomenon—the cooperative enterprise. The two owners of a small cheese shop sold the business to their employees in 1971, and it has been a worker-owned and -run cooperative since, relying on a shared work ethic, high standards, and

The Produce Center building at Shattuck and Vine.

decisions reached through democratic debate. Another example was the trend-setting Berkeley Co-op (Consumer's Cooperative of Berkeley), which was founded during the Depression and folded in the late 1980s. A new Berkeley Student Food Collective was founded in 2010.

Walk along Shattuck toward Vine Street, noting the giant monkey puzzle tree (araucaria) in front of Chez Panisse and the sign designed by David Lance Goines. Stop at the corner of Shattuck and Vine. The North Shattuck commercial area was developed in 1878, when the steam railroad line was extended from its first terminus at Shattuck near Center Street in downtown Berkeley, to this corner, with a railway yard just beyond. A further impetus for residential and commercial development came with the arrival of electric trains around 1910. Many settlers in the North Shattuck area were railroad men and their families, and this was their shopping area. From 1900 to 1910, Berkeley was one of the fastest-growing cities in the United States, getting a boost from the exodus from San Francisco after the 1906 earthquake and fire.

The Squire's block, built in 1895 on the southeast corner of Shattuck and Vine, is a remnant of those days, although it was modernized and later restored to a more historic appearance.

Cross both Shattuck and Vine to the northeast corner. Look back to the **⑮ Produce Center** (southwest corner), a city landmark located in probably the oldest commercial building (1891) still standing along north Shattuck. Note the small, porticoed side entrance for second-floor residences on Vine. This building was originally Cole's hardware store; the builder and likely designer was the prolific A. H. Broad, who designed many early Berkeley schools as well as homes and commercial buildings. From 1920 to 1971, this was the Capitol Market, with a butcher shop and grocery operated by two generations of the same family. Although it is a Victorian building—note the fish-scale shingles and turret with witch's hat—it has some Colonial Revival features, such as the side entrance.

Walk east up Vine toward the hills to the **⑯ Vine Street Pumping Plant**, on the left at 2113 Vine. Water-supply battles were common in Berkeley's early days, with various companies merging to maintain monopolies on East Bay water (and not necessarily supplying a high-quality product). After several failed initiatives, state legislation in 1923 allowed their acquisition by a public company, the East Bay Municipal Utility District (EBMUD), which subsequently brought high-quality water from the Mokelumne River through a 94-mile pipeline. This was the first and most elaborate of EBMUD's pumping stations. Although it is unobtrusive and utilitarian, this elegant building now serves up another liquid: high-quality but moderately priced wines.

On the opposite side of Vine, note the two-story, Colonial Revival mixed-use building from 1902. It was designed by William Wharff, a Civil War veteran who became a prolific architect later in life and lived to be over 100. Peet's Coffee and Tea was founded here in 1966. Alfred Peet, who learned the coffee trade in his native Holland, was a pioneer in the US gourmet coffee industry, among the first to roast beans different times for different tastes, to sell a variety of coffee beans, and to make coffee beverages to order. Peet's was the model for Starbucks; in fact, Alfred Peet was a mentor to the founder of Starbucks and the source of that firm's original coffee bean supply. After several changes of ownership, a large German consumer-products company bought the Peet's chain in 2012.

Return to Shattuck and turn right, passing Books Inc. Note the appealing shop fronts here, followed by the unfriendly concrete block wall of CVS (originally a grocery store). By contrast, the Safeway across the street was improved in 2013 by a major renovation, which added windows facing the street. On Thursday afternoons, Shattuck is closed off here for an all-organic farmers market, one of three city farmers markets run by the Ecology Center. At the corner of Rose Street, cross Shattuck to the left and continue to Henry; at the signal, cross Rose to the right and walk north on Henry.

As you walk along Henry, note (across the street) the **⓱ brown-shingle townhouse condominiums** built by Alan Wofsy & Associates (circa 1973). Townhouses conserve space and materials and are

David Lance Goines's poster for Peet's Coffee and Tea.

common in many cities, though there are few in Berkeley. In the median, double-flowering cherry blossom trees bloom in April.

Cross Berryman Street and walk to **⑱ Codornices Court** at 1225–37 Henry, developed and designed circa 1985 by Mui Ho of UC Berkeley. The nine townhouses have the feeling of single-family units, with innovative placement of walks and driveways and a large, mature conifer. When this development was first proposed, one opponent turned many neighbors against this project. Looking now at this quiet little development, which fits well into the neighborhood, it is hard to imagine the pitched battles and threats that caused the developer to hire a bodyguard—but land use is often the most controversial of local political issues. The landscaping features native ceanothus with sprays of tiny blue flowers in February and March.

Walk back to Berryman. Across the street, on the southeast corner at 1301 Henry, is the commune and winter home of **⑲ Wavy Gravy's Camp Winnarainbow**, a circus and performing camp for all ages and abilities. Wavy Gravy (a.k.a. Hugh Romney) was an announcer at the original Woodstock and is a beloved clown and comic, writer, and promoter of social causes. Ben & Jerry's named a flavor after him; in return, he received free ice cream for life, and he often hits the local Ben & Jerry's store to secure dessert when it's his turn to cook for the 40-odd people who reportedly live here.

Turn left and walk up Berryman. On the left side, at 2033 Berryman, is a large gray-shingle house designed by Henry Gutterson that was the home of Rebecca Howell, a leading figure in the Berkeley theater scene in the 1910s and 1920s; she reportedly used the living room as an impromptu performance space. The **⑳ Live Oak Condominiums** (built circa 1979) are at 2043–51 Berryman and around the corner (turn left) at 1230–34 Shattuck. At least one house on this block of Shattuck is a remodeled older home and another is a renovated duplex, while other units are more recently built. The higher-density condo project makes an amenity of Codornices Creek by keeping it out of a culvert and visible from the windows of most units. You can see the creek from the stone wall on Shattuck.

These homes and many others in the area were built in a style known as Berkeley brown-shingle, particularly popular between 1895 and 1915, when it defined the town with its emphasis on Arts and Crafts style, simplicity, and harmony with nature. The style fell out of favor after the devastating 1923 Berkeley fire, but can still be found in many areas of the city, compatible with a woodsy style of urbanism.

Before entering Live Oak Park, walk north along the west side of Shattuck toward the corner. The science fiction writer Philip K. Dick (whose stories were the basis for movies such as *Blade Runner* and *Total Recall*) lived on the other side of the park on Walnut (as well as elsewhere in Berkeley).

Near the end of the block, **㉑ 1210, 1208, and 1200 Shattuck**, are three homes designed by Bernard Maybeck, in concordance with his philosophy of building in harmony with nature. Near the corner of Eunice Street, 1200 Shattuck was built in 1900 for Isaac Flagg (the UC professor who first lived in the "blue bottle" Victorian at Milvia and Francisco streets). In the early 1920s, it was the home of Dr. Clarence Wills and his family. They had a daughter named Helen Wills (later Helen Wills Moody). Not long after moving here, she launched her tennis career and became the first American woman to be an international sports superstar. Between 1922 and 1938, Moody won 31 Grand Slam titles, including 8 Wimbledon Championships, and 2 Olympic gold medals. She was famous for her lack of emotion on the court, tremendous power, and reclusive personality. The garden at 1210 has lovely azaleas in February and March.

Turn back on Shattuck, carefully cross the street before the stone walls over Codornices Creek, and walk into Live Oak Park. In 1914, with the City Beautiful movement in full swing but Berkeley lacking parks, Live Oak Park was designated the city's second public park (after San Pablo Park in southwest Berkeley). The site had been privately held and subdivided but was mostly undeveloped, while the creek remained unculverted. The city acquired the property and added the Walnut Street bridge in 1915, the giant fireplace in 1917, and the community center in 1955. A plan to connect this park along the creek uphill to Codornices Park was never realized.

Codornices Creek (*codornices* means "quail" in Spanish) is the least-culverted creek in Berkeley. It flows through parks and backyards and even has waterfalls on its upper reaches (see Walk 7, Codornices Creek). Enjoy wandering through Live Oak Park toward Walnut Street and looking at the creek from the bridges. The numerous redwood trees and native live oaks retain their leaves all year. Cross the stone bridge to the south side and take the path up and to the left to Walnut or walk under the road bridge.

Either way, continue into the next park segment east of Walnut. If the Berkeley Art Center is open, drop in or take in more of the creek. Then take the upper walkway to Oxford Street; go left and cross in the crosswalk; turn right on the other side, peeking over the wall for a view of the creek. Farther along, a historical plaque is just off the sidewalk before the driveway for ㉒ **Congregation Beth El**, a Reform Jewish community, at 1301 Oxford.

In 1873, entrepreneur Henry Berryman purchased this site from Napoleon Bonaparte Byrne, who bought 827 acres around Codornices Creek after moving here from Missouri in 1858. When the Byrne family left Berkeley for the San Francisco Bay Delta, they left behind two freed slaves—the first African Americans in Berkeley. The original Byrne house of 1868, one of Berkeley's oldest homes, was lost to arson fires in 1988. In the early 2000s, there was considerable controversy over the congregation's plans for the site, including parking and the building's relationship to the creek. In the end, the creek was restored with native plants that are now maturing.

Continue south on Oxford (with the synagogue to your left). 1315 Oxford has a wisteria vine and pink crabapple tree that bloom together in March. At the signal, cross Rose, then cross Oxford to the southwest corner. Continue south along the west side of Oxford, noticing the small but attractive street-side Japanese maple trees. As you near Vine, notice the side of the ㉓ **Andrew Weir House**, at 2163 Vine but best viewed from the Oxford side. This 1885–95 Stick-Eastlake Victorian cottage has a raised basement and spindled front porch. The long side on Oxford includes squared bays, exposed wood features, stick work, geometric friezes, and sunbursts.

Turn right on Vine at the signal and walk west past evergreen magnolia trees, with their shiny dark leaves, to the corner of Walnut and Vine streets. On this side of Walnut, on the northeast corner, the Friends Meeting Hall (2151 Vine), with warm brown shingles, has been here since 1923. Built in 1911, it was originally the Wesley M. E. Church. A renovation in 2013–14 connected the building with a former private home to the east. On the southeast corner is the Church of Jesus Christ of Latter-day Saints, in Spanish style with Moderne elements, from around 1935. Notice how these churches have a scale and relation to the sidewalk that allows them to fit comfortably next to the commercial zone.

An apartment building at 1517–19 Walnut.

Turn left (south) on Walnut, noting Walnut Square on the right, a 1972 development of shops along an L-shaped pedestrian way, with another entrance on Vine. Ronald Dean Senna's use of existing buildings and new construction was considered quite innovative at the time.

A little farther along on the left side, at 1517–19 Walnut, a pair of charming apartment buildings is in the same style with different design features, including bays and small balconies. Across at 1518 Walnut, the brown-shingle has a small bottle collection in a front window. On the left, at 1525 Walnut, the **24** **Daniel Fraser House**, an Italianate-style early Victorian from 1878, is the oldest house in the neighborhood (best seen from the driveway south of the house). At some point, it was resurfaced in Berkeley brown-shingle and expanded. From 1881 until 1915 or so, it was the home of Meldon LeRoy Hanscom, who became city auditor. His daughter Adelaide Hanscom Leeson was an important figure in the pictorialist movement in photography; her photo illustrations for a 1905 edition of *The Rubaiyat of Omar Khayyam* won national acclaim.

Continue on Walnut and cross Cedar carefully, as there are no stop signs. On the southeast corner, the delightful **25** **Christ Church** (originally North Berkeley Congregational Church and subsequently used by other congregations) was the first commission in private practice for architect James Plachek. The 1913 Arts and Crafts–style structure, a city landmark, includes a large trellis over columns at the entrance and a set of windows above with an ascending shape. If it is open, look inside to see exposed wooden trusses and organ pipes.

Across the street, 1602 Walnut was the home of Emily Pitchford in the early 1900s; she was a well-known pictorialist photographer, whose studio was in downtown Berkeley on Oxford. A large Colonial Revival house is next to the church at 1607 Walnut and an ornate Victorian is directly across the street at 1608 Walnut. Farther along on the left, 1623 Walnut has Colonial Revival elements as well as unusual windows and uncommon design elements. Some of the older houses and apartments along this block are attractive— including 1631–33 Walnut, called Sunny Gables—with numerous individual front entrances from the driveway.

At the corner of Walnut and Virginia streets, the **26 UC student organic garden** has a lovely sculpted metal gateway adorned with plants, bugs, and birds. Cross Virginia carefully (there is no stop sign). The west side of the block is lined with older and newer apartment buildings. On the left beyond the garden, additional land is used for experimental agriculture, followed by several UC Berkeley agricultural research facilities, including an insectary for studying live insects, a quarantine greenhouse, and the **27 Natural Resource Laboratory**.

When Walnut ends at Hearst, look across the street and to the left to see the large, modern, **28 Helios Building**. Opened in 2012, it houses the Energy Biosciences Institute (EBI), a collaboration of UC, Lawrence Berkeley National Laboratory, and the University of Illinois. EBI seeks to develop new sources of energy and reduce the impact of energy consumption, with controversial and major funding from BP (British Petroleum). The building has some intriguing design elements but it does not relate well to the public sidewalk. Unfortunately, the entrance was placed in the middle of the block facing a large surface parking lot, which UC Berkeley is planning to replace with a high-rise academic building.

Turn right on Hearst and walk one block to return to the starting point.

✳ ✳ ✳

WALK 7

CODORNICES CREEK

✳ ✳ ✳

Overview: This walk, with steep uphill portions, explores the watershed of Codornices Creek as it runs from the North Berkeley hills to the San Francisco Bay. The creek winds through parks and between homes, forms a small waterfall that plunges toward street level to emerge below, and burbles through restored riparian habitat in the Berkeley flatlands.

Highlights:

- Berkeley's most free-flowing creek
- A watershed
- An urban waterfall

Distance: 2.3–10 miles*

Time: 1.5–6 hours

Elevation gain: 370–800 feet

Loop walks:

2.3 miles: Start and return at Rose Walk (upper reaches of creek)

4.0 miles: Start in and return to downtown Berkeley (upper reaches of creek)

10.0 miles: Start in and return to downtown Berkeley (upper and lower reaches of creek)

Transit return:

7.5 miles: Start in downtown Berkeley and return by bus (upper and lower reaches of creek); if more than one person is walking, you may want to leave a car at both ends and shuttle back and forth.

When planning your outing, keep in mind that the shorter options (2.3 and 4.0 miles) are loops that explore the upper reaches of the creek, while the longer options (7.5 and 10.0 miles)—from downtown to headwaters to bay—allow for taking transit or walking back to the start.

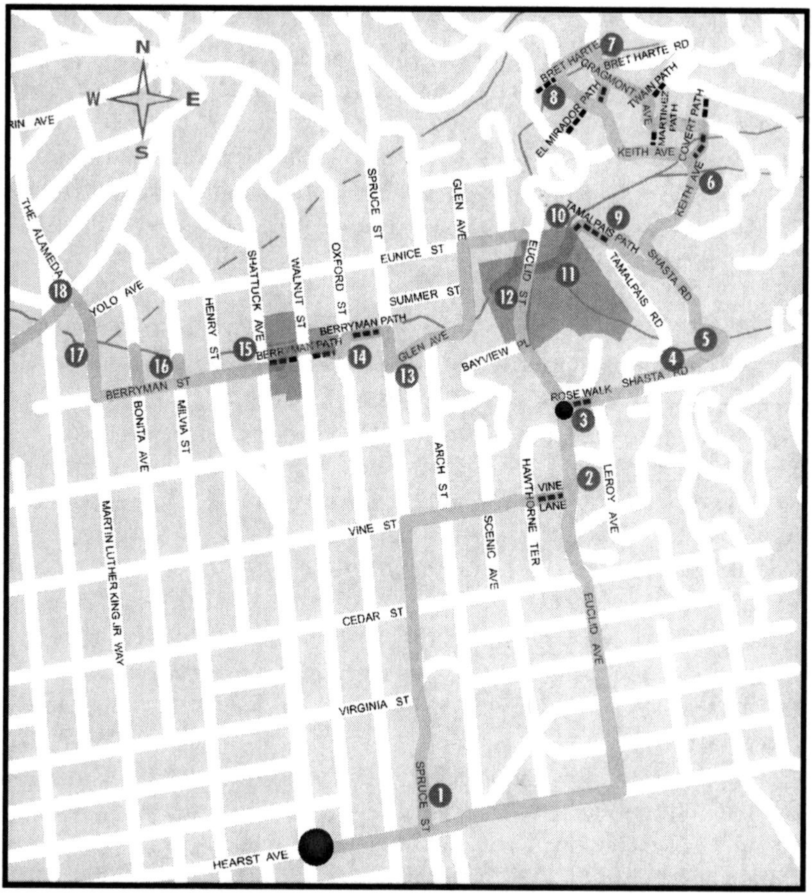

Please note: This is the first of three maps in this chapter showing the route of the Codornices Creek walk. The other maps are on pages 105 and 108.

❋ ❋ ❋

For the 2.3-mile walk option, drive or take AC Transit 65 to Rose Walk on Euclid Avenue. Start at ❸ below. For the 4.0-, 7.5-, or 10.0-mile walk options, start at Hearst and Shattuck avenues in front of Bistro Liaison at 1849 Shattuck, four blocks north of the Downtown Berkeley BART station.

Walk up Hearst to Spruce Street and turn left. On the right, ❶ **Normandy Village** (1781–1851 Spruce), also called Thornburg Village, was designed in 1927–29 by William R. Yelland, who studied at the École des Beaux-Arts in Paris but was more impressed with the architecture he saw in the French countryside. Yelland was hired by developer Jack Thornburg, who designed several storybook homes in Berkeley and some parts of Normandy Village. The village features gargoyles, exaggerated gables, interesting stairways, spiral chimneys, frescoes, and unusual stonework. The center building at 1815 Spruce was constructed later, in the 1950s, and its architecture and quality of materials are inferior to the Yelland designs.

Continue on Spruce, crossing Cedar at the stop sign. After one block, turn right up Vine Street, which hosts a stylish collection of Tudor, Colonial, and Berkeley brown-shingle homes. The red oak trees along Vine add color to the street in autumn.

Where steep Vine ends at Hawthorne Terrace, cross to go up Vine Lane path. Peek through the fence and shrubbery into the front yard of the first house on the left to catch a glimpse of Schoolhouse Creek, a long-lost stream that is now mostly culverted. Continue up Vine Lane to Euclid, noting the pretty entryway arch at the top.

Turn left on Euclid. Across the street at 1495 Euclid, Walter Ratcliff, Jr., designed the large ❷ **English Tudor–style home** with an impressive garden in 1929. Continue past the first two intersections with Hawthorne to a crosswalk and cross Euclid to Rose Walk.

A plaque near the steps describes how ❸ **Rose Walk** was laid out by architect Bernard Maybeck and funded by neighbors. As you ascend, notice how well these homes, designed by Henry Gutterson, relate to each other and how the attractive central communal space unifies the homes. Follow the sidewalk (right fork) up between the houses. Continue to the right, up the steps and through redwoods. Turn left on the sidewalk at the top.

When this part of Berkeley was laid out, a conscious effort was made to have streets follow the contours of the hills (rather than shooting straight up, as Marin Avenue does). The public paths and steps allowed pedestrians to reach transit lines or to escape in an emergency, and they may have also been designed to follow main sewer lines downhill. The contour pattern helps explain why Codornices is the least-culverted creek in Berkeley.

At the curve where Tamalpais Road meets Rose Street, turn left. A few steps farther, cross and go right up Shasta Road. Use the sidewalk on the left side, which eventually turns into a path. Native blue ceanothus and tiny gooseberry flowers bloom in February and March. After the fence ends, and just past a sculpted stone feature that looks like a simple rose window in a church, walk out on the ❹ **level area** to get a view of the creek. Continue on the path and watch your step, as the creek ravine plunges down to the left.

Rose Walk, laid out by Bernard Maybeck.

Walk around the large ❺ **Swiss chalet-style house** at 2645 Shasta, with an extensive garden and the creek emerging from a culvert underneath. Originally built in 1911, the home was later renovated by Maybeck and significantly expanded. You may see chickens or a goat in front, as well as some animal and gnome sculptures.

Continue up Shasta, keeping to the left and watching for traffic on this narrow, curvy street. Go past Tamalpais on the left. After the curve, turn left on Keith Avenue (named for William Keith, a Berkeley painter famous for his California landscapes).

John Hudson Thomas designed the large house on the right, at ❻ **1185 Keith**, just after the descent. Continue to a waterfall on the right that steps down the ivy-clad slope next to 1179–81 Keith; the waterfall generally runs year-round and can be dramatic after significant rainfall. Codornices Creek has about five forks in the hills; this is one of the largest. On the opposite side of the street, the creek emerges and goes under a wooden footbridge in the front garden of a house.

Walk along Keith. To the right of two modern houses at 1173 and 1175 Keith, an intermittent stream flows only during the rainy winter season. There are two alternatives from here that both lead to the same place, one steep and challenging **(A)** and one more moderate **(B)**.

(A) Ascend on El Mirador Path on a steep stairway amid redwoods; next to the mailbox for 1119 Keith, a metal signpost and stepping stones mark the path. This (private-seeming) public path uses wooden railroad ties for steps, It passes around a big redwood to the left and rises over 100 steps to Cragmont Avenue. Turn left at the top and continue to Bret Harte Road, which ascends to the right.

(B) Walk on Keith to Bret Harte Road (not Bret Harte Path) and turn right, going uphill. At Cragmont, turn right for a few steps to the continuation of Bret Harte, which goes left uphill.

The stepped waterfall of Codornices Creek on Keith Avenue.

Ascend Bret Harte along a hedge and fence on the left to a **❼ Japanese-style wooden gate** at 131 Bret Harte. Peek through the gate to see a house accessed by a long footbridge that crosses another fork of Codornices Creek.

Descend back to Cragmont and turn right. On the right, look through the fence next to a gate (in the lower yard of the house with the long footbridge) to see the stream running through a small, human-made cascade. Turn left on Bret Harte; down the block just where the left sidewalk ends and past a redwood, the creek emerges from a culvert and goes under an angled footbridge. Turn left on Keith; on the right side, just past **❽ 1104 Keith**, you might be able to see or hear the creek through the hedge as it descends to the right of the next house.

Continue on Keith, passing the stepped waterfall again, and turn right to go down Shasta, which you previously traveled. This time, turn right on Tamalpais after the curve; proceed with care, as this remote, windy, narrow street has limited sidewalks. At the next sharp curve, on the right, is **❾ 149 Tamalpais**, a large house designed by John Hudson Thomas in 1906 in brown-shingle, stone, and stucco. On the left side of that house, descend Tamalpais Path down the extremely steep stairs with a helpful handrail. A fork of Codornices Creek runs free in Benner Canyon to the right.

After about 180 steps and an S-curved stairway, you will arrive at **❿ Codornices Park**. At the bottom of the path, look across and above the private bridge on the right. From 1940 to 1965, the lower building was the studio (later expanded as a residence), and higher up the hill was the home of documentary photographer and photojournalist Dorothea Lange and her husband, UC Berkeley economics professor Paul Schuster Taylor. Lange is best known for her Depression-era photography documenting migrant workers; she also took numerous photos of the large oak next to the upper house. Architect John White (Bernard Maybeck's brother-in-law) originally designed the home for himself in 1910.

Facing the park, walk toward the second bridge over the creek (do not cross it). From here there are two options:

(A) Walk left on the path next to the wooden railing about 50 to 60 paces to the steep path that descends, taking care around an eroded section near the top, until you arrive at the paved area between the playground and where the creek enters a culvert.

Trees by Dorothea Lange, who lived near Codornices Park.

(B) If the first descending path is too steep or muddy, proceed another 50 paces along the path to where concrete steps go back down to the right, emerging at the same place between the playground and the culvert.

Head left on the paved path around the playground, past another playground and the spectacular **⓫ 40-foot concrete slide** (feel free to give it a go—but not without cardboard), until you reach a fence where the south fork of Codornices Creek cascades over rocks and enters another culvert.

Turn around toward the road (looking west) and take the paved path to the right side of the basketball court. Walk through the pedestrian tunnel under Euclid. After you emerge, walk to the left past the public restrooms. Continue on past the tennis courts and picnic tables to a gate in a high fence on the right. This is the entrance to the **⓬ Berkeley Rose Garden**. Go through the gate and walk toward the trellis for a view of the bay.

This delightful amphitheater was built as a New Deal Works Progress Administration project in 1937. Descend the steps, enjoying the roses if they are in season. At the bottom, the creek, the two forks of which have converged underground, emerges in a concrete channel before flowing into private gardens (a third fork enters the park from the north unseen). This area was formerly a marshy confluence of creeks with a wooden trestle for a streetcar line where the raised embankment of Euclid is now.

Return uphill through the same gate and turn left, passing again between the restroom and tennis courts. This time, take the steps up to the left toward the street instead of going through the tunnel. There are several options from here:

(A) Take the 65 bus back to downtown Berkeley. The bus stop is near the top of the steps, by the corner of Euclid and Eunice Street.

(B) To return to the starting point at Rose Walk (a 2.3-mile walk), turn right (south) on Euclid and walk about two blocks.

(C) To return to the starting point in downtown Berkeley (a 4.0-mile walk), turn right (south) on Euclid and walk to Hearst. Turn right on Hearst and walk to Shattuck. To get to the nearest BART station, turn left and walk four blocks on Shattuck to the Downtown Berkeley BART station.

To continue exploring on the 7.5- or 10.0-mile walk, turn left on Euclid and left again on Eunice. Descend and turn left on the first street on the left, Glen Avenue. After passing Summer Street on the right, look to the left just beyond 1239 Glen to hear the creek as it emerges from behind the house.

Follow Glen as it angles right; the road narrows and there is no sidewalk here. (Codornices Creek flows through the back yards of many houses on the right but cannot be seen from the street.) On the southeast corner of Spruce and Glen, the **13 large Craftsman** at 2204 Glen has a witch's-hat turret. The house was built in 1908 to withstand earthquakes on the nearby Hayward Fault after owner Roy R. Dempster lost his home near Lake Merritt in the 1906 earthquake.

Cross Spruce in the crosswalk, turn right, and take Berryman Path to the left, just beyond Congregation Beth El, which has a garden and gaga pit to the left of the path. (Gaga is an Israeli dodgeball-style game, played in an octagonal court; this one is made of wood.) During planning for its move to this site in the early 2000s, **14 Congregation Beth El** was at the center of a citywide controversy, in part over Codornices Creek. To resolve the controversy, a parking area originally designated for above the creek culvert (where the garden is now) was moved, and the steep open portion was restored with native plants.

At Oxford Street, turn left and look over the cement fence to see the creek. There is an informational plaque about this historic property just beyond the creek at the synagogue's driveway entrance.

Go back to the crosswalk at Berryman Path and cross Oxford. Turn left and take the metal ramp and then the path on the right down into Live Oak Park; follow the creek downstream amid native oak, redwood, and buckeye trees and nonnative flowering plums. The Berkeley Art Center, a nonprofit museum with public programs and classes, is creekside. Pass under Walnut Street beyond the art center or go up and cross at street level. Walk down through the park, crossing the bridges to enjoy the stream and more trees, including bay laurels. Opened in 1916, Live Oak Park was the second public park in Berkeley (San Pablo Park was the first). Community festivals are held on the lawn to the north of the creek throughout the year, and there is a theater and recreation center to the south.

Across Shattuck, look over the wall to where **⓯ Codornices Creek** emerges amid a group of houses and duplexes, designed during the 1970s in an effort to bring together old and new structures with the creek as a central feature.

Turn right to walk down Berryman. At the southeast corner with Henry Street, on the left with the large peace sign, is the communal home of Wavy Gravy (née Hugh Romney) and the seasonal headquarters of his Camp Winnarainbow. Wavy Gravy is a professional hippie, entertainer, political activist, global philanthropist, and the inspiration for a Ben & Jerry's ice cream flavor.

Cross Henry carefully in the crosswalk (cars tend to speed here) and continue down Berryman past St. Mary Magdalen Church and school on the right. Cross Milvia Street and turn right on Milvia down the hill—you might smell the perfumed flowers of winter daphne in late winter or early spring—and look on the left side where the **⓰ creek emerges** after the apartment building and goes around a big live oak and under several bridges.

Walk back to Berryman, passing the quirky older apartment building on the corner, and turn right, then turn right again on Bonita Avenue. At the bottom of the hill, the creek is open on both sides; one side is just beyond a large, handsome brown-shingle house on the right. The creek is very natural looking here, but it can be hard to discern through the hedge across the street. The confluence with a northern fork of Codornices Creek is in the middle of this block, though difficult to see.

Return again to Berryman and turn right. Cross Martin Luther King, Jr., (MLK) Way at the stop sign and turn right (the street name changes to The Alameda here). Just before the **⑰ storybook house** at 1214 The Alameda, the creek goes under the garage. Cross Hopkins Street at the signal to the front of the **⑱ Berkeley Public Library North Branch**, built in 1936.

Turn left and walk down Hopkins. The creek crosses Hopkins unseen near Josephine Street, then flows openly behind the houses on the right side of Hopkins. You may be able to see a line of tall trees that follows the stream. Hopkins is lined with mature London plane (sycamore) trees, which form a green tunnel in spring and summer.

Turn right on Colusa Avenue. You can see the creek on the right side, just past an angled garage at **⑲ 1215 Colusa**. The creek flows under rustic bridges, ducks under the garage, and emerges again at the concrete wall across the street at 1230 Colusa.

Return to Hopkins and continue to a busy neighborhood shopping area that intersects Monterey Avenue. Turn right on Monterey, and walk a half-block to see the **⑳ creek** on the right side, lined

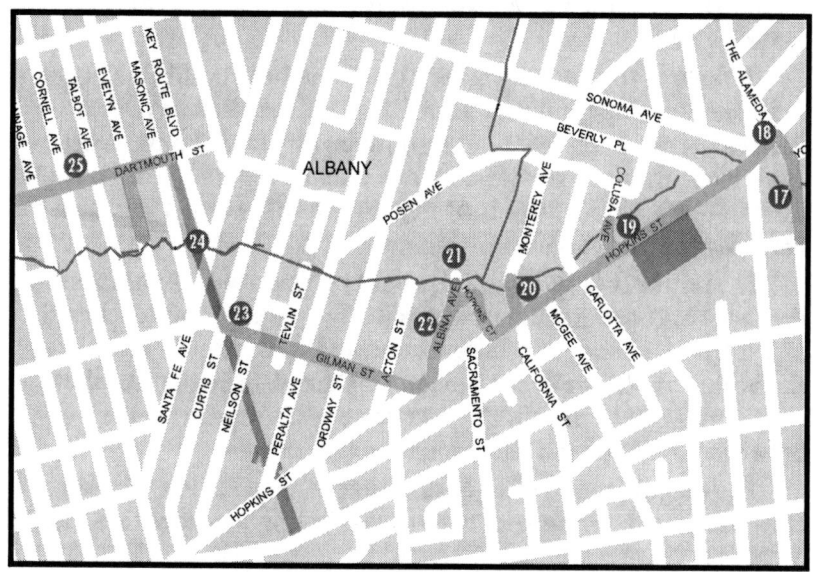

Berkeley Public Library North Branch.

with native alder, bay laurel, and (less-common) box elder trees. Return to the stop sign at Hopkins, turn right to cross Monterey, and continue on Hopkins to Hopkins Court. Turn right, following Hopkins Court as it curves left, then go right on Albina Avenue to the bridge, where you can see **㉑ Saint Mary's College High School**, a private school just over the border in Albany. From this point to the bay, the creek forms the boundary between the cities of Berkeley and Albany.

In the late 1800s, Maurice B. Curtis sought to build an elegant, exclusive development in this area. The multiturreted Peralta Park Hotel was completed in 1889, but only 13 large homes were completed around it before Curtis went bankrupt in 1900. The hotel was used as a school from 1903 to 1959, when it was demolished; the Saint Mary's campus is here now.

The house at 1296 Albina was built on concrete pilings close to the creek and has erosion issues that affect both the creek's health and the house's stability. Turn around and walk directly away from the bridge on Albina to see a plaque for the historic 1841 Peralta Adobe, the first home built by a nonnative (European) in Berkeley, between 1302 and 1304 Albina, under a small tree.

The magnificent **㉒ Lueders House** at 1330 Albina, an 1889 Queen Anne Victorian with turrets, was lovingly restored and added onto by second owners Thomas E. Roe and Stephen Johnson over the course of nearly 40 years. Believed to have only three owners in its long history, this is the most impressive of the five remaining Peralta Park Victorians.

Continue to Hopkins and turn right, and then bear right onto Gilman Street at the stop sign. In the autumn, look right, down Ordway Street, to enjoy colorful Chinese pistache trees. In the summer, the purple-flowering jacaranda trees lining Gilman are lovely. The **㉓ Westbrae commercial district** goes from Peralta to Santa Fe avenues, with a grocery, restaurant, bagel store, florist, and beer garden.

Just after crossing Curtis Street at the stop sign, bear right onto the Ohlone Greenway, a miles-long bicycle and pedestrian path that follows the elevated BART tracks and old railroad rights-of-way all the way to Richmond (see Walk 16, Ohlone Greenway). Cross Santa Fe in the crosswalk; just beyond is a tall railing on the left where the **㉔ creek emerges from a culvert**, with several mature native cottonwood trees and box elder. Volunteers from Friends of Five Creeks, a local nonprofit organization, built the structure, restored the native plants, and commissioned the quail sculptures (*codornices* means "quail" in Spanish). Crabapple and plum trees flower in March on the north bank.

Continue on Ohlone Greenway to the next intersection, Dartmouth Street (no street sign), and turn left. Avid creek enthusiasts can turn left on Evelyn Avenue and walk a block to see the creek between 1145 and 1203 Evelyn, as well as a very large tree. Several redbud trees bloom in March near the southwest corner of Evelyn and Dartmouth. Continue down Dartmouth west to Talbot Avenue. At the northwest corner, the **㉕ tot playground** has equipment built from recycled materials. Continue on Dartmouth to San Pablo Avenue, turn right, and cross at the Monroe Street signal to enter **㉖ University (UC) Village**.

For thousands of years, the Huchuin Indians used nets and other means to trap fish and birds among the native cordgrass and pickleweed that grew in the wetlands here. The area became part of the huge Peralta land grant of 1820, and Jose Domingo Peralta grazed cattle here until the 1850s. By the 1870s, slaughterhouses, tanneries, and other foul-smelling enterprises had moved in to take advantage of the freshwater creek, which was reduced to a straight channel with little native vegetation by the 1930s.

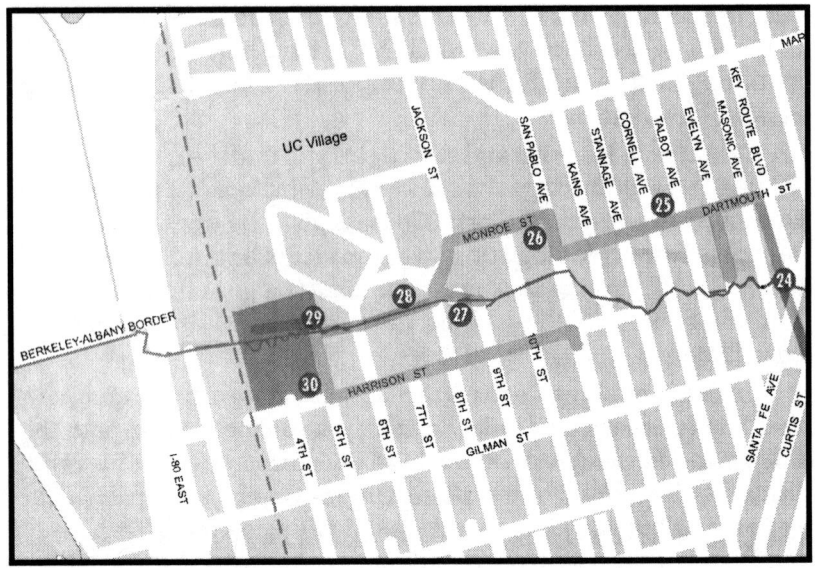

The development here now began as a federal housing project for workers during World War II, especially employees of the Kaiser Shipyards in Richmond; after the war, returning servicemen and women and their families were housed here. UC acquired the units in 1956, and, between the mid-1990s and late 2000s, replaced most of the old, unsafe housing with new apartments. The residences are primarily for students with families as well as postdoctoral fellows and visiting scholars.

Continue down Monroe and turn left at Jackson Street, which curves and connects with 8th Street. Go through the gate to the left on a dirt trail to see a **㉗ restored creek** segment that is heavily shaded by fast-growing native trees—mainly willows as well as alders, buckeyes, oaks, bay laurels, and California grapevines. In the mid-1990s—at a cost of about $35,000—this segment was daylighted (removed from its underground concrete culvert and restored) thanks to efforts by Richard Register (founder of Ecocity Builders), Carole Schemmerling (founder of the Urban Creeks Council), and numerous creek advocates and community members.

When the office building at 1101 8th Street was built, creekside restoration work was done, perhaps as environmental mitigation, though that side is fenced off from public access. Explore a bit around here (the dirt path goes to a ball field at 9th Street), then return to 8th and cross over.

Take the path on the left side of the bridge, with a **㉘ small sandy sitting area,** just down from the street and log benches. The city of Albany received about $2.5 million in funding—linked in part to the renovation of UC Village—to fully daylight and restore this reach between 6th and 8th streets, with the primary goal of creating habitat for native fish. The creek's flood plain was reconfigured to allow it to meander, and the banks were planted with native trees, shrubs, and perennial flowers. There are several small cascades in this delightful stretch of restored creek, and informational panels along the path describe the area's history and environment. However, the concrete block wall on the south side of the path is unsightly; perhaps the US Postal Service will remove it some day.

Thanks to restoration efforts, steelhead trout have spawned in the creek for several years, although the marshy area at the bay may have discouraged them from entering this stretch long before Anglo settlers changed the creek. Frogs, crayfish, stickleback, and other aquatic animals are plentiful, and endangered steelhead trout have been spotted here.

Take the path past 6th Street. Willows shade the creek here. At 5th Street, the **㉙ pedestrian bridge** is a good place to look for creek life or just enjoy the flow. The trail turns into a dirt path that continues on to another bridge, joining playing fields on the north and south sides (a joint project of Berkeley, Albany, and UC).

Beyond this, railroad tracks prevent pedestrians from following the creek any farther. Codornices Creek skirts the back side of Target (just visible past the playing fields) and enters a culvert, eventually joining the bay near Golden Gate Fields.

To see the **㉚ Berkeley Skate Park**—with its ledges, ramps, and boarders going through their paces—return to the bridge at 5th and turn right (south) past the playing field. From 5th, return to San Pablo on Harrison Street or walk back on the stream trail through UC Village. Check *511.org* for the quickest public transit route back to downtown Berkeley (a 7.5 mile walk), or walk back on the Ohlone Greenway, or a route of your choosing, for the 10-mile walk.

❋ ❋ ❋

WALK 8
HOPKINS AND MONTEREY MARKET

✻ ✻ ✻

Overview: This walk explores a neighborhood of historic homes, a unique shopping district, a trend-setting school garden, a yard full of delightful found object sculptures, and the site of an unsuccessful early Victorian residential development. There are moderate ups and downs with no steep sections.

Highlights:
- Historic Peralta Park
- Found-objects sculpture garden
- Edible Schoolyard, Hopkins Street shopping area

Distance: 3.5 miles
Time: 2–2.5 hours
Elevation gain: 260 feet

✻ ✻ ✻

Start at Vine and Milvia streets, which is a short walk from the North Berkeley or Downtown Berkeley BART stations; you can also take AC Transit 7 or 18, get off at Shattuck Avenue and Vine, and walk two blocks west (away from the hills) to Milvia. Parking is available on nearby streets, with restrictions.

The neighborhoods in this walk were all part of the 44,800-acre Rancho San Antonio, granted in 1820 by the Spanish crown to Luis María Peralta. In 1842, Peralta divided the rancho among his four sons; José Domingo Peralta received what is now Berkeley and Albany, and his adobe home was located on Albina Street, which is

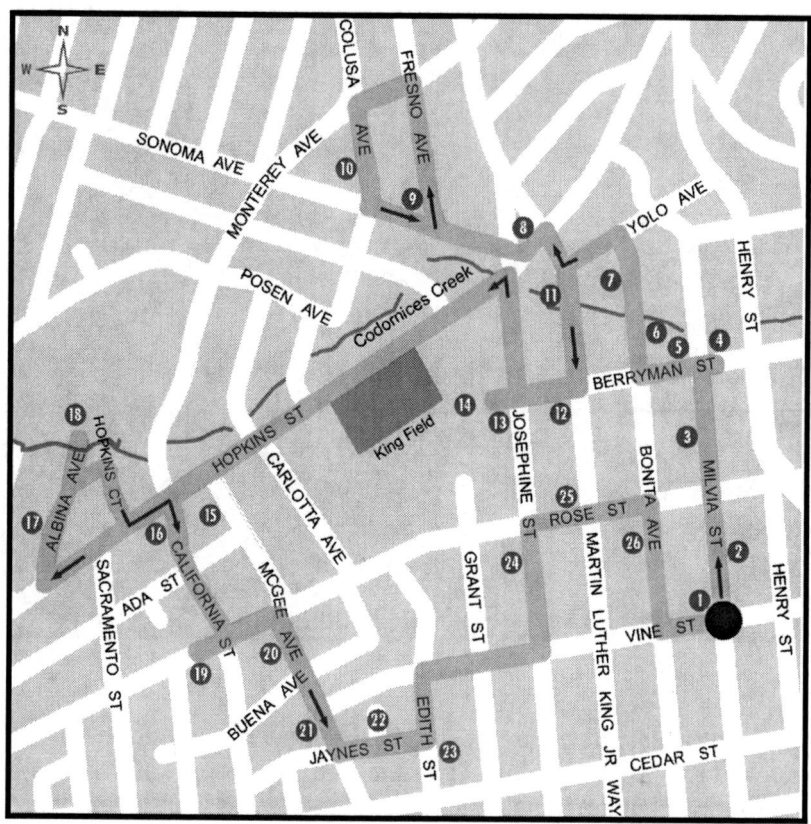

in this walk. Streets in the northern part of the walk (including the Northbrae and Peralta Park tracts) veer off diagonally from the rest of Berkeley's street grid because of the way the Peralta family subdivided and sold off the land grant over the years.

The ❶ **Queen Anne Victorian** at 1941 Vine (northwest corner), with sunburst and geometric designs in the gables and roof dormers, was built in 1888 and is typical of homes belonging to railway employees at that time.

Walk north on Milvia (with the hills to your right). In February, lots of pink and white plum trees bloom here. Another Queen Anne cottage from the 1890s is at 1434 Milvia; this one has been renovated.

Farther along and across the street, 1425 Milvia is an ❷ **Italianate house** from 1880, one of the earliest homes in the

A Queen Anne Victorian at 1941 Vine Street.

area, with characteristic arch-headed window forms and a low-pitched roof. It has a colorful paint job, although some of the ornamentation is not original. The Italianate style was popular early in the Victorian era and is less common in Berkeley than the Queen Anne style. The 1888 house at 1414 Milvia has elements of Italianate but seems to represent a transition to the later Victorian style.

Proceed on along Milvia and cross Rose Street carefully (cross traffic does not have a stop sign); continue toward Berryman Street, noting 1960s-era apartment buildings that do not fit well with the late-19th-century homes along the way. At ❸ **1322 Milvia**, a hedge has been pruned to resemble an automobile.

At Berryman, ❹ **St. Mary Magdalen Church** is on the northeast corner, built in 1924 in Mission Revival style on land formerly owned by the Southern Pacific Railroad.

On the northwest corner of Berryman and Milvia, opposite the church, the ❺ **1904 apartment building** was designed as an individualized interpretation of Mission Revival style, with a turret and rather strange proportions. Nevertheless, it is a fun building and the apartments have varied layouts as the building steps down the slope. The side and rear have unique details as well, including top-floor sunrooms.

Cross the street and walk west (away from the hills) one block on Berryman to Bonita Avenue and turn right. 1235 Bonita, built in 1915, has half-timbering in an unusual combination with Chinese ceramic tiles. Across the street, 1234 Bonita is a brown-shingle house with its entrance on the south side and an unusual pattern of shingles and horizontal wood siding facing the street. It has a pleasant feeling of simplicity and age. At 1231 Bonita, an impressive ❻ **Berkeley brown-shingle house** has a large gable and green shutters; just beyond the house, Codornices Creek is visible from the sidewalk. The least culverted of Berkeley's creeks, Codornices Creek gathers from several forks in the hills and enters the bay near Golden Gate Fields (see Walk 7, Codornices Creek); Coho salmon and steelhead trout have been spotted in its waters.

The unusual house at ❼ **1210 Bonita** was reportedly built before 1921; Carr Jones remodeled it in 1944 and added the unique brick facade that gives it so much character. Jones trained as an engineer but also designed many storybook homes in the East Bay. He renovated the house he lived in, across the street at 1211 Bonita.

Walk up Bonita to Yolo Avenue and turn left. This is part of the 700-acre Northbrae subdivision of 1907 developed by the Mason-McDuffie real estate company, which also developed the Claremont and Uplands neighborhoods. Northbrae was developed in six different tracts, so there is some confusion about the boundaries. Broadly, it centers on the Marin Circle.

At The Alameda (which turns into Martin Luther King, Jr., [MLK] Way), turn right to pass the gas station on the corner, built in Spanish style and the oldest still in use in the city. At the corner of Hopkins Street (at the traffic light), cross The Alameda and Hopkins to the northwest corner in front of the ❽ **Berkeley Public Library North Branch**. Built in 1936, this branch was designed by the architectural firm of James Plachek, which also designed Berkeley's main library downtown and the Claremont Branch.

As part of a voter-approved bond issue, Berkeley's four branch libraries received seismic upgrades and improvements in the early 2010s. Amid some controversy, the South and West Branches were demolished and rebuilt, but the landmarked North Branch was renovated, with a modest new addition on the back. If the library is open, go inside to view the domed entry area and two historic

The G. E. DeVries House.

wings with beautiful stenciled beam ceilings, revealed in all their glory after the removal of modern lighting fixtures and other features that had partly obscured them. Brick fireplaces frame the ends of the wings.

Upon exiting the library, turn right, and then turn right again at the corner onto Sonoma Avenue, crossing Josephine Street. The large ❾ **G. E. De Vries House**, designed in 1921 by B. E. Remmel, is set up high on the Fresno Avenue corner at 1825 Sonoma. This unique design combines Craftsman and other styles with separate wall treatments such as shingles on the lower floor and stucco and half-timbering on the upper floor. Other appealing features include the bay with tall windows, projecting second floor, and entry stairway.

Turn right on Fresno, walking past several early 20th-century bungalows. (The word "bungalow" is derived from the Indian word *bangalo*, which refers to being built in the Bengali style during the British Raj; this word now generally refers to a detached house that is one or one and a half floors with a veranda.) The street is lined with plane (sycamore) trees, replacements for elms that were removed due to disease. White dogwoods bloom here in March.

At Monterey Avenue, turn left and walk one short block to Colusa Avenue, noting the older and larger trees lining the street. Turn left on Colusa, walking down the right (west) side of the street; on the opposite side, some old California oaks are unusually short for the size of their trunks.

The 1913 ❿ **Craftsman bungalow** at 1118 Colusa has an intriguing sculpture garden that includes a Japanese samurai with armor made from disposable lighters and a figure composed of fishnet floats. According to the artist (carpenter Mark Olivier), the sculptures are made almost entirely from objects found at or near the shoreline—a great example of creative reuse. Some neighboring homes also have sculptures from the same innovative artist.

Turn left at Sonoma; 1813, 1815, and 1819 Sonoma have walls made from local stone along their walkways. Camphor trees line this block on both sides; their bright green (sometimes red) leaves are fragrant when crushed. After crossing two streets and turning left at Hopkins, you are back at the front of the North Branch library. Cross Hopkins, turning right at the signal, to proceed south on The Alameda. The right (west) side is lined with large plane trees and the east side has tall ash trees that continue all the way to University Avenue.

About midblock, two ⓫ **storybook houses** are at 1214 The Alameda and 1225 The Alameda. To the left of 1214 The Alameda, a garage is built over Codornices Creek. The street name changes to MLK Way at number 1239.

At the southwest corner of Berryman Street, 1300 MLK Way is where architect ⓬ **Bernard Maybeck first lived in Berkeley** and began experimenting with design, as he expanded the small 1892 house (now apartments) and discussed ideas with his students. The house is a city landmark, although it is much altered since Maybeck's time.

Turn right on Berryman, passing a row of Craftsman houses on the right with subtle design elements of Swiss chalets. At the southwest corner at ⓭ **1304 Josephine Street**, James Plachek designed the large 1917 house with an inset porch. Cross the street and proceed to the end of Berryman. The school district does not want visitors to enter the garden, but from here you can see the ⓮ **Edible Schoolyard**.

The Edible Schoolyard was founded in 1995 by Alice Waters in partnership with the Berkeley Unified School District. Students at Martin Luther King, Jr., Middle School not only plant, tend, and harvest the farm; they also learn to prepare food from the garden in the classroom kitchen and eat food from the garden together as a community. The garden includes vegetables, fruits, flowers, chickens, and ducks. It is integrated into the school curriculum— from math to science to social studies—and the concept has been emulated at schools throughout the nation. The henhouse is to the right. (Check with the middle school about public tours.)

Return to Josephine, turn left, and then go left on Hopkins. Mature plane trees line both sides of the street; their high branches make a sylvan tunnel. Continue past the track, playground, and tennis courts. Across the street, the large Victorian at 1675 Hopkins is one of only five remaining from an early development called Peralta Park. In the next block on the right, the historic storefronts have clerestory windows placed high above eye level to allow natural light inside.

As you cross McGee Avenue, notice ⓯ **Berkeley Horticultural Nursery**, with entrances on McGee and California Street. Founded in 1922 by George Budgen and still family owned, the nursery takes up most of the block and features a wide variety of plants in a compact space and a rock garden with dwarf conifers; it is also known for native plants. Take a side trip through the nursery, unless you're there on a Thursday, when it's closed. McGee is lined with large sweetgum trees that have vibrant colors in late autumn and early winter and sometimes well into January.

Back on Hopkins, walk past the row of mainly food-oriented shops. The street is lined with graceful curving Chinese elm trees. Between the real estate office (1600 Hopkins) and the liquor and wine shop (1590 Hopkins), walk a few steps into an alleyway. Two things are of note: the shop is only 10 feet wide here and the rear of the retail building curves outward, reflecting the streetcar right-of-way of the spur that went up Hopkins.

This shopping district was the hub of a major streetcar stop, and the stores fulfilled the daily needs of local residents. Berkeley is a community of "foodies," and these shops and the neighborhood's ambience draw people from all over town. The grid of streets and sidewalks makes this a walkable neighborhood, where people can still easily go on foot or by bicycle to do their grocery shopping— especially handy because parking spots are often hard to come by. Continuing on Hopkins, you will pass a pizzeria, a bakery, a fish market, a restaurant, a cheese and tea and coffee purveyor, and a butcher; it is like stepping back into the era before giant supermarkets.

The store on the corner, currently Magnani's Poultry (1576 Hopkins), was the original location of ⓰ **Monterey Market**, which is now across the street. Tom and Mary Fujimoto opened Monterey Foods, a shop specializing in local produce, in 1961. The store became a Berkeley tradition, a harbinger of numerous markets in town featuring sustainable, local, and organic products.

Cross catty-corner at the stop sign and continue left down Hopkins on the opposite (northwest) side. Along this part of Hopkins, look for two of the remaining early Victorian houses from the Peralta Park subdivision (hint: there is one on each side). The one on the left has a tall, white dogwood blooming in late March. After the signal, turn right on Albina Avenue. At 1330 Albina, **⓱ Lueders House** is a grand Victorian designed in 1889 by Ira A. Boynton; it was in the family of Edward Lueders, the original owner, until 1972. Thomas E. Roe and Stephen Johnson bought it at that time, when it needed substantial maintenance; it became a commune and then suffered a disastrous fire in 1974. Roe and many others worked on restoring and adding to the house over several decades. (Roe passed away in 2011.) A giant monkey puzzle, or araucaria, tree is in the front yard. Several large American elm trees still line the street, but this noble species is being lost to disease.

Just a bit farther along on the right side of the driveway at 1304 Albina, a plaque on the ground commemorates the site of the 1841 adobe of José Domingo Peralta, whose father had the 1820 land grant that covered most of today's Alameda County. Walk a bit farther along Albina to the bridge at the entrance to **⓲ Saint Mary's College High School**.

In 1889, Maurice B. Curtis (a.k.a. Mauritz Strelinger), who made a fortune as a comic actor, bought the Peralta Park tract of undeveloped land in this area and subdivided it. He established a horse-car line (a streetcar pulled by a horse on rails, before electric ones) and built the grand Peralta Park Hotel as the focal point of the subdivision. However, only a dozen or so of the grand Victorian homes were built, and Curtis ended up gong bankrupt defending himself in a series of trials in which he was charged with killing the San Francisco policeman who arrested him on drunken behavior (eventually he was found innocent). Five of the original Victorians remain, including 1330 Albina and the three on Hopkins that you passed earlier. The hotel building subsequently housed Catholic school facilities, including the Saint Joseph's Academy for Boys from 1903 and Saint Mary's College High School from 1927, both operated by the Christian Brothers. In 1959, Saint Mary's tore down the historic building and replaced it with a newer structure, visible from the bridge over Codornices Creek. On the left before the bridge, notice how close the house at 1296 Albina is to the creek; Berkeley now restricts construction near creeks to protect the waterway from pollution, prevent erosion, and limit the flooding of residences.

From the bridge, backtrack and turn left on Hopkins Court, walk to Hopkins, and turn left. At the stop sign, cross Hopkins to California Street and walk on the sidewalk adjoining the Monterey

Market parking lot. Continue past Ada Street; just past the corner on the right, the duplex at 1330–32 California extends back at a long diagonal. This was part of the former streetcar right-of-way (extending from behind the liquor store on Monterey). Continue up the hill to Rose Street, cross in the crosswalk, and turn right. If you look closely, you can see a concrete projection on each side of the street; this is actually a bridge. The **⑲ California streetcar line** avoided the hill you just climbed by going through a tunnel; if you peek through the shrubbery along the bridge, you can see the railway cut in backyards on this side (the cut is slightly visible from the bridge's north side).

Turn around and walk back up Rose (east toward the hills). Go one block beyond California to McGee and turn right. The first block includes a number of **⑳ Craftsman houses** built between 1906 and 1920, including 1412 McGee and 1419 McGee, both brown-shingles. The Craftsman style was influenced by the British Arts and Crafts movement, a reaction to ornate Victorian style. Craftsman homes are usually simply designed in wood or wood and

A Craftsman house at 1516 McGee.

stucco and usually include moderately pitched roofs and extending eaves, prominent rafters and brackets, front porches, the upper parts of windows divided into smaller lites (segments), and simple wood ornamentation. Cross Buena Avenue and pass more Craftsmans, most notably **㉑ 1514 and 1516 McGee.** Turn left on Jaynes Street, which has more Craftsmans; walk into the cul-de-sac North Street on the **㉒ left side of Jaynes** to see several more. Continue on Jaynes, noting the Japanese maple and ginkgo trees, which have brilliant hues in late autumn.

At Edith Street, look across to the right at 1533 Edith; the **㉓ brown-shingle** has a wide, finely detailed, second-floor dormer. Turn left on Edith, which has more Craftsmans, such as at 1518, as well as a high-peaked Colonial Revival house with brown shingles across the street at 1511. A more recent house (1973) at 1508 Edith mixes Craftsman and other styles, perhaps overdoing it.

Turn right on Vine, walk two blocks to the corner of Josephine, and cross left to proceed on Josephine. 1410 Josephine is an appealing **㉔ brown-shingle Craftsman.** A Berkeley architect designed a second-floor addition in an extremely sensitive fashion, preserving the house's character but giving residents the space they wanted.

Turn right on Rose. At the signal for MLK Way, **㉕ Fatapple's restaurant** is popular for its burgers, pie, and big breakfasts. Mr. Mopps' Children's Books and Toys, on the opposite side, has been selling a variety of toys here since 1962.

Cross MLK Way at the signal, walk one block to Bonita (lined with sweetgums, with brilliant autumn colors), and turn right. A large **㉖ Queen Anne Victorian** at 1410 Bonita dates to around 1892 and is attributed to Ira A. Boynton. This was once a senior convalescent home; in 1971, it became the first residential-style psychiatric halfway house in the county, called Bonita House. A Victorian at 1418 Bonita has colored glass sections in the windows. At Vine Street, turn left and walk one block to the starting point.

❊ ❊ ❊

WALK 9

SOUTHAMPTON AND THOUSAND OAKS

❋ ❋ ❋

Overview: Southampton and Thousand Oaks are two upscale neighborhoods developed by John Hopkins Spring in the early 20th century. The tree-lined streets are quiet with a pleasing variety of architecture. There are a few stretches of steep up and downhill.

Highlights:
- Tree-lined residential streets and architectural gems
- Cascades on Blackberry Creek
- John Hinkel and Great Stoneface parks

Distance: 3.0–3.5 miles
Walking time: 1.5–2.5 hours
Elevation Gain: 470–676 feet

❋ ❋ ❋

By car, take Arlington Avenue, turn right on Santa Barbara Road, and park around 670–83 Santa Barbara. By AC Transit, take the 67 Spruce bus to the stop at 619–25 Spruce (Acacia Path). Walk in the same direction as the bus, and cross Spruce Street at the crosswalk; turn right and then left down Northampton Avenue to the starting point at Santa Barbara. Or take the 7 Arlington bus and get off at San Luis Road. If you take the Arlington bus, skip sites ❶ and ❷ and begin with ❸; at the end, you will walk past ❶ and ❷ to return to Arlington.

The first stop is in front of ❶ **656 Santa Barbara,** downhill behind a wooden fence, with brick and wood walls in varied

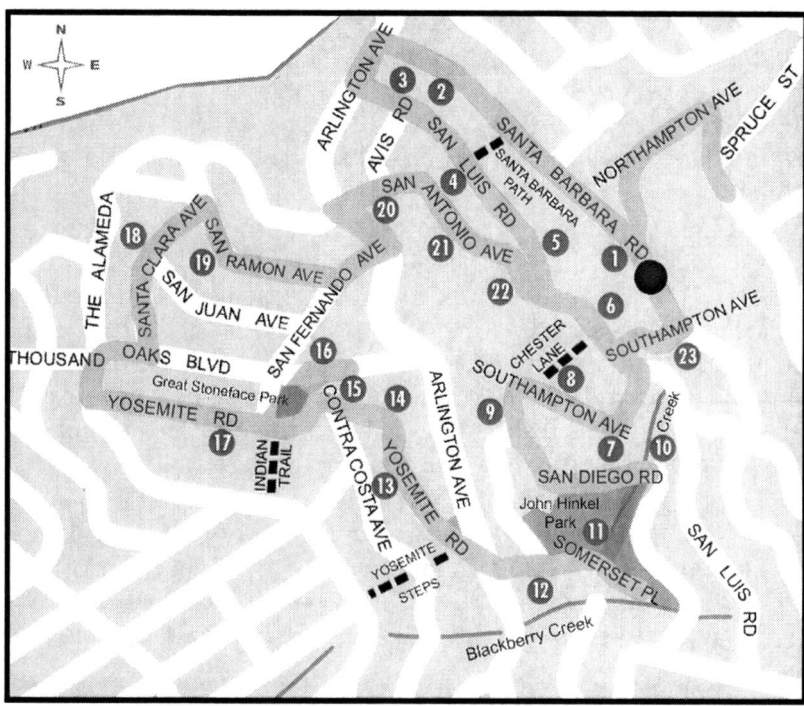

patterns, a wooden shake roof, and a diamond-pane window projecting out next to the garage. Walk downhill (with house numbers descending) on Santa Barbara, enjoying the ambience of diverse gardens as well as a mixture of homes, including generic Mediterranean, Tudor, Craftsman, and English cottage. More than 40 pink flowering plum trees may be lining the street in January and February, as well as some Japanese cherry blossoms and crabapples in March. On the left, ❷ **530 Santa Barbara** is a notable two-story house with Craftsman details, including intricate window designs, large brackets, and wood-and-stucco siding.

At the end of the long block, descend the steep steps and turn left on Arlington. Walk to the next street, San Luis, and turn left. Walk up this street, with homes of various styles from the 1920s to 1940s as well as some recent modern homes. The street is lined with camphor trees with glossy leaves. The fallen leaves that still have color have an intriguing fragrance when crushed. Unfortunately, the roots are disruptive to sidewalks.

On the left, 527 San Luis has extensive ❸ **gardens and a Japanese-style gate**. A more recent version of the traditional

Craftsman homes built in the early 20th century is at 575 San Luis. On the opposite side, ❹ **600 San Luis** has several extremely tall pine trees (perhaps ponderosa). Farther along, at 661 San Luis, the ❺ **huge, dark, layered rock** next to the driveway seems different from light-colored volcanic rhyolite seen in most other outcrops of this area.

After San Antonio Avenue joins from the right, 683 San Luis on the left has a castle-like garage. Next door, ❻ **687 San Luis** has a projecting bay at the second-floor corner that looks like it would be a delightful place to read a book or enjoy a view of the trees and the street. Across the street at 690 San Luis, architect Edwin Lewis Snyder—who studied in Berkeley and Paris—designed the brick-and-wood Tudor Revival from 1931. In the front garden, the large Japanese cherry blossom is lovely in March.

Continue past the first intersection with Southampton Avenue to the second, cross over, and turn right down Southampton. This area was developed by John Hopkins Spring, who made and lost fortunes, and who planned the Southampton development as a location for others to build lavish villas. This street also has many camphor trees.

The bright orange house on the left at 180 Southampton—it's hard to miss—was vastly expanded and remodeled in recent years. (It seems to lack a unifying style among the various design elements.)

On the right, the house at 175 Southampton, with a wooden balcony, was also designed by Edwin Snyder. Here he worked in another period style that some call Monterey Revival, reflecting early Spanish/Mexican influence in that California city.

At the bend in the road, 168 Southampton, ❼ **designed by Bernard Maybeck,** has stucco walls and copper sheets under the eaves. Maybeck sought to integrate fireproof materials after the great Berkeley fire of 1923, the year this house was designed; subsequent owners made alterations, especially to the windows. The unconventional chimney designs are characteristic of Maybeck, who liked to build the chimneys himself on many of his projects.

Farther down the street on the right, at 131 Southampton, is a grand house from 1927 by W. W. Dixon in the style of an ❽ **English country manor** with Tudor elements. It faces in a northerly direction onto a large, sloping lot, with a water feature resembling a natural stream flowing down through rocks—although the stream

131 Southampton resembles an English country manor.

can generally only be heard and not seen from the sidewalk. This was the home of Luis Alvarez, a Nobel Prize winner in physics with wide-ranging achievements, including being one of the three original proponents of the theory that a meteor impact caused the dinosaur extinction. Across the street a bit farther down at 116 Southampton, a dead tree trunk in front of the big house is carved with a family of bears, and there's a fiddler on the roof.

A large arched window on a Spanish-style house with a central turret (best seen from where the driveway crosses the sidewalk) stands at 117 Southampton. Next to it and set farther back from the street at 111 Southampton, another Spanish-style house from 1927 has a three-story tower (often hidden by dense foliage) that was apparently meant to emulate a rural farmhouse; it has a sheltered patio as well. At the intersection with San Diego Road, **❾ 89 Southampton**, a recently remodeled, midcentury, modern house, turns inward for privacy, leaving mostly walls facing the street.

Cross the street to the left and walk up San Diego on the right side, passing some attractive houses and a large rhyolite outcrop in one yard. On the right, as you pass John Hinkel Park, is a wooden Boy Scouts clubhouse, with a stone chimney.

On the left at 771 San Diego, just beyond the ravine, is the
⑩ Helen and Donald Olsen House. Olsen taught architecture
at UC from 1954 to 1990 and designed quite a few modern homes,
including his own, which is now a city landmark. The house is
simple and elegant, of modest size but practical in its interior
design. It seems to float among the trees on the hillside; contrast
this to the heavy and boxy house on the left. Olsen also designed
the modern house to the right. A small stream flows by on the left
side of Olsen's house, a fork of Blackberry Creek.

Back downhill, a bit opposite 767 San Diego, walk down the steep
steps next to the stream into **⑪ John Hinkel Park**; use the handrail,
as the first part is unusually steep. The park has mainly native oak
and bay laurel trees, with fragrant, long, narrow leaves, as well as
California redwoods (the latter were probably planted here).

A human-made cement cascade is on the right, and the giant
base of a multitrunked bay laurel is on the left. Below the cascade,
the stream is natural, though mostly overgrown with ivy. Follow the
steps and path down, keeping to the left side of the stream. Turn left
and then right down the next set of steps, left near where the stream
crosses the path, and right down more steps to the bridge, where
there is a nice view of the stream, especially lively in the rainy
season. Descend the steps, following the stream on the left.

Arrive at the bottom of the park to a flat open area with an
amphitheater on the right. A project of the Civil Works Administration (a New Deal agency), the amphitheater was built during the
Great Depression in 1934; it was used for summer movies and is still
a venue for occasional live performances. A landmark plaque is on
the left side of the seating terraces.

Exit the park to the street ahead and follow it up to the left a
short distance for views of another fork of Blackberry Creek and a
garage over the creek; the house for this garage is on the other side.
This fork joins the cascading one you saw earlier (which tunnels
underground past the amphitheater) down in the ravine, but it's not
accessible by a public path.

Now turn back and follow this street, Somerset Place, with the
park to the right as the road circles around an old oak. Stop at the
gate of **⑫ 2 Somerset** on the left (opposite where Southampton
comes in on the right) to see an impressive house in rural English
style designed in 1925 by Walter Ratcliff, Jr., who designed many
ecclesiastical structures in Berkeley. This house features stucco

Spotlight: John Hudson Thomas (1878–1945)

Best known for residential architecture, John Hudson Thomas was adept at working in a variety of architectural styles, often mixing design details and giving them his own personal stamp. Unusual massing and window treatments and thoughtful siting are noteworthy elements of his work. A prolific architect, he designed hundreds of buildings throughout California.

The First Bay Tradition (practitioners included Bernard Maybeck, John Galen Howard, Willis Polk, and Ernest Coxhead) was an important influence on Thomas, as were contemporary European designers such as Charles Rennie Mackintosh, Charles Voysey (Arts and Crafts), and Otto Wagner (Vienna Secession).

Thomas designed at least 116 buildings in Berkeley, 15 in Oakland, 9 in Piedmont, and several in other California cities. In the East Bay, Thomas's most prominent designs include the Spring Mansion above Arlington Avenue at 1960 San Antonio Avenue, Hume Castle (also known as Hume Cloister) at 2900 Buena Vista Way; Loring House at 1730 Spruce Street; and Captain Maury House near Live Oak Park (1335 Shattuck Ave.). All are Berkeley landmarks, and Loring House is on the National Register of Historic Places. His only known commercial building design is in downtown Berkeley at 2136–40 Shattuck—also a city landmark.

Born in Nevada in 1878, Thomas grew up in the Bay Area and attended Yale University before returning to Berkeley to study at UC in 1902 under Maybeck and Howard. He worked in Howard's office from 1904 to 1906 before entering a four-year partnership with George T. Plowman and then setting up his own practice in 1910. He was an active member of Berkeley's Hillside Club, which promoted an aesthetic that emphasized harmony with nature and eschewed excessive ornamentation.

After 1915, Thomas's designs became less whimsical and more literal, probably mirroring architectural trends in the Bay Area, but they always included unique touches such as original window designs or varied massing. His signature, a block of four squares and/or two vertical lines, can be spotted on many of his Berkeley homes, including the Spring Mansion and Loring House. ✳✳

and stone walls, slate roof tiles, and leaded windows. On the right, the fine living room has windows on three sides. The house was recently renovated. In March, fragrant wisteria blooms along the front garden wall.

Nearby on Southampton is the home of Daniel L. McFadden, who taught at UC Berkeley for many years and was awarded the Nobel Prize in Economic Sciences in 2000.

Continue ahead to Arlington, lined on one side by sweetgum trees with brilliant colors in late autumn. Cross Southampton to the right and proceed a short distance to steps on the left leading down to a crosswalk at Arlington. Be careful here, as traffic moves fast and sight lines are short. Continue downhill on Yosemite Road, crossing it to descend on the left side.

You are now in Thousand Oaks, another John Hopkins Spring development. Yosemite offers varied architecture and is lined with camphor trees. At Yosemite Path, on the left, the wooden fence visible down the steps has poems by various writers posted for passers-by to read; feel free to peruse them and then return to continue on Yosemite Road. The big Tudor and Jacobean Revival house at 1972 Yosemite has highly decorative half-timbering and a large bay window.

Farther along is **⓭ 1962 Yosemite**, a symmetrical residence from 1920 that was designed by Julia Morgan, the first woman to attend the esteemed École des Beaux-Arts in Paris. Morgan designed this house at about the same time that she started Hearst Castle in San Simeon. The unique and elegant house features gables and a central dormer, window boxes, graceful half-timbering underneath the second-floor windows, translucent first-floor central

windows, and sun porches on each side. Across the street and back a few steps, at 1967 Yosemite, note the boxy house made more appealing by its pattern of windows on both levels, with elements of Prairie School design.

1962 Yosemite, by Julia Morgan.

Proceed to the row of four houses on the opposite side, at 1941–47 Yosemite. John Hudson Thomas designed these charming 1928 **⑭ houses in the style of English cottages**, utilizing a similar style, and similar materials and stylistic elements that relate well to each other despite individualized designs. In a clever design solution, two of the houses share a central garage structure.

At the T intersection, cross Contra Costa Avenue and continue to the right, which is the continuation of Yosemite. Around the bend on the opposite side and uphill is the rear of another **⑮ John Hudson Thomas house**, with elements of Spanish style but with an eclectic and original approach. It is well-sited among large live oaks, rocks, and a huge magnolia. The stucco house has a big arched entryway with an unusual wooden section on the top floor painted blue. Though impressive, this is the rear entrance, where there is a ballroom (sometimes used for musical performances). Next to this house on the left is a house with Japanese-influenced design in both the residence and the garden, which incorporates tall rock outcrops.

Cross this street carefully (listen for cars coming around the curve) and proceed up paved Great Stoneface Path, next to the fence, for a better look at the house and garden. To the left is Great Stoneface Park, one of many small "rock parks" in this area of Berkeley. Many of these outcroppings of the volcanic rock rhyolite were incorporated into yards in the neighborhood or quarried for use in retaining walls and steps. Great Stoneface Park was a gift to the city from John Hopkins Spring during the development of Thousand Oaks; the feature that gave the park its name is now hard to discern.

At the street on the other side of the park, cross and turn right, noting at 1923 Thousand Oaks Boulevard a **⑯ brick house**—not particularly common in Berkeley. The design is influenced by American Colonial style, different from typical 20th-century Colonial Revival. Just past the big rocks next door, at 1937 Thousand Oaks, is another sensitive Julia Morgan design, built for a congressman. The Spanish-influenced house is placed to take advantage of the trees and rocks, with one rock right in front of the entrance. Look up from where the steps meet the sidewalk to notice the angled facade; apparently none of the rooms are rectangular in shape.

Directly across the street, at 1936 Thousand Oaks, is the front of the John Hudson Thomas house, site **⑮**, with the large, arched rear entry that you saw earlier from Yosemite; it almost seems like a different house. Thomas put his signature on many of his designs, in this case, the incised or raised vertical lines and pattern of four small squares (can you find them?).

Cross the street toward the Hudson house and return back to the right. At the park, cross left diagonally on the grass toward the big urn at the far corner, taking time to notice the patina of rust from iron oxides, as well as lichens and moss on the rocks; perhaps you can detect the layered flow patterns of the lava. A plaque explains the 20 original urns placed by the developer. All but one were subsequently lost, but the Thousand Oaks Neighborhood Association has re-created the one here and several others. The trees in the park are mostly California live oaks, which keep their leaves all winter; found throughout the neighborhood, they gave Thousand Oaks its name.

At the corner, cross Yosemite and walk to the right along the long, low stone fence, which extends all the way to 1844 Yosemite. Just beyond Indian Trail on the left (a fun detour) are two houses built for families of developer John Hopkins Spring; the two sons-in-law worked in his real estate business. The first house is hard to see through the shrubbery, but the second, at **17** **1874 Yosemite** (best seen from just past the gray gate), is a 1911 John Hudson Thomas design. The architect was highly skilled at adapting various styles and mixing elements to make unique buildings. In this case, there are elements of English Tudor Gothic, with Dutch-style gables and a harmonious blend of brick, stucco, and half-timbering.

Next on the left at 1864 Yosemite is a 1910 shingled house with Swiss chalet elements, one of the earliest homes in the area. It was built for Mark Daniels; accounts vary on whether Daniels himself or architect A. W. Smith designed it. The house is built up against Shasta Rock; rumor has it that a smoke-darkened cave used by Native Americans is on the property. In front of the house, there are several Bradford pear trees with intense leaf colors in late autumn/ early winter and white flowers in March.

Daniels was a landscape architect who laid out the Thousand Oaks neighborhood and its contoured streets to be in tune with nature and to protect native oaks and rock outcroppings. He briefly worked as a landscape engineer for Yosemite National Park; for a year and half, he was the general superintendent and landscape engineer for the National Park Service. Daniels also designed the

Forest Hill and Sea Cliff neighborhoods in San Francisco and helped lay out 17-Mile Drive on the Monterey Peninsula. At one point he moved to Southern California and helped lay out Bel Air. He returned to the Bay Area and worked on the design of the Golden Gate International Exposition (1939–40).

The Mediterranean-style house next door at 1844 Yosemite, built in 1922, has extensive gardens and rock outcrops. It began as a small, honeymoon cottage but has been added onto numerous times.

Continue down Yosemite to the end, cross to the right through the little island (with another urn), and proceed on The Alameda toward the stop signs. Cross the street straight ahead and turn right on Thousand Oaks and then left on Santa Clara Avenue. As you pass the large **18 Tudor-style house** at 570 Santa Clara, stop before the driveway gate to view the house to its right, at 564. This is another John Hudson Thomas house in yet another style, this time with elements of the Prairie School style, popularized by Frank Lloyd Wright, as well as Craftsman and northern European design features. The corner room on the main floor has wonderful windows, and the brackets under the eaves are impressive.

Continue up Santa Clara to San Ramon Avenue and turn right. In the long wooden fence along the right side there are charming carved openings. On the right, 1840 San Ramon looks like an **19 English cottage**. The curve on top of the front door is repeated in the roof segment above. Next door at 1844 San Ramon, the huge wisteria over the gateway is full of blossoms and very fragrant in March.

Turn left at San Fernando Avenue and proceed uphill one block to Arlington. Cross Arlington in the crosswalk, looking for fast-moving traffic. Turn left and walk one short block to San Antonio Avenue. On the corner of San Antonio, 611 Arlington is a 1930 **20 English Tudor–inspired design** by Francis H. Slocombe. Look at the front from Arlington and the side from San Antonio to notice how the stone, brick, stucco, half-timbering, and leaded windows combine to create a style known as "storybook."

Look across San Antonio to the opposite (northeast) corner; the sizable house at 1901 San Antonio, designed by John Hudson Thomas, was home of the chief gardener for the John Hopkins Spring estate. (It has been altered over the years.) Another large wisteria is on the Arlington side.

Walk up San Antonio; notice the garage behind 611 Arlington (the corner house), which has an English look that complements the house. Ignore the "Not a Through Street" sign just past Avis Road.

On the right side, at the entrance to 1930 San Antonio, is a cork oak tree, one of several along this stretch; the spongy bark of this European species has been harvested for wine corks and other uses for centuries. San Antonio was once a private road for the estate of John Hopkins Spring. At 1940 San Antonio, the Pueblo Revival house (in stucco, not real adobe) is a style not commonly seen in Berkeley. It has a water feature that can be heard but is hidden by the tall hedge. Across the street at 1939 San Antonio, the Craftsman has an unusual shingle pattern, and the three-story house next door at 1945 San Antonio is built over a huge rock.

The **㉑ Spring Mansion** of the John Hopkins Spring estate is on the right behind an iron fence at 1960 San Antonio. Finished in 1912, this was John Hudson Thomas's largest commission. The classical design, influenced by a palace on the Mediterranean island of Corfu built for the Empress of Austria, has numerous personal touches by Hudson. The house faces west toward Arlington; even the rear, with its large porte cochere for vehicles, is sumptuous. Spring originally had a 20-acre estate here as part of his Southampton villa development, but the advent of World War I, financial difficulties, and divorce led him to subdivide the estate, leaving four acres for the main house, which he sold. The Cora L. Williams's Institute of Creative Development, a private, progressive school, was based here from 1917 for five decades; author and screenwriter Irving Wallace was among William's students.

The cost of maintaining the house made it difficult for subsequent owners to finish a restoration, and a company that bought the house with the intention of subdividing the property also gave up; at this writing, the house is empty and off the market. It is a designated city landmark, which affords some protection for the exterior. It has 12,000 square feet of space with a skylighted central

The trunk of a cork oak tree.

The Spring Mansion, 1960 San Antonio, by John Hudson Thomas. This view of the mansion cannot be seen from the street.

atrium, eight bedrooms, and six baths.

Giant Australian blue gum trees line the street. On the left, a recent modern house seems to project out in different directions. The Spring Mansion carriage house at 1984 San Antonio, on the right, was sold off and renovated as a separate dwelling. Beyond this on the right are a Norman Revival house at 1988 San Antonio with a round turret, and a house in Spanish style at **㉒ 1998 San Antonio**. The homes in this area belong to a neighborhood association (and the street is technically private), with a clubhouse and pool (out of sight) midblock.

When the street joins up with San Luis, continue to the right. Turn left up curving Southampton. At 260 Santa Barbara, note the large **㉓ Italian Renaissance–style house** on the southwest corner, situated with a creek running through the front yard and a bridge from the garage area to the front of the house.

Turn left on Santa Barbara to return to the starting point; if your walk started at Arlington, continue down Santa Barbara to see the first two stops on the left. To catch the 67 bus toward downtown Berkeley, proceed up to the right on Northampton to Spruce and then turn right.

✸ ✸ ✸

THE ROCK PARKS

Overview: Northeast Berkeley has a higher concentration of rock outcroppings—mainly volcanic rhyolite—than other Bay Area locales, and the way these rocks were integrated into the landscape is unique. This walk visits seven small rock parks and passes several striking residences, as well as large garden rocks and rock walls. Some steep uphill walking is involved.

Highlights:
- Seven rock parks, fascinating geology
- Paths and stairways, California live oaks
- Lovely homes and gardens

Distance: 3–5 miles
Time: 2–4 hours
Elevation gain: 470–1,100 feet

Start at the northeast corner of Solano Avenue and The Alameda. Street parking is available nearby (read signs carefully) or take AC Transit bus lines 7, 18, or 25 from the Downtown Berkeley BART station or other locations.

Walk north on The Alameda, with the hills to your right, for about five blocks. The right side of the first few blocks is lined with London plane (sycamore) trees, with large, maple-like leaves, and sweetgums, with bright colors in late autumn, line part of the left side. A tall Canary Island palm is at Tacoma Avenue on the southwest corner. After Capistrano Avenue, there are four *Melaleuca linariifolia*, or paperbark trees, along the sidewalk. With soft, spongy bark and small leaves, they look almost coniferous; their sprays

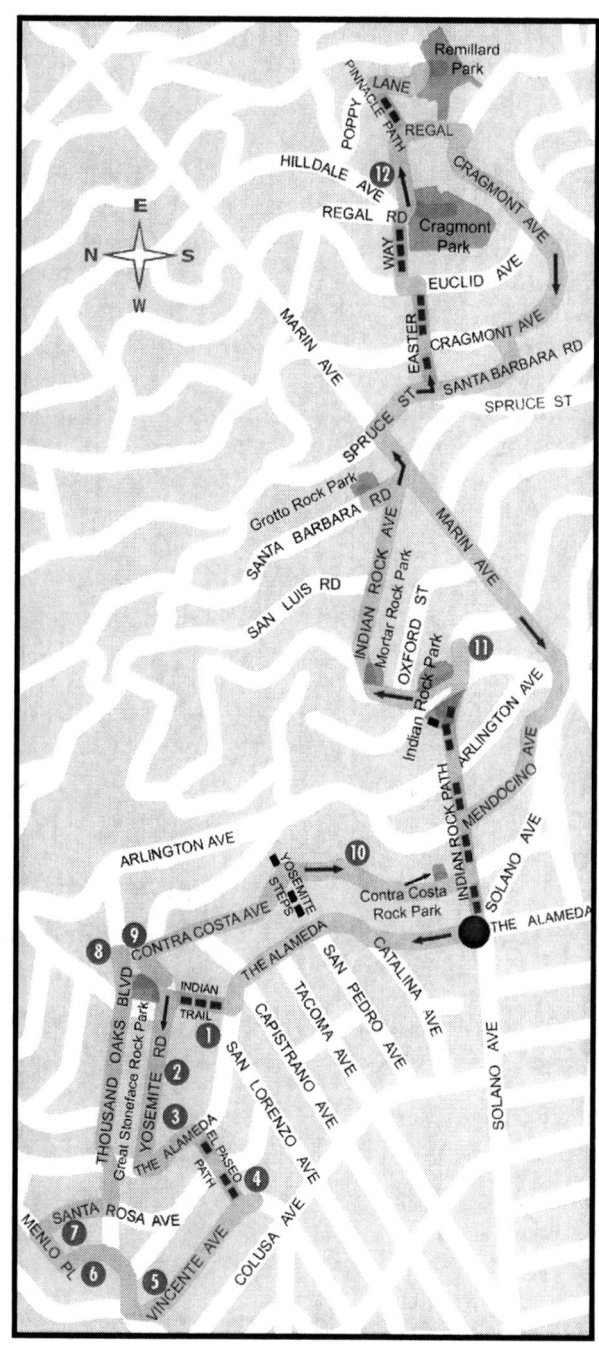

of white flowers in the summer remind one of broccoli dipped in cream. ❶ **Indian Trail** is on the right, just past 717 The Alameda.

The original developers of this area placed the urn at the beginning of Indian Trail path as part of their landscaping, which also included stone street markers. This is the only original urn of 20 that were placed in this neighborhood around 1911; the community recently replaced several. The developers also brought streetcar trains to the area in the 1910s as an inducement to homebuyers.

To avoid the rigid street patterns found in lower Berkeley and in the San Francisco hills, the roads in the Thousand Oaks neighborhood were contoured to follow the natural hillsides. Pathways and stairs were built for pedestrians to walk to the streetcar or to use as escape routes; one theory is that the paths were built to follow main sewer lines (allowing maintenance access). These paths are now a city treasure.

Carefully ascend the steep trail, which has large, rough-hewn rock steps. This fascinating and unusual trail goes up between two impressive homes—on the left, at 715 The Alameda, a red-brick, Georgian-style house by Henry Gutterson, and on the right, at 717 The Alameda, a house modified by John Hudson Thomas in 1917. There are many California live oaks (with leaves all year) in this area and along the path—thus the name Thousand Oaks.

At the top of Indian Trail, cross the street to Great Stoneface Park (see the East Bay Geology box near the end of this walk), which was designated a public park as part of the Thousand Oaks development in 1921. It is only 0.73 acre, or 31,800 square feet, and the feature that gave the park its name is now hard to see due to shrubbery. In the rock outcropping nearest the corner, the rust color is derived from iron oxides and the yellowish brown from limonite (another iron oxide), while the green is from lichen and moss. If you look carefully, you may also see bands from repeated volcanic flows.

After exploring the park, walk back toward Indian Trail and cross Yosemite Road. Turn right on the side-

An urn marks the start of Indian Trail.

Thousand Oaks and Northbrae

In 1907, a civic effort was launched to entice the state capital to move to Berkeley from Sacramento. The Thousand Oaks and Northbrae areas were laid out with street names of California counties (Alameda, Marin, Solano, etc.), and major urban enhancements were made. However, the citizens voted in 1908 not to move the capital.

The same year, in a related move, Berkeley's civic leaders promoted the idea of a public park just to the north of the planned capital. The city planned to buy 980 acres at $1,000 per acre in the area that became the Thousand Oaks neighborhood to create a regional park. Although the chamber of commerce, developers, the UC president, and others enthusiastically campaigned for the enabling ballot measure (also in the 1908 election), it received only 60 percent of the vote. Because the parks measure needed a two-thirds majority to pass, the land was promptly sold off to John Hopkins Spring and Duncan McDuffie. These two developers, who catered primarily to higher-income households, contributed significantly to the overall look and feel of these neighborhoods. ✴✴

---

walk, strolling past impressive houses in different styles with rock walls at the sidewalk.

Stop at the second house from the trail, 1874 Yosemite, a huge Gothic Tudor with Dutch and fairy-tale elements in brick, stucco, and half-timbering. It was designed by John Hudson Thomas in 1911 for the family of Robert Newell, John Spring's son-in-law and a partner in the real estate firm promoting Thousand Oaks. The family of Percy Murdock, another Spring son-in-law, lived in the European-style house next door on the left, though it is hard to see that house through the foliage.

Just past 1874 Yosemite, 1864 Yosemite (best seen from the gate) was the ❷ **home of Mark Daniels**, a civil engineer and landscape architect who built this home in 1910, one of the first in Thousand Oaks to promote the idea of building with nature; he worked with Spring on the layout of the entire development. The Swiss chalet-style house—believed to be designed by Daniels and architect A. W. Smith of Oakland—incorporates many boulders (including Shasta Rock), some of which press up against the lower side of the house while others bolster the retaining walls and steps. This was a challenging site because there are rocks all over it. A rock outcropping is visible against the left side of the house, and there are rumors of a smoke-darkened cave with Native American implements. Daniels, who worked briefly as landscape engineer for Yosemite National Park and as general superintendent and landscape engineer for the national park service, also designed the neighborhoods at Forest Hills and Sea Cliff in San Francisco and helped lay out Monterey's 17-Mile Drive and Bel Air in Southern California.

Continue downhill on Yosemite and turn left on The Alameda. Just after a rock wall–lined driveway, tall Guardian (or Sentry) Rock stands in a landscaped private garden; there is a cleft with a path through the rock (not open to the public). This rock is in the garden of a grand Italian Renaissance house, 641 The Alameda, which can be viewed from just past the rock; the house is called ❸ **Villa Felice** and dates to 1934.

Cross the street toward 640 The Alameda, where a red-flowering gum tree is brilliant in summer, and then go left a bit and turn right down rock-lined El Paseo Path, crossing one street (Santa Rosa Avenue, which is not marked) and continuing another block down the path until it ends at Vincente Avenue.

On Vincente, virtually every lot has at least one rock outcrop, though many are hidden from the street in backyards or even in basements. Turn left to see the house at ❹ **683 Vincente**, with large rocks in the front yard, a sinuous wrought-iron handrail, stairway lantern, built-in mailbox, and a charming light fixture in the shape of a miniature lighthouse (it might be covered in ivy).

Turn around, cross the street, and walk right (north) up Vincente, noting first 680 Vincente, with a collection of ceramic planting pots in front. Proceed to 636 Vincente, a brown-shingle with a huge wisteria vine across the front that blooms in March and April. Continue on to ❺ **619 Vincente** on the right side; this house was built over a giant rock and includes siding of a different kind of rock. Half the garage/basement is taken up with a large outcropping. On the left side, 616 Vincente is built up against an outcrop called Tamalpais Rock, which has a deck on top of it.

Cross Thousand Oaks Boulevard at the stop sign and turn right to walk uphill. In February, lovely pink flowering plum trees are in full bloom along many streets in this area, particularly on Thousand Oaks. After one block, bear left on Menlo Place to see a big rock on the left that almost hides ❻ **11 Menlo** (with a big spruce growing at one side). After the curve, turn right on Santa Rosa to see ❼ **Picnic**

The deck over Tamalpais Rock.

Rock, a city landmark, on the right. At one time, public access was allowed to the rock, but a new owner halted this (except by permission) due to liability concerns.

Continue on Santa Rosa and turn left up Thousand Oaks, crossing The Alameda then Santa Clara Avenue (on the northeast corner a native ceanothus shrub has fragrant sprays of blue flowers in February and March). Continue past San Fernando Avenue and Great Stoneface Park. Julia Morgan, one of the Bay Area's most famous architects, designed ❽ **1937 Thousand Oaks**, a Mediterranean-style house framed by rock outcrops; no rooms have all four corners at 90 degrees. Live oaks and big boulders surround the 1915 residence.

Cross the street toward ❾ **1936 Thousand Oaks**; the front of this house, designed by John Hudson Thomas and dating to 1913, includes his signature of four squares and two parallel vertical lines. Return right to Great Stoneface Park and descend left down paved Great Stoneface Path, which passes a residence and its garden fence. Cross the street carefully and turn left on Yosemite Road.

From across the street, note the Japanese-influenced house and garden that you just passed, with impressive rocks, including a large rhyolite plinth; some pink crabapple and other trees bloom here in spring. The house to its right contains another large rock in the yard. With its high stucco wall and arched rear entranceway, this house is actually the same one you saw on Thousand Oaks designed by Thomas. Note how different it looks from this side, as well as the fine oaks and large magnolia tree.

Keep walking around the curve to the right. The street becomes Contra Costa Avenue as Yosemite veers to the left. Keep walking straight ahead on Contra Costa past Capistrano Avenue. Contra Costa is lined with Japanese maples, which often have brilliant autumn colors depending on ground moisture. Blackberry Creek is visible on the left, just past 825 Contra Costa. The creek was restored with native plants, and there are some nice rocks upstream. Just beyond, ⑩ **841 Contra Costa** is reminiscent of a Japanese temple. The huge oak on the right side of the street—some call it Hercules because of its mighty branches—is believed to be one of the oldest oaks in Berkeley.

Continue walking on the left to Contra Costa Rock Park, a gift to the City of Berkeley from the Mason-McDuffie real estate company during its development of the Northbrae area. Dedicated in 1917, the park is a tiny 0.17 acres, or 7,410 square feet. If you wish, proceed carefully up the steps cut into the rock's left (north) side to a lookout with a view (there will be an even better view later). Take the rock's back steps down, ducking under the oak branches. Note small, cave-like erosion features as you circle around clockwise on a return path to the street.

Walk left along Contra Costa to Indian Rock Path. The Berkeley Path Wanderers Association (BPWA) advocates for these paths, and its volunteers have devoted many hours to constructing paths that were originally designated as public rights-of-way but were not built. (BPWA sells an excellent map of all public steps and paths in Berkeley; you can purchase one in local bookstores or at www.berkeleypaths.org.) Proceed left uphill on the path, cross Mendocino Avenue, and walk up another block. Cross Arlington carefully and continue up the path until you reach Indian Rock; at the rock face, bear right.

On the left going up the south side, about 50 access steps are cut into the rock, leading to the top (the first step is a bit of a challenge, but the rest are relatively easy). The view from the top is panoramic, and many people come here to watch the sun set over the bay. Be aware of a steep drop-off on the far side.

Indian Rock Park was also a gift to the City of Berkeley from Mason-McDuffie during its development of Northbrae. The park was dedicated in 1917 with 1.18 acres, or 51,400 square feet, including a portion across the street.

Dick Leonard (known as the father of technical climbing), David Brower, Jules Eichorn, Bestor Robinson, and other members of the Cragmont Climbing Club practiced at Indian, Cragmont, and Pinnacle rocks in the 1930s to prepare for climbing the difficult cliffs of Yosemite. They pioneered dynamic belaying, the use of nylon rope, and other innovations, transforming the sport. Beginning and experienced climbers often practice in Berkeley: top-roping at Cragmont and Pinnacle rocks, bouldering with no ropes or equipment at Indian and Mortar rocks, and rappelling at Cragmont Rock. Brower used his knowledge of rock climbing to prepare training manuals during World War II that proved critical in enabling the 86th Regiment of the US Army to surprise the Germans at Riva Ridge in the North Apennines in Italy; the successful attack disrupted German supply lines in southern Europe.

Steps leading up Indian Rock.

After returning to the ground via the same steps, walk up through the park to Indian Rock Avenue and turn right. At the intersection with Shattuck Avenue, look catty-corner across the street to three **⑪ John Hudson Thomas houses** in a row (800 Shattuck and 859 and 861 Indian Rock). These all-gray stucco homes were designed in a style called Vienna Secession (seceding from dull traditional architecture, as the proponents saw it). Cross Indian Rock and walk straight ahead on Shattuck to 811/811A Shattuck, built over a rock. Next door, 813 Shattuck has a huge oak on top of a front-yard rock (how did the roots reach the ground?).

Return back toward Indian Rock Avenue. At the corner, walk up the 10 steps to the right and take the path through the upper part of Indian Rock Park. The path is lined with oaks and tall blue gum trees, one of many Australian eucalyptus varieties. At the next corner, turn right on the sidewalk and up Indian Rock Avenue past Oxford Street to Mortar Rock Park. This park was another gift to the City of Berkeley from Mason-McDuffie, dedicated in 1917 with 0.39 acres, or 16,990 square feet.

Steps are cut into the main rock from the south side; the view from the top of the rock is mostly obscured, and there is not much space at the top. At the steps, a plaque discusses Native Americans and plants. Do take the steps and path between the rocks to the left side of the main rock outcropping, noting native oak and buckeye trees, the latter sprouting plumes of fragrant white flowers in late spring. Beyond the large rocks, take the right fork to low rock outcroppings, where mortar holes can be found near the main rock face and to the right. Native Americans ground acorns and other foods in these holes.

If you want to cut the walk short, return to the starting point by walking back the way you came to Indian Rock, walking around the rock, and descending Indian Rock Path four blocks to the starting point at Solano and The Alameda.

To see three more rock parks, continue on the path to the northeast from the mortar holes. Walk down four steps to the street (the upper part of Indian Rock Avenue) and turn right; a couple of blocks up, you may see goats on the steep slopes across the street at 828 Indian Rock. At the end of Indian Rock, turn left onto Santa Barbara Road; when you see the stone steps on the right, cross over into Grotto Rock Park. Another gift to the City of Berkeley from Mason-

Native American mortar holes.

McDuffie, this park was dedicated in 1917 with 0.31 acres, or 13,500 square feet.

Grotto Rock Park once had a natural spring that provided the park's name. Steps between the sidewalk and the rock lead up to a gravel and dirt path. Many native plants are in front of the rock, including purple-flowered ceanothus, yellow-flowered fremontia trees, sagebrush, manzanita, and fragrant black sage. Circle the rock in either direction; on the south side, about 33 steps carved in the rock lead to a view (the steps do not go all the way to the top).

After exploring, return to Santa Barbara, turn left, and walk down to Marin Avenue, where a large but squat Canary Island palm is on the corner. Turn left, up steep Marin to Spruce Street, crossing both streets to the southeast corner. Walk southeast on Spruce, looking carefully for a sign on the left marking Easter Way, just past 933 Spruce. Walk up Easter Way to Cragmont Avenue, cross the street, and walk up another block on the steep path to Euclid Avenue. Cross Euclid carefully (there is no stop sign on this busy street) and go left about 30 yards to continue up Easter Way just past the bus stop sign. The path ends at Cragmont Rock Park. At Regal Road, turn right into the park. Take the paved path to the park's upper section, where there are picnic tables.

Cragmont Rock is mainly rhyolite but was formed from agglomerates of hardened ash, volcanic glass, and pebbles—different than flows on other rocks on this walk. Neighborhood residents bought the land from the Cragmont Land Company and donated it to the city of Berkeley; it was dedicated in 1920 and covers three acres, or 130,680 square feet. Using the techniques he honed at Cragmont Rock Park, Dick Leonard planned the first technical rock climb (that is, one aided by devices such as pitons, carabiners, and ropes) in Yosemite in 1934. He eventually led over one hundred expeditions and climbs in the Sierra Nevada, making many first ascents on mountains thought impossible to climb.

Walk around the flat upper area, which sits on the rock faces, to see the views: a partially obstructed view of the bay from the pavilion; the UC campus, Oakland, and the South Bay from the low rock wall across the upper lawn; and a favorite rock-climbing cliff, seen through the shrubs past the stone bench to the left.

Go back down to the street, noting the **12 Spanish-style "village"** across the street, with various living units and faux ruins.

The Spanish-style "village" near Cragmont Park.

East Bay Geology

In relatively recent geologic time (about 25 to 29 million years ago), the heavier Pacific Plate began creating California by diving under the lighter Continental Plate. In the process, the Pacific Plate scraped the edge of the Continental landmass, resulting in a jumbled mélange of diverse rocks—fascinating, but a nightmare for geologists to decipher—called the Franciscan Complex. Heat, pressure, earthquakes, and volcanoes further transformed the rocks.

The rocks in the majority of Berkeley's outcroppings are rhyolite, a volcanic rock that erupted about 8 to 12 million years ago. Unlike granite, which is formed underground, rhyolite was formed by surface eruptions and has small crystals and layers—flow bands from successive outpourings of volcanic material. Rhyolite flowed slower than basalt (the more familiar lava), rather like molasses. The bands are 1 to 3 inches thick at Indian Rock and at Great Stoneface, quite thin compared with, for example, basalt lava flows in Hawaii. It is unclear if the numerous rocks in the area join up underground, but certainly much is below the surface. Violent explosions also distributed rhyolite. The rock tends to be cream, pale yellow, or gray.

Some geologists believe the source volcanoes for Berkeley's rocks were near Sibley Regional Park, while others believe they were near Hollister (southeast of San Jose). The Hayward Fault carried the rocks here, and similar rocks can be found near Hollister and near Mount Burdell in Marin County. Geologists continue to study and ponder.

Graywacke is another local rock, in this case, sedimentary sandstone. Fairly soft, it was commonly used in decorative columns along streets in this area. Many rocks are now covered with ivy; exposed, they greatly enhance gardens. Immigrant Italian stonemasons and others used local rock for dry walls (fitted together without mortar). Lovely blueschist is globally rare but fairly common here, to the delight of geologists. There are many rock quarries in the East Bay dating to the mid-19th-century Gold Rush days, including Cerrito Canyon at the end of Vincente Avenue as well as at locations in South Berkeley, El Cerrito, and Oakland.

Although most of the East Bay landscape would be unrecognizable to Native Americans, Berkeley's large rocks are unchanged. Petroglyphs up to 8,000 years old have been found on some of the rocks, which some Native Americans consider sacred. Although Native Americans lived nearby, no one knows for sure what their population was and where permanent settlements were, since few artifacts remain. Various rocks were used for different purposes, and tribes often traded rocks quarried from their areas with other tribes. Rocks were used for making tools as well as for charm stones—pendant-like stones found in burial sites. Native people also heated stones to use in cooking.

Berkeley's prominent rocks served as landmarks in Spanish/Mexican times (about 1769 to 1848) as well as the early period of American settlement. For example, Monument Rock was the northeast corner boundary of the huge Peralta land grant of 46,000 acres, which covered most of the land from San Leandro to El Cerrito. ❋❋

Walk down Regal Road to the right, looking for Pinnacle Path on the left, where "983" is painted on the curb. Ascend Pinnacle Path, noting the ceramics embedded in the retaining wall, a family gift to the mother who lived in the house above. At Poppy Lane, turn right and walk to Remillard Park, the seventh and final rock park.

Lillian Remillard Dandini, heiress of the Remillard Brick Company, donated this property, which includes Pinnacle Rock, to the city of Berkeley in 1963. The city purchased additional acreage in 1969–70. The area of park is 5.9 acres, or 257,000 square feet. Its most notable feature is that the rock is very different from that in the other parks both in its spire-like appearance and its composition: the reddish rock here is not rhyolite, as in the other six parks, but rock from deep in the Earth's mantle believed to have formed 140 million years ago during the Jurassic Period (think dinosaurs). Pinnacle Rock is popular with climbers, with or without ropes. The park also has a number of tall blue gum (eucalyptus) trees.

To get back to the starting point, return along the street to descend Pinnacle Path. Turn left to go downhill on Regal Road and turn right on Cragmont to Euclid. Cross Euclid carefully and continue down Cragmont to Santa Barbara. Turn left on Santa Barbara and walk to Spruce Street. Go right on Spruce and continue to Marin. Descend steep Marin, which was laid out for a cable car that was never installed and is lined with plane (sycamore) trees that form a canopy. At Marin Circle, walk counterclockwise and turn right on Mendocino Avenue. Finally, turn left down Indian Rock Path and walk two blocks to the starting point.

(Alternatively, for a quieter route with less traffic, one block down from Spruce on Marin turn right on Santa Barbara and left on Indian Rock Avenue. At Indian Rock Park, walk around the main outcropping and pick up Indian Rock Path. Walk four blocks down to the starting point.)

Part III
South Berkeley

✳✳✳

WALK 11
THE ELMWOOD

✳ ✳ ✳

Overview: See the charming neighborhood where Bill and Hillary Clinton lived, Patty Hearst was kidnapped, and the Unabomber holed up when he was a UC lecturer. In addition, this walk offers superb architecture, lovely gardens, tree-lined streets, and the lively Elmwood shopping district. This is a relatively flat walk with minimal traffic.

Highlights:
- Vibrant commercial district
- Classic Berkeley homes on tree-lined avenues, including many Julia Morgan designs
- Homes of the Unabomber, Bill and Hillary Clinton, Pauline Kael, and other celebrities

Distance: 2.4–3.4 miles
Time: 2–3 hours
Elevation gain: 110–170 feet

✳ ✳ ✳

Start at the northwest corner of College and Ashby avenues in front of  **2956 College**. The 51 AC Transit bus runs frequently from the Downtown Berkeley and Rockridge BART stations. Drivers should take note of parking restrictions in the area.

An electric streetcar was installed on College in 1903; in 1905, groundbreaking for the Elmwood Park subdivision was marked with stone gates that still stand on the northeast and southeast corners of this intersection. The 1906 San Francisco earthquake spurred the rapid development of the residential area and its commercial center along College.

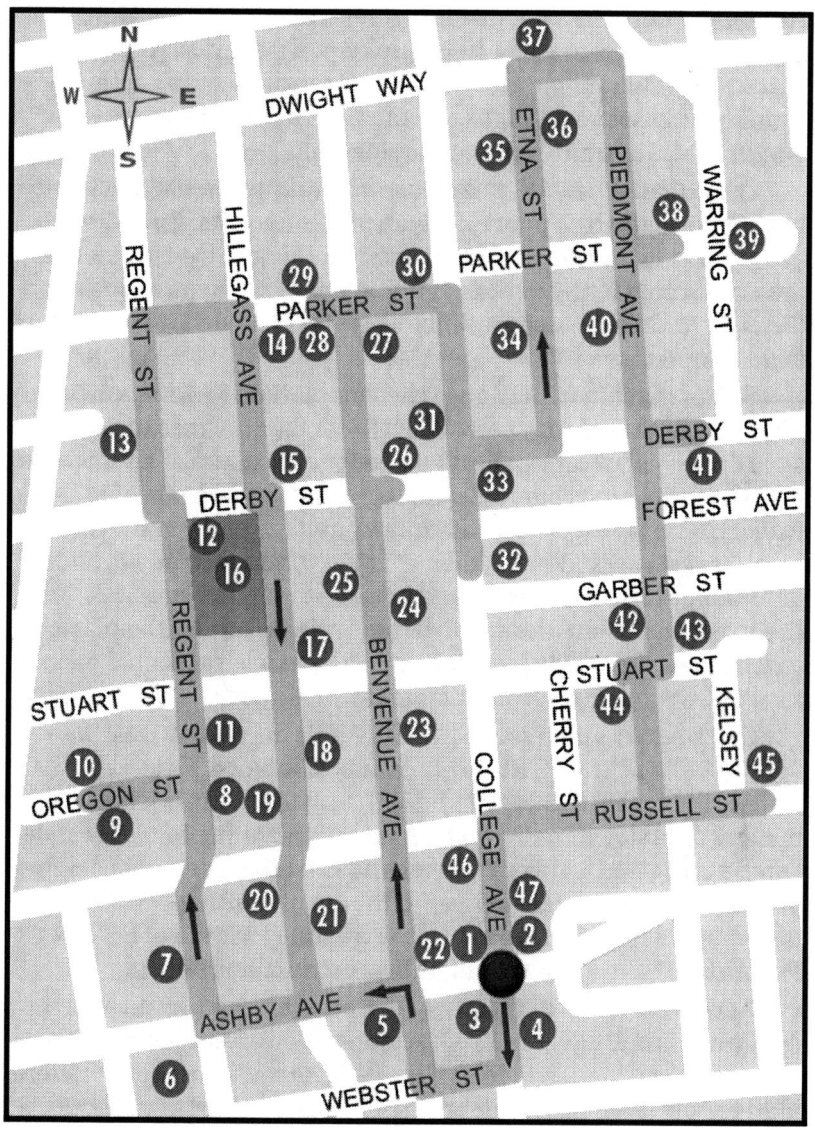

The Elmwood is a compact but robust local shopping district, partly due to neighborhood pressure on city zoning rules to limit the number of restaurants so that diverse retail businesses can thrive. In addition to numerous restaurants and cafes (Chinese, Indian, Mediterranean, burritos, craft ice cream), the (nonchain) retail stores sell books, toys, clothing, jewelry, wine, gifts, and more.

Although College is a busy thoroughfare, the pedestrian ambience is pleasant thanks to street trees (ginkgos, with fan-shaped leaves that turn golden yellow around November), parked cars acting as a buffer between pedestrians and moving traffic, and stores with windows and entrances lining the sidewalk.

The Colonial Revival, mixed-use building at the starting point has shops on the first floor and apartments upstairs. Built around 1907, this is likely the oldest surviving building in the commercial area, according to the Berkeley Architectural Heritage Association (BAHA). Its attractive second-floor bays and fine detailing benefited from a 2008 renovation.

Walter Ratcliff, Jr., designed the landmarked **2 Mercantile Trust Company** of 1925 (now Wells Fargo Bank) across the street at 2959 College. Ratcliff was best known for ecclesiastical architecture, often in Tudor style, but this building includes elements of Mission Revival, with lavish ornamentation around the entry in the middle arch. Looking west down Ashby, at 2629–35 you can see a former auto-repair shop that has been renovated into retail stores. Across the street on the left, the small deli/grocery, Ashby Marketplace, is a welcome recent addition in an era when many traditional main streets have lost their grocery stores to supermarkets.

Cross Ashby going south (with the hills to your left) and walk to 2966 College, the **3 Rialto Cinemas Elmwood**. Originally the Strand, the movie theater was built in 1914 in a Prairie School design but was remodeled in 1947 to its current Streamline Moderne style. Offering an eclectic mix of movies and live broadcasts, this neighborhood movie theater survives in the era of multiplexes. A plaque next door at 2980 College marks the original location of Berkeley Repertory Theatre, which had its first productions here in 1968.

Across the street at **4 2979–95 College**, each commercial storefront is outlined in a bright-colored, floral, terra-cotta pattern; the clerestory (high) windows have delicate mullions; and different kinds of tile were used under the shop windows and entries. Continue walking to 2992–98 College, a retail building from 1922 with large arches, a high clerestory, and colored ornamental tiles, creating a pleasing rhythmic effect. (The rug store claims it has also been here since 1922.)

Turn right on Webster Street and right again on Benvenue Avenue. On the left at the end of the block (2940 Benvenue), James Plachek designed the **5 Claremont Branch of the Berkeley**

Public Library in 1924. A small addition was made during a major renovation in 2012. If the library is open, feel free to go in and take a look.

Tiled storefronts on College Avenue.

Cross Ashby in the crosswalk (traffic does not have a stop sign), and immediately turn left and walk two blocks along Ashby to Regent Street. Nurse Alta Alice Miner Bates founded the Alta Bates Sanatorium on Dwight Way in 1905; it offered eight beds to care for women and their infants. Development of this campus, now known as ➏ **Alta Bates Summit Medical Center**, began in 1907; the current main structure dates from 1985. In 2000, Alta Bates merged with Oakland's Summit Medical Center and Sutter Health. The combined not-for-profit medical center has about 630 beds; the Berkeley location specializes in birthing, infant care, mental health, and emergency care. The surrounding neighborhood hosts many medical buildings.

Turn right (north) on Regent. This neighborhood is appealing for its variety of building styles and richly landscaped small front yards. At 2918 Regent, on the opposite side, the ➐ **Berkeley Presbyterian Mission Houses** are in a cul-de-sac. Established in 1937, the center provides housing and support for international church professionals pursuing advanced degrees at the Graduate Theological Union in Berkeley. The residential complex consists of seven charming two- and three-bedroom cottages, six apartment units, and two homes, one of which houses five residents in shared housing.

At 2917 Regent, the brown-shingle house has not one but two octagonal turrets, flaring eaves, and a densely landscaped garden. Continue to 2901 Regent (southeast corner with Russell Street), designed by A. Dodge Coplin of Oakland, a talented architect who died at age 39 in 1908. According to an account in *The Architect and Engineer* magazine, he was killed in a freak accident when a pistol fell out of his pocket while he was returning to Berkeley from an automobile outing with a young woman (he was divorced at the time). The house has large brackets under the eaves and exposed beams with carved ends that resemble jigsaw-puzzle pieces. The next few blocks of Regent have white and pink plum trees that flower in late January or February.

In the next block, ❽ **2827 Regent** is a brown-shingle-and-board Craftsman from 1909, with flower boxes and a wide pop-up dormer. The 1908 Tudor house next door at 2821 Regent has a beautiful large oak in the front, brickwork below the first-floor windows, half-timbering, and a rhythmic pattern of gables around the roof.

Cross over and turn left (west) on Oregon Street. On the left, at 2430 Oregon was the ❾ **home of artist Chiura Obata**, who taught at UC and was celebrated for his introduction of Japanese art techniques and aesthetics to the United States, both in his teaching and by example in his prints and paintings. Obata was a keen observer who loved nature and promoted a blending of Japanese and Western techniques. His wife, Haruko Kohashi, was a noted teacher of Japanese ikebana flower arranging, and his son, Gyo, is an architect who cofounded the global architecture-engineering firm HOK (formerly Hellmuth, Obata + Kassabaum). A big white magnolia blooms in front of the house in late winter.

Farther down and across the street, at 2419 Oregon, a simple brown-shingle is next to a neoclassical house with large columns that looks like a plantation mansion. From 1955 to 1964, the brown-shingle was the ❿ **home of film critic Pauline Kael**. Petaluma-born and a graduate of UC Berkeley, Kael managed the two-screen Cinema Guild at Telegraph Avenue and Haste Street, where she showed American and European films that were rarely seen elsewhere. From 1968 to 1991, she was film critic for *The New Yorker* magazine. She had a profound influence on American attitudes toward cinema. Inside the home are murals by San Francisco artist Jess Collins.

Return to Regent. At the northwest corner with Oregon, 2820 Regent—with two corner turrets and an imposing entrance—has been significantly altered. The fence is out of sync with the neighborhood pattern of open gardens.

Turn left at Regent; 2812–14 Regent is a large brown-shingle with centered steep gables, carved-leaf brackets, and a front bay. The house was moved from Telegraph Avenue in 1949, when Berkeley purchased numerous properties to accommodate the expansion of play areas for Willard Middle School; the house is now subdivided into three residential units. Opposite, at 2815 Regent, incongruously plopped down, a building of condominiums looks like a 1960s medical building; to its left, **⓫ 2811 Regent** is a Colonial Revival with a Victorian-style turret.

Continue on Regent, crossing Stuart Street. Willard Middle School, a Berkeley public school founded in 1916, is on the left. Continue past the little circle and take the path between the tennis courts and school grounds to Derby Street. Look right to see a **⓬ cast-cement mosaic wall** produced by Andrew Wervy as a community project 1978.

Cross Derby at the crosswalk and continue north on the left side of Regent, which jogs a bit to the west. Several tall magnolias line the left (west) side of this block; they are adorned with large, shiny, green leaves and white flowers that bloom from late spring to early summer. On the left, behind the brown-shingle home at 2626 Regent, the small cottage at 2628A was the **⓭ home of Theodore John "Ted" Kaczynski**, also known as the Unabomber. Kaczynski taught for two years at UC Berkeley; he was the youngest professor hired by UC at the time but he was not popular with students. He eventually moved to a remote cabin in Montana where, between 1978 and 1995, he sent 16 homemade bombs to airlines, computer stores, and universities, killing three people and injuring 23. In 1995, he sent the media a 35,000-word antitechnology manifesto rife with clues that led to his capture and arrest.

At Parker Street, you can see Sather Tower (also known as the Campanile) on the UC campus, in the distance to the north. Student dorms, apartments, and subdivided old homes increasingly dominate the area between here and campus.

Turn right at Parker and right again at Hillegass Avenue. The **⓮ Marshall-Lindblom House** on the southeast corner (2601–03 Hillegass) is a Berkeley landmark. The lovely Colonial Revival was designed by the architectural firm of Cunningham Bros. and completed in 1897. The L-shaped porch, Ionian columns, corner pilasters, elaborate brackets, and ornamented oval windows create an aura of elegance. Now a duplex, it is well maintained thanks

Spotlight: Julia Morgan (1872-1957)

Julia Morgan was the first woman admitted to the architecture program of the École des Beaux-Arts in Paris and the first female licensed architect in California. Born in San Francisco, she grew up and lived most of her life in Oakland. While working on a civil engineering degree at UC she met Bernard Maybeck, who encouraged her to go to Paris to study architecture.

Persistence enabled Morgan to realize this dream, despite formidable barriers against women in architecture. Repeated attempts, including dressing as a man, helped her to finally gain entry to the École des Beaux-Arts. On her return to California, Morgan worked with John Galen Howard to design part of the Hearst Memorial Mining Building and most of the Greek Theatre on the UC campus. In 1904, she opened an office in San Francisco, where she gained clients in the wake of the 1906 earthquake. She eventually designed more than 700 buildings in a career spanning almost 50 years.

Morgan was renowned for her ability to borrow from different styles while forging her own, and she was meticulous about craftsmanship. Her designs could be extremely sensitive and subtle, as in many Berkeley homes, or flamboyant, as in Hearst Castle at San Simeon. She made particular use of local California styles, such as Mission Revival and Bay Area Arts and Crafts.

William Randolph Hearst's mother (Phoebe Apperson Hearst) introduced Morgan to her son, and he became a key client. His first commission was the Los Angeles Herald Examiner building; his most famous was Hearst Castle, which Morgan worked on for nearly 30 years (1919–47). She supervised every aspect of construction—even the placement of artworks.

For the Young Women's Christian Association, Morgan designed the Asilomar Conference Grounds in Pacific Grove and other California YWCA buildings. She did numerous assignments for Mills College, the first women's college west of the Rockies.

Walter T. Steilberg, another talented Berkeley architect, worked for Morgan for a year after his graduation in 1910 and joined her practice in 1918, working or consulting with her into the 1930s and playing a key role in both office and project management.

In addition to numerous Berkeley residences (often built in harmonious pairs), Morgan designed the Craftsman-style St. John's Presbyterian Church (now Julia Morgan Theater) at 2727 College Avenue, Berkeley Women's City Club (2315 Durant Ave.), Phoebe Apperson Hearst Memorial Gymnasium for Women (with Maybeck) on the UC campus, and a key Berkeley Baptist Divinity School building on the corner of Dwight Way and Hillegass Avenue.

In 2014, Morgan was posthumously awarded the American Institute of Architects' Gold Medal—the first woman to have this honor. ❀❀

partly to the benefits of landmarking and the Mills Act, which provides tax deductions for the maintenance and improvement of historic properties.

Continue to 2613–15 Hillegass, a large Colonial Revival house painted in bright colors. At the northeast corner of Hillegass and Derby, 2601 Derby was **15 designed by Bernard Maybeck** early in his career and completed in 1900. Charles Keeler, who promoted simple homes without ornamentation and in harmony with nature, supervised the construction. It has lively massing, an unusual third-floor balcony with windows above French doors, and a medieval-looking steep gable. Recently, the shingles were painted charcoal and dark brown with white and yellow trim, a departure from the traditional unpainted Berkeley brown-shingle.

Cross Derby at the crosswalk and walk to the entrance of **16 Willard Park**, faced by a pleasing row of homes along Hillegass and containing a grove of large redwoods near the corner. The city purchased and demolished homes in the 1960s to create the park; when it opened in 1971, during the Vietnam War, community activists opposing the war called it Ho Chi Minh Park. In 1982, the park was officially named in honor of Frances Willard, a suffragist, educator, and temperance leader. Neighborhood activists spear-headed various improvements during the 1990s, including reno-vation of the busy tot lot. A few latter-day hippies hang out here, and its broad lawns and shade trees are popular with students and families; dogs run off leash in the park's grassy central area. The clubhouse at the southeast corner is the busy base for after-school programs and camps.

Walk either on the Hillegass sidewalk or through the park heading south. Across the street from the clubhouse, 2731 Hillegass has a corner turret and charming window mullions. At the northeast corner with Hillegass, **17 2747 Stuart** is a George B. McDougall design from 1905 featuring a round turret at the corner, two oval windows over the entrance, a delightful mullion pattern in the upper parts of windows, and dentils under the eaves.

At the northwest corner of this same intersection, the Rumi Apartments are hard to miss (cross Stuart Street and turn around). This building with six stories over a parking garage was completed in 1958 and provides an excellent lesson in how not to develop high-density residences. The architecture is reminiscent of a tacky seaside development, while the scale is out of sync with the surrounding houses. Architecture ages differently depending on construction; apartment buildings from this era often appear to be in worse condition than historic homes from much earlier.

Cross Hillegass to walk along the left (east) side. Notice the colorful and amusing sculptures and signage at 2811 Hillegass. At 2821 Hillegass, George Rushforth of Wright & Rush-forth designed the ⑱ **Hillegass Court Apartments** in 1915 for G. A. Mattern, a clothing manufacturer who was reportedly inspired by illustrations of a European resort hotel. This is one of the most attractive apartment buildings in Berkeley, with variation in the roofline and plenty of windows, many of which are triplets with curved cutouts above. There are also lattice mullions, ornamentation over the three entrances and on the inner corner bays, a landscaped entry court, and garage entrances nestled under the wings. Best of all, the structure fits comfortably with the scale of the surrounding single-family homes. With 34 bedrooms, it provides even more housing than the Rumi Apartments, which has 24 bedrooms.

Farther along, at 2827 Hillegass, a 1905 brown-shingle has a tall roof sweeping up over the second and third floors, a wide

2828 Hillegas combines Craftsman and Prairie styles.

second-floor dormer, and two small dormers on the third floor. The entryway features wood and clinker brick. Across the street at 2828 Hillegass, a 1909 house combines **19 Craftsman and Prairie School elements**, the latter in its horizontality, low-hipped roof, and bands of windows. The structure of this house is emphasized by carpentry outlines, as well as by the porch design and juxtaposition of shingles and wood-board siding on different floors.

A few doors down on the left, 2835 Hillegass is a quirky brown-shingle with a high gable and tiny attic window, leaded mullions, classical porch columns, and a Palladian window. At the intersection with Russell Street, 2842 Hillegass (northwest corner) was Walter Ratcliff, Jr.'s, first commission. Built in 1904, this three-story brown-shingle has big brackets in the gables, a third-floor balcony, and highly varied roof designs.

Cross Russell, and on the southeast corner of the intersection, 2901 Hillegass is an apartment building designed by James Plachek in 1913. There are some Prairie School elements in the horizontal emphasis, window layout, and fine detailing around the windows and doors. The shallow window bays contribute to the elegant design.

Look across Hillegass to see the final **20 home of poet Ina Coolbrith** at 2902 Hillegass, on the southwest corner, a simple brown-shingle. Coolbrith was California's first poet laureate (and the first poet laureate of any US state); she promoted the literary career of Joaquin Miller and served as Oakland's city librarian for 19 years, where she mentored Jack London and Isadora Duncan. Her last years were spent here with her niece in the mid-1920s; she died in 1928 just before her 87th birthday.

A few doors down at **21 2909–11 Hillegass**, a Colonial Revival from 1908 has varied window bays, small pilaster-like columns on the window framing, dentils in cornices over the windows, and a shell design in the dormer. Next door, 2915 Hillegass has very blue front steps and the same shell design. The west side of the street is lined with two large, squat Canary Island palms and three tall California Washingtonia fan palms, the latter native to California desert springs.

A. Dodge Coplin designed the 1906 Craftsman across the street and a few doors down, at 2920 Hillegass, with an intersecting, hipped roof, shelves for the smaller windows, leaded panes, and a mix of boards, shingles, and brick. There are a number of other fine Craftsman-style houses on this street.

Turn left on Ashby. After one block, cross Benvenue, turn left, and walk a few steps to 2933 Benvenue, a charming 1907 bungalow named **㉒ Flotsam and Jetsam**. Also designed by Coplin, it has large brackets, is sided in shingles and boards, and features a brick chimney. Continue to 2917 Benvenue, which has a turret, a large brick porch, and a huge Canary Island palm in the side yard. Down the block, at 2905 Benvenue, is a house designed by John Hudson Thomas

California desert fan palms on Hillegass.

and George T. Plowman that has a half-hipped roof over the porch that looks like a hood or cap, and a similar gable behind it, over the bay. The 1909 house combines brown- shingle, stucco, and half-timbering.

At 2901 Benvenue (southeast corner with Russell), the house has attractive latticework on the windows and multiple gables. Cross Russell, noting the deep orange-yellow exterior at 2835 Benvenue, on the northeast corner, with a third-floor pop-up room and a bright red door. On the opposite side, 2832 Benvenue has a roof over the porch and another over the bay that have an Oriental flair, lending charm to an American Foursquare design.

The 1904 Colonial Revival–style house at 2823 Benvenue is appealing in its asymmetry and finely detailed bay, presumably at an internal stair landing. The porch entry on the side and other details give an air of urban elegance. 2815 Benvenue has a wisteria, with prolific bloom in March, all across the front.

Next door is 2811 Benvenue, the **㉓ (Charles A.) Westenberg House**. This 1903 Berkeley landmark was designed by Coplin, and is a treasure that stops passersby in their tracks. For the best view, pause at the garden to see the front and south sides. The steep gables of this three-story home—two large ones on the south side and one big and one small gable facing the street—have a fascinating rhythm, and the shingles on the upper floor versus boards on the lower floors are handsome, as are the window treatments and jigsaw-puzzle beam ends and bargeboards. The garden includes an Art Nouveau, wrought-iron gateway. Coplin went all out on this house—the first on its block—for Westenberg, a former minister who became a successful businessman.

The Westenberg House and several others in this neighborhood have main entrances on the side rather than the street. This urban design approach for larger homes is also often seen in San Francisco's Pacific Heights.

Across the street and just a bit farther back south, the brown-shingle at 2812 Benvenue was for a time the home of noted 20th-century painter Richard Diebenkorn, an early abstract expressionist and later part of the Bay Area Figurative Movement. His bridging of these artistic styles resulted in his most famous paintings, including the Ocean Park series. Diebenkorn lived and worked in Berkeley from 1953 to 1966 and then moved to Southern California; he returned to Berkeley late in life, moving with his wife to this house and another one near Healdsburg. He spent his final months in poor health, still sketching, and passed away here in March 1993. The large jacaranda in front is covered in lavender blossoms in early June.

In the next block, 2733 Benvenue is a **24 John Hudson Thomas design** from 1909 with a complex roof and leaded window; one room of the house projects forward, although the entrance and the main mass are farther back. This house is an example of the early use of stucco.

On the opposite side a little farther on, 2722 Benvenue is a **25 Georgian-style brown-shingle** attributed to Ernest Coxhead from 1903 and built as a home. The Bentley School was here from the 1930s; The Academy, another private school, has been in the building since 1969 (with an ownership change in 2014). At 2717 Benvenue, note the sculptures in the garden and the blue glass collection in the windows.

Cross Derby, turn right, and continue to 2667–71 Derby, **26 Bill Clinton and Hillary Rodham**'s home in the summer of 1971, as their relationship blossomed but well before their marriage or any hint of future political doings. According to the Berkeley Historical Plaque Project, "During a summer break from Yale Law School, they shared the apartment of Hillary's mother's half-sister, Adeline Rosenberg. Hillary clerked for Oakland attorney Mal Burnstein while Bill hung out, reading and exploring the area."

Walk back to Benvenue, turn right, and continue to the rather nondescript brown-shingle apartment building at 2603 Benvenue, where the ㉗ **Symbionese Liberation Army (SLA) kidnapped Patty Hearst** on February 4, 1974. Patty was the granddaughter of William Randolph Hearst—publisher of newspapers and builder of Hearst Castle in San Simeon—and the sensational crime and its aftermath enthralled the nation for years. As ransom, the SLA demanded that Patty's father donate food to needy California families. Saying Hearst's subsequent $6 million food donation was of poor quality, the kidnappers held Patty captive for 19 months. During that time, she was brainwashed and tortured and committed several crimes on behalf of the SLA (including armed bank robbery). She was ultimately captured and sentenced to 35 years in prison. After serving 22 months, her sentence was commuted by President Jimmy Carter. President Bill Clinton pardoned her in 2001.

Across the street at 2600 Benvenue (corner with Parker Street), are the ㉘ **Lindblom Apartments,** designed by George Anderson and completed in 1911. This attractive building (a blend of Mediterranean and classical elements) is set amid trees and has rich ornamentation, including dentils, geometric designs in the window boxes, carved plant designs in the window outlines, and ornamental balconies over the three entrances. The apartments fit well in a neighborhood of primarily single-family homes.

Turn left on Parker and walk along the north side of the Lindblom Apartments. In 1905, ㉙ **Julia Morgan designed the trio of houses** across the street at 2615, 2617, and 2619 Parker. This ensemble was developed for one client to be sold speculatively, but the buildings relate well to each other, with all entrances facing a central open area and the middle house set back. The middle house is the only one that seems to have undergone significant alteration.

Walk back up Parker (toward the hills) and continue past Benvenue to College. Pulitzer Prize–winning playwright and novelist ㉚ **Thornton Wilder** (who wrote the oft-performed play *Our Town*) lived on the northwest corner at 2598 College as a middle school student in Berkeley around 1906–10; the house has been altered and is now a frat house (Sigma Epsilon Omega), but some of the 1898 historic residence remains.

St. John's Presbyterian Church.

Turn right and walk to the ㉛ **Julia Morgan Theater** at 2640 College. Designed by Julia Morgan, the building is a sterling expression of Bay Area Arts and Crafts design. Originally built for St. John's Presbyterian Church (now up the block), the complex includes the Fellowship Hall (1908) on the right, the sanctuary (1910) on the left, and the Sunday school in the rear (1916). The sanctuary has clerestory windows; a shingled and wood-plank exterior; and exposed, stained wood on the interior. The congregation did much of the construction to save on costs. When the church moved to its current, much larger location in the 1960s, a major effort was made to save the building, which led to the formation of the Berkeley Architectural Heritage Association. The building became a theater for live performances, now called Berkeley Playhouse. The Sunday school is rented out for arts-related education, and the Fellowship Hall is now Heart's Leap preschool.

Walk on College past Derby to see the newer ㉜ **St. John's Presbyterian Church** across the street. Built in 1964, its architecture is modern, but features such as unpainted wood, pergolas, and spacious grounds fit nicely into the neighborhood. (To shorten the walk, continue on College to return to the starting point.)

To see more of the Elmwood, backtrack on College. In front of the Julia Morgan Theater, cross College at the stop sign at Derby. From the northeast corner of Derby and College, there is a good view of the stucco ㉝ **Danbert Apartments** (originally called Marguerite Apartments) at 2704 Derby. Built in 1915, the building features small balconies, bay windows, and fine window detailing.

Continue up Derby. At 2716 Derby, the Berkeley Masjid (mosque) was purchased around 2000 and gradually renovated as funds became available. The building was originally constructed in 1915 for the Twentieth Century Club of Berkeley. An attractive apartment building with a gabled bay over the entrance is to the right, between Berkeley Masjid and The Danbert.

Walk to Etna Street and turn left. On the corner, at 2719 Derby/2644 Etna, is a Charles W. McCall-designed brown-shingle duplex with varied bays and porches built in 1905. Julia Morgan designed ❸❹ **2618 and 2616 Etna** in a Dutch Colonial style with brown shingles; the attractive fence came later.

Cross Parker. On the next block, in a row of Colonial Revival houses, ❸❺ **2516 Etna** is a high-peaked version of this style in yellow and white with lovely leaded mullions. Julia Morgan did the finely detailed brown-shingle with brick chimney at 2514. Bernard Maybeck designed the house across the street, 2515 Etna. This ❸❻ **charming 1921 cottage** is set back in the trees behind a fence; peek through the gate to glimpse the house. The studio room was nicknamed the "barn" because Maybeck remodeled it from a barn. The original owner, Cedric Wright, was a violinist and photographer (the mentor of Ansel Adams) who participated in 33 Sierra Club trips. The studio was popular for musical evenings and parties for Sierra Club members in the 1920s and 1930s.

At Dwight Way, notice the highly varied shingle pattern across the street at 2727 Dwight; you can see the original stucco on the side. Designed by Willis Polk and completed in 1891, ❸❼ **Gorrill House** is now a 12-bedroom residence for UC students.

Turn right on Dwight and then right on Piedmont Avenue, where you will pass several older, attractive apartment buildings and some newer ones. The 1896 house at 2528 Piedmont has well-kept shingles, numerous gables, a front pergola, and diamond window panes.

Continue and turn left to 2811 Parker, a well-restored ❸❽ **Italianate cottage** with discreet charm from 1883 (quite old for this area of Berkeley). Up the street, you can see UC's ❸❾ **Clark Kerr Campus**, formerly the California School for the Deaf and Blind. The campus has Mediterranean-style buildings, designed mainly by George B. McDougall and Alfred Eichler (no relation to the subdivision developer Joseph Eichler), who both worked in the California Office of the State Architect. The Clark Kerr Campus was built in the 1920s; buildings were added in the 1950s.

Return to Piedmont and turn left. The large 1902 brown-shingle at 2625-27 Piedmont has twin gables with Gothic arched windows. On the opposite side at **40 2620 Piedmont**, a 1905 house was constructed by a civil engineer of concrete blocks that look like stone over reinforced concrete, an early example of this kind of construction in Berkeley. Notice the amusing roof over the turret and the porch.

Farther along, at 2630 Piedmont, is a fascinating design by Coplin (who designed the Westerberg house on Benvenue) from 1905, with varied gables, an oval window in the front gable, and a porch with columns that narrow as they go up. The 1909 Mission Revival at 2647 Piedmont (corner of Derby) is not common in this area and is a refreshing sight after all the brown-shingles.

Cross Derby and turn left to 2814 and 2816 Derby, a pair of 1908 **41 Julia Morgan houses** with entries facing each other. They are harmonious despite differing designs; she often created pairs. The ornamentation on the bay of the house on the right is striking. Morgan's designs were refined and subtle but could be flamboyant, as in Hearst Castle at San Simeon. By contrast, a graceless 1960s apartment building is opposite the houses.

Return to Piedmont and turn left. When you cross Forest Avenue, note the large London plane (sycamore) trees lining the street in both directions, although those on the south side have been hacked to accommodate utility lines. After passing Emerson Elementary School, look up Garber Street (or take a short detour) to the left, where there is a miniature version of San Francisco's twisty Lombard Street. (Beyond that, Garber slopes down to the east with attractive houses described in Walk 13, Rockridge to Claremont.)

At the southwest corner, 2746 Garber is a **42 rare Gothic Revival** from the 19th century, added onto (and lovingly renovated). The original section is probably one of the oldest structures in this part of Berkeley (along with the Italianate cottage at 2811 Parker). The large redwoods on the east side of Piedmont were an unusual choice for street trees in the narrow planting strip; the trunks are too broad for the space and the sidewalk is buckling.

On the left at **43 2799 Piedmont** (corner with Stuart), the 1911 brown-shingle with an asymmetrical gable and squarish dormers is by William Knowles; note the wisteria across the front intertwined with a climbing rose. Cross Stuart and turn right, then continue just past Piedmont to 2800 Piedmont (on the corner) and 2732 and 2730 Stuart. These **44** **three residences** were designed by Leola Hall. Although not formally trained in architecture, from 1907 to 1912 she designed, developed, built, and sold a number of highly regarded Craftsman-style houses in Berkeley at a time when few women carried on such work. Ten of her designs are within a block of here. She was also a painter and an outspoken suffragist.

Return to Piedmont and turn right to continue south toward Russell. Piedmont and Russell are lined with attractive pink and white flowering plums in February. Near the northeast corner with Russell, a plaque commemorates historic Kelsey Ranch, which was more of a nursery with an orchard and ornamental plants.

Walk left (east) up Russell to the corner of Kelsey Street to see the exuberant, large house at 2827 Russell. Completed around 1910 from a popular design in one of Henry L. Wilson's bungalow books, which provided sample illustrations and floor plans, this is an **45** **over-the-top Mission Revival** with swooping curves on its Spanish-style gable. The original owner was Edward M. Marquis, a hardware-store proprietor who became a busy developer in the Elmwood district after moving to Berkeley; he took out 151 building permits during the 1920s. The living room extends the width of the first floor. The house is also notable for stately Canary Island palms and an impressive display on Halloween. Although many streets from College to Claremont are closed off at Halloween to accommodate the crowds admiring extravagantly decorated homes, Russell

Street is regarded as "the" place to be that night. Just past the east edge of the property in the next yard, the large rhododendron has brilliant red flowers in full bloom in early spring.

Turn back toward Piedmont. Across the street, William Wurster, who

A Mission Revival extravaganza at 2827 Russell.

became dean of the UC Berkeley School of Architecture, designed 2812 Russell. The French Regency design features an original house from 1927 framed by a front studio structure from 1931, creating a simple and elegant courtyard with a fine iron gate.

Walk down Russell. At Cherry Street, 2717 Russell, on the northwest corner, was the family home of Elmer Bischoff, a leading painter in the Bay Area Figurative Movement and an art teacher; the house was designed and built by his father in 1919. Elmer graduated from Berkeley High in 1935; he and his wife Jean later lived in an apartment above where the Elmwood Cafe is now, at College and Russell.

At College, cross at the stop sign and turn left. The **46 storefronts** at 2900–36 College, built in 1922 with second-floor apartments, have an unusual arched clerestory (such high windows are a popular feature in the Elmwood). In 2010, the busy Elmwood Cafe on the corner replaced Ozzie's Soda Fountain, a neighborhood institution for nearly 90 years. (The original Ozzie's sign is still over the door.) Mrs. Dalloway's bookstore opened here in 2004 at 2904 College.

Toward the end of the block and across the street, 2947–53 College is another Berkeley landmark, a **47 storefront designed by William H. Weeks** from 1923. For decades it was home to Bolfing's Elmwood Hardware. In the mid-2000s, the owners sought to put in senior apartments and office space above the store—which the Landmarks Preservation Commission was willing to approve—but ultimately the planning department rejected the plan due to zoning rules, and the store closed in 2007. The owners renovated the property in 2008 and other retail is now at this location. This block is lined with ginkgo trees.

The walk ends where it began at Ashby and College. To celebrate completing the walk, treat yourself to ice cream at Ici, a Dreyer's cone at the Beanery, donuts at Dream Fluff (around the corner on Ashby), a pastry at the Elmwood Cafe, or one of the many other gastronomic pleasures available in the Elmwood.

✳ ✳ ✳

PIEDMONT AVENUE TO PANORAMIC HILL

Overview: Frederick Law Olmstead laid out Piedmont Avenue, south of the UC campus, specifically for grand homes; the area later was taken over by some of the college's fraternities and sororities. From the historic International House, this walk moves up the hill, where you will explore historic neighborhoods with architecture by Julia Morgan and others, and get some stairway exercise.

Highlights:
- Grand homes turned into Greek societies
- International House, Cal Memorial Stadium
- National historic district of Panoramic Hill

Distance: 1.5–3 miles
Time: 1.5–3 hours
Elevation gain: 175–530 feet

Start at the northwest corner of Dwight Way and Piedmont Avenue. The AC Transit 51 bus stops one block away at Dwight and College Avenue.

On this corner, **❶ Alpha Sigma Phi fraternity** at 2498 Piedmont is a large, shingled house (built in 1893) with a gambrel roof, setting the pattern for this area—large residences that became UC fraternity/sorority houses or apartment buildings.

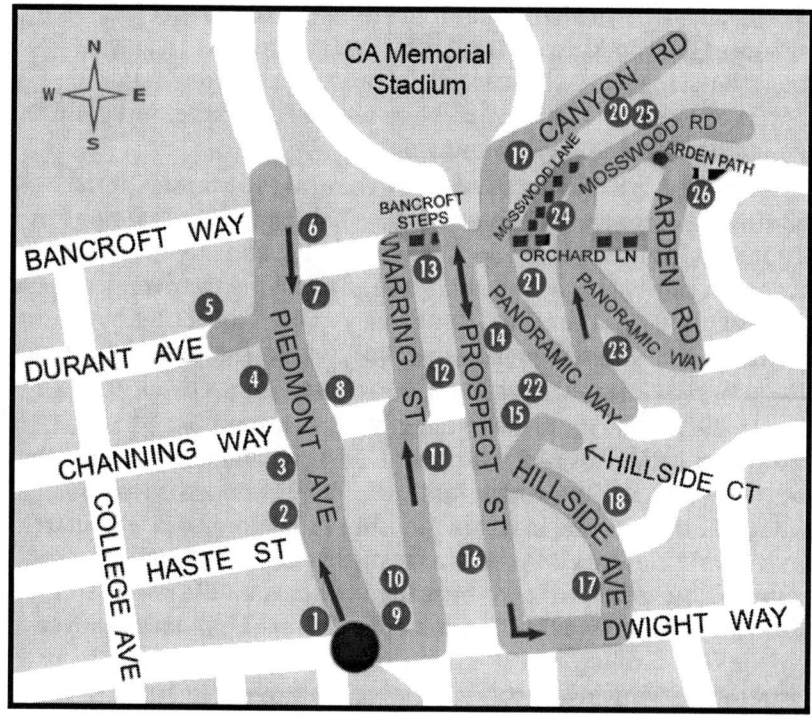

Frederick Law Olmstead—who developed the master plans for UC Berkeley and Stanford and designed New York City's Central Park and dozens of other parks around the country—laid out the Piedmont Avenue area (but not Panoramic Hill) in 1865 as part of a plan for the College of California, which became UC. His designs strived for harmony with nature; landscaped open spaces are surrounded by curving streets that follow the contours of the hills. The neighborhood became a model for other well-to-do residential areas in communities around the country.

This area bloomed during the East Bay's rapid growth after the 1906 San Francisco earthquake and fire, and the grand houses were built for businessmen and UC professors. The construction of Memorial Stadium in 1923 and the International House in 1928 resulted in the demolition of numerous homes and caused many remaining homeowners to move in search of more tranquil surroundings. As a result, many large homes were sold or rented out to student groups.

Head north on Piedmont on the left side. At the first intersection, ❷ **2747 Haste Street** (northwest corner) is an apartment building with whimsical features such as turrets, a gothic entranceway with medallions above on the Haste side, and gothic window grills on the Piedmont side.

The ❸ **Alpha Delta Pi sorority** at 2400 Piedmont is at the southwest corner with Channing Way. This charming 1931 English Tudor–style home has bricks, half-timbering, and pleasing dormers. Its south side was added onto without destroying the overall appeal. Typical of many in the area, this home replaced an earlier house, in this case, one where Phoebe Apperson Hearst—mother of William Randolph Hearst and a major UC benefactor—once lived.

In the middle of the next block, 2336 Piedmont is a ❹ **1915 house by Julia Morgan**, who designed many houses in this neighborhood. Originally a single-family home, this house is reasonably intact, unlike the one to its left, another Julia Morgan design marred by a poorly conceived 1950s-era facade. Notice the ceramic tiles of ships on the front wall and the leaded window on the porch. In 1974, Casa Joaquin, a residence for Chicano/Latino UC students, moved in; the Greenlining Institute, a multiethnic residential leadership program serving low-income students, acquired it in 2004.

Next door, 2328 Piedmont is the Kappa Kappa Gamma house. This dignified Georgian edifice with ornate entry, including Corinthian columns, was originally a brown-shingle designed by Julia Morgan in 1905, but it was drastically altered in 1948.

At Durant Avenue, cross and walk a bit to the left to 2735 Durant, a ❺ **1908 house designed by the firm of Maybeck and White**. A typical early Maybeck, this Swiss chalet–style house has unpainted redwood with Craftsman features. The porch was probably subsequently glassed in with a skylight, with a nice effect. At one time, the house had a sweeping view of the bay, but trees and buildings now block the vista.

Return to Piedmont, walk left, and cross Bancroft Way. Just past the bench, look across the way to see California Memorial Stadium, a John Galen Howard design of 1923 that is on the National Register of Historic Places. Home of the Cal Golden Bears football team, the stadium is an elegant example of a neoclassical bowl stadium, with arches reminiscent of the Roman Colosseum. Neighbors joined Howard, who was UC's campus architect, in opposition to placing

California Memorial Stadium.

the stadium here, directly on top of the Hayward fault and Strawberry Creek.

The stadium was gutted for a seismic retrofit and major renovation, completed in 2012. Controversy was intense again: for more than two years, protesters objecting to the planned razing of mature oaks sat in them, until a court order allowed the university to remove the tree-sitters. Some trees were cut down to make way for the new Student-Athlete High Performance Center in front of the building (which does not detract from the classic stadium exterior). An architectural controversy focused on the large, modern structure placed on top for luxury boxes and a press center. Many of the live oaks were retained on the slope in front of the stadium, and the new structure on top of the stadium is fairly light and airy.

Backtrack a little to the corner of Bancroft; directly across the street is the **❻ International House**, or I-House, a 1928 George W. Kelham design with later additions. The imposing building was the first co-ed campus housing on the West Coast and was built with a donation from John D. Rockefeller, Jr., to promote cross-cultural experiences and interracial understanding (although at the time, many people were upset at the idea of multiethnic housing). About

600 students from 70 countries live here during the academic year; alumni include entrepreneurs, ambassadors, Nobel laureates, and California governor Jerry Brown. The architecture combines Mediterranean and Mission Revival elements with an Indian stupa-shaped tower. There is a cafe and restrooms inside.

Cross Piedmont at the crosswalk and turn right on the east side. Just beyond Bancroft is the **❼ Thorsen House** at 2307 Piedmont, among the most architecturally significant in the area. The brothers Charles Sumner Greene and Henry Mather Greene (Greene and Greene) designed the house in 1908–10, in the heyday of their Craftsman residential design period. Often considered the ultimate bungalows, these were not in fact bungalows but fair-sized homes custom built with fastidious attention to the design and production of every element inside and out, from wooden railings to light fixtures to furniture. The brothers had studied metal and woodworking as well as architecture; in 1893, they moved from the Midwest to Pasadena, where the bulk of their work was done.

Built for William Randolph Thorsen, a lumberman, the house has unpainted wood, with Japanese and Gothic design elements; stained glass in the beautiful door; fascinating mullions in the

The Thorsen House, designed by Greene and Greene.

2395 Piedmont, in Italian Renaissance Revival style.

bands of windows; metal and glass light fixtures on the porch and over the gateways; copper gutters and downspouts; a garage on the side in the same style and gable as the house; and wrought-iron gates. The retaining walls, foundation, and chimney feature "rough" brick that gives a rustic look. In 1943, Sigma Phi Society, the second-oldest college fraternity in the United States, purchased the house; it has done an extraordinary job of maintaining this historic property. The house is occasionally open for tours, and the wood paneling and details inside are magnificent.

To the right of the Thorsen House, 2311 Piedmont is another example of a Julia Morgan house destroyed by an insensitive "modernization." Farther along at 2325 Piedmont, Pi Beta Phi sorority is beautifully maintained. The 1908 mansion by Charles Kaiser features a balcony with an arched colonnade, gables, leaded-glass windows on the first floor, and an attractive pattern in the half-timbering. At the northeast corner of Piedmont and Channing, 2395 Piedmont is the **8 Phi Gamma Delta fraternity house**, an Italian Renaissance Revival with gleaming-white cement columns and balustrades, brick and woodwork, arched windows, and a tile roof. The house is angled to dominate the corner.

Olmstead designed medians on Piedmont to provide land-scaped open space; however, they were used for parking for many years. Citizen outcry led to chain fencing and tree planting during the mid-2000s to restore Olmstead's design.

Continue two blocks to 2499 Piedmont, at the northeast corner of Dwight, to see the **9 Theta Chi fraternity house**. Walter Ratcliff, Jr., designed this imposing corner house in 1913, in Mediterranean style with leaded windows on the upper portion of the first-floor windows, simple decoration, and a tile roof.

Turn left on Dwight, then left again on Warring Street. Ratcliff also designed the 1913 house at **10 2438 Warring**, with curving segments in the half-timbering. A large, evergreen araucaria tree from the South Pacific is in front.

Many houses on this block have been altered or replaced, but on the right, 2409 Warring is an exception. Designed by Ratcliff, this well-preserved **11 Tudor house** from 1936 has painted-brick, stucco, half-timbering, and diamond-paned windows.

At the intersection, look across to the northeast corner of Channing and Warring at **12 2901 Channing**, a large, brown-shingle house with an elongated roof dormer by Julia Morgan from 1905. Built for William E. Colby, a long-time Sierra Club leader, it combines formality in the arrangement of windows with a rustic feel.

Cross Channing and continue on Warring, which jogs a bit. At the end, take the Bancroft Steps on the right, a classic among the many public stairways and paths in Berkeley. As you ascend, a large Julia Morgan house from 1913 in brick and stucco (later enlarged) is on the left, partly hidden by foliage. On the right is the 1926 **13 Alpha Phi sorority house**, designed by Ratcliff in Spanish Colonial Revival style.

At the top, turn right on Prospect Street (Memorial Stadium is to the left). Noteworthy houses on the uphill side of this block include **14 2317 Prospect**, another Ratcliff design, with a charming top floor and interesting gables. The brown-shingle house two lots down at 2347 Prospect, dating to 1908, is now the African American Theme House of the Berkeley Student Cooperative.

Directly across from the theme house, look through a gap in the ivy-grown fence into a yard. There used to be a house here where playwright Thornton Wilder lived with his family from 1913 to 1915 while he attended Berkeley High. Wilder was already writing plays as a teenager; he later won two Pulitzer Prizes for drama and one

Spotlight: Walter Ratcliff, Jr. (1881–1973)

As Berkeley's first city architect, Walter Ratcliff, Jr., designed numerous civic buildings, as well as commercial and residential structures all over town; his work had a long-lasting impact on Berkeley's overall look and feel. Ratcliff's style was less flamboyant than that of Bernard Maybeck or John Hudson Thomas, but he showed an impressive ability to take styles from Tudor to Mediterranean to Swiss chalet and give them harmonious proportions with subtle and elegant details.

The son of a clergyman, Ratcliff was born in England and came to the United States in 1894 as a teenager, arriving in Berkeley in 1897. While studying chemistry at UC, he began designing simple homes with a partner, Charles Louis McFarland. After graduation, he decided to make a career in architecture, and an uncle underwrote a grand tour of Europe, including six months of architectural study in Rome. Ratcliff partnered briefly with John Galen Howard back in Berkeley and then opened his own practice in 1908.

Ratcliff was the primary designer for Bay Area real estate developer Duncan McDuffie. In 1913, he was named Berkeley's first city architect, a position that included overseeing the construction of Berkeley schools and firehouses. With McFarland, Ratcliff founded Fidelity Savings and Loan (in a lovely building downtown that he designed, at 2323 Shattuck Ave.). He designed the 12-story Chamber of Commerce building (now the Wells Fargo Building), Berkeley's first skyscraper, at Shattuck and Center Street. In the Piedmont area of Berkeley, he designed an impressive corner house on Piedmont Way as well as five other residences in various styles.

Ratcliff was comfortable with the collegiate Gothic style and designed ecclesiastical buildings at the Berkeley Baptist Divinity School (2606 Dwight Way) and the Pacific School of Religion at 1798 Scenic Avenue (notably Holbrook Hall). The city landmark Wells Fargo Bank at College and Ashby and the Mason-McDuffie building downtown at 2102 Shattuck Avenue (now Scandinavian Designs) are excellent examples of his commercial work. He also designed the Elks Club (2018 Allston Way) and Armstrong College at 2210 Harold Way (now both part of the Nyingma Institute/Dharma College); some Mills College buildings, where he was supervising architect; and a host of residences. His son and grandson carried on his architectural firm, Ratcliff Architects, which is located in Emeryville and still going strong today. ❉❉

for a novel, and was awarded the Presidential Medal of Freedom, among other honors. Wilder's *Our Town* is by some accounts the most-performed drama in the United States.

Continue down Prospect. At Hillside Avenue, turn left, and then turn immediately left again up steep **⑮ Hillside Court**, which is rather like an alley. There is no sidewalk but little traffic on this delightful cul-de-sac, which features houses that feel far from the bustling campus area. All were built from 1906 to 1909 and have not been greatly altered. On the left, 11 Hillside Court was originally the carriage house for a large residence on Prospect. An early John Hudson Thomas design is at 15 Hillside Court, with narrow wood shingles. Next door, the impressive Julia Morgan house at 19 Hillside Court (home of Berkeley Bayit—Jewish cooperative student housing) is a brown-shingle with Classical elements and a two-story arch over the balcony. The walls seem to angle out slightly as they go down. On the left side and in front, the giant sequoia was probably planted by the original owner, Joseph Nisbet LeConte, Sierra Nevada explorer and second president of the Sierra Club.

The charming brown-shingle house at 21 Hillside Court is by A. H. Broad, a builder who designed and constructed many early Berkeley schools. There is a large stucco and half-timbered house at 23 Hillside Court; the first owners used a private creekside path (which still exists) to get down to Hillside Avenue.

On the south side, 18 and 14 Hillside Court, both designed by John Hudson Thomas, share a courtyard, although the main entry for 14 is on the street. Vienna Secession, a movement that protested the formality of traditional architecture, influenced the style. Thomas liked to "sign" his houses with a pattern of four squares and/or two vertical lines; here the four squares are repeated in many windows of both houses. At 18, an unusual storeroom door is on a corner. There is a Gothic window and a pleasant, three-sided, glassed-in room above; 14 has a Gothic entry and door.

Continue down Hillside Court, turn right on Hillside Avenue, then immediately left on Prospect, and proceed toward Dwight. On the right, 2436 Prospect is a very strange clubhouse from 1960 that seems to be half-buried in the ground. The architectural firm Skidmore, Owings & Merrill designed it for **⑯ Skull and Keys**, an upperclassmen society of the Theta Nu Epsilon fraternity founded in 1892 by novelist Frank Norris and others. For many years, members met semimonthly in this facility, called the Tomb. Farther along, 2446 Prospect is a considerably more charming, shingled, Georgian-style residence.

To end the walk here, turn right on Dwight to return to the starting point. Otherwise, turn left on Dwight and walk uphill. On the right is UC Berkeley's Clark Kerr Campus, formerly the California School for the Deaf and Blind.

Turn left at Hillside Avenue. On the right, the minipark belongs to UC's Smyth Fernwald student-family housing, farther up the hill. This area was once Fernwald, the estate of English inventor William H. Smyth. He built a late-1860s Victorian house, which was altered by Julia Morgan in a Tudor Gothic design in 1911. You can catch sight of part of the house from this street in the northeast corner of the minipark, sadly abandoned and boarded up with a razor-wire fence. Smyth willed the property to UC, which constructed dorms on the uphill side of the park after World War II. Neighborhood pressure forced the university to retain the open space for the public.

At 2444 Hillside (one house from the corner), the **17 early Julia Morgan home** from 1905 is simple and elegant, with a welcoming

porch and entryway. Morgan also designed the brown-shingle house next door at 2440 Hillside. Up the street and to the right, you can see part of the imposing **18 1890 house** at 2425 Hillside, originally a Victorian, which was altered to a brick neo-Georgian style for a fraternity in 1927. Since 1971, it has been a retreat center, called Padma Ling, for the Tibetan Nyingma Institute, located north of campus. Decked out with colorful prayer flags, the building is quite a contrast to the subdued Julia Morgan brown-shingles around it.

Detail of 19 Hillside Court, by Julia Morgan.

A little farther along, the bridge was the result of a 1903 petition by Smyth and neighbors to stop the city from culverting the stream below (Derby Creek). The rough stone and sylvan stream banks are rustic for such an urban location. Smyth and an Italian stonemason built the facing of the bridge as well as fine stone walls for the Fernwald estate and other nearby properties.

At Prospect, turn right and walk back to where the road turns right. Carefully cross in the diagonal crosswalk to walk up through the upper portion of the stadium cul-de-sac parking area that parallels the street.

Just after the parking lane turns left, look across the street to a concrete stairway for residents to access 1 and 9 Canyon Road; Julia Morgan designed 9. Just beyond these, **⑲ 15 Canyon**, a four-story brown-shingle with leaded windows and dormers designed by Ernest Coxhead, sits above a high, concrete retaining wall.

Where the parking lane ends at a fence, carefully cross the traffic street toward the corner of the concrete retaining wall and walk to the left next to the wall, looking up to see another interesting facade of the Coxhead house at 15 Canyon. Turn into Canyon Road as it bears right, near a "Not a Through Street" sign. Witter Field, home of Cal Rugby, is on the left, followed by the Strawberry Canyon Recreation Area, which includes a softball field, outdoor pool, ropes course, and clubhouse for UC students and employees.

On the right side, this shady cul-de-sac features contemporary and historic brown-shingle homes on the steep, wooded side of Strawberry Canyon. (Strawberry Creek is buried here in a culvert beneath the UC fields and pool.) Rustic houses on the right, at **⑳ 45–51 Canyon**, are reminiscent of cabins at a state park. At the end of the street, a trail leads up to the Strawberry Canyon fire trail, a popular route for walkers, runners, and dog walkers.

Go back down Canyon Road and return carefully across to the walkway next to the stadium fence, keeping your eyes and ears open for speeding cars. Go left between the fence and stanchions and continue down through the parking area as it curves back toward the Bancroft Steps. This time, cross in the diagonal crosswalk (where the road turns into Prospect) and turn left.

Walk a short distance uphill from the bend in the road at Prospect and then right onto Panoramic Way.

The lower part of this area, called the Panoramic Hill historic district, is on the National Register of Historic Places thanks to efforts by residents to document and apply for the status in 2005. The sidewalks on Panoramic appear and disappear; be mindful of fast-moving traffic (despite the curves) and stay to the side. Uphill on the left, 1 Orchard Lane, whose address is on the public stairway, is an impressive 1922 Walter T. Steilberg house with an octagonal tower (you will walk these stairs and get a closer look later). Steilberg was the chief draftsman in Julia Morgan's practice for years and a key figure in managing the office and design projects; he consulted with Morgan even after he set up his own practice.

The large English Tudor apartment house with myriad windows from 1912 at **㉑ 5–11 Panoramic** is by Julia Morgan. Next door, 23 Panoramic is an early Bernard Maybeck house from 1901 that signifies his embrace of the Arts and Crafts design movement. Inside, sliding panels allow the living and dining areas to be combined, a radical idea for that time. The structural elements, including the thick siding boards crossing each other at the ends, are evident on this simple but handsome house.

Farther along on the right, Steilberg designed **㉒ 38 Panoramic** and lived there for a time. The house goes from one story on the

5–11 Panoramic, an apartment building designed by Julia Morgan.

street to three stories down the slope. After 48 Panoramic there is a cul-de-sac to the right; cross this and continue uphill around the hairpin curve. Inside the hairpin to the left, 59/61 Panoramic is another Steilberg design. A different architect added the second floor in 1954, which complements the design.

On the right at 72 Panoramic (the number may be missing; it's the next house after 70), the stairway on the left side of the house has a **㉓ sculptured water feature** derived from a natural spring.

At the next hairpin turn, go straight on Mosswood Road rather than turning to the right to continue on Panoramic. Immediately on the left, at 11 Mosswood, with a gate just at the turn, is a Julia Morgan house that was the **㉔ home of Professor Willis Linn Jepson**, renowned for his definitive manual of California plants (*The Jepson Manual*). Mosswood, like Canyon Road, is on a north-facing slope and is heavily wooded with live oaks, redwoods, and some nonnative trees. The houses feel like they're in a forest rather than a city.

On the right, the houses at 6, 8, and 10 Mosswood in various styles share an attractive common entry stairway. On the left at the curve, 13 Mosswood, built in 1975, is based on a 1939 design by Frank Lloyd Wright. The owners purchased the plans long after Wright's death in 1959; the foundation he established at Taliesin West in Arizona offered his plans for sale.

A Frank Lloyd Wright design at 13 Mosswood.

Across the street, 14 Mosswood has a nice residential unit over a garage. Up the steep hill, ㉕ **37 Mosswood** (the number is on an oak tree beyond the brick entryway on the left) is a big house overlooking the canyon, designed in 1911 by Walter Ratcliff, Jr., with numerous tall gables and brown shingles.

At this point, you can return the way you came on Mosswood (toward the Wright house); if you do so, skip the next three paragraphs.

If you want to get a workout, opposite 37 Mosswood take the steep Arden Steps to Arden Road. On the left, the brown-shingle house at ㉖ **100 Arden** has a brick retaining wall and steps, as well as ceramic planting urns.

Head to the right, down Arden, and look for the Orchard Lane sign and the number 59 painted on the curb on the right. These steps go down to Panoramic; there are more than 160 steps and numerous landings with mostly no handrails, so descend carefully. Go right at the bottom and continue straight onto Mosswood.

To avoid going down the Orchard Lane stairs, stay on Arden until you reach Panoramic, then turn right and continue until you pass the lower end of the Orchard Lane stairs and reach the earlier hairpin turn. Continue straight on Mosswood.

On the downhill side of Mosswood Road, between the Wright house at 15 and two mailboxes marked 33A and 33B, look for the sign to Mosswood Lane; the actual lane is between the mailboxes and a garage to the right when you are facing them. Take this charming dirt path (which descends around the Frank Lloyd Wright house) with high brick walls on the left and a row of redwood trees on the right, passing between backyards. Toward the end, it feels like an overgrown garden path.

Mosswood Lane ends at a lower section of Orchard Lane, at a grand staircase built in 1911 with broad concrete stairs and balustrades designed by Warren Cheney, developer of the lower Panoramic Hill residential area. On the right as you descend the stairs is the Walter Steilberg–designed house at 1 Orchard Lane that was noted earlier, as you started up Panoramic Way. It features an octagonal tower, varied window designs, and Chinese ceramic tiles.

At the end of the steps, turn right on Panoramic, and then briefly left down Bancroft Way. Go left on Prospect Street, continue to Dwight, and turn right to return to the starting point.

✳✳✳

ROCKRIDGE TO CLAREMONT

Overview: Starting in Oakland, this walk takes in some of Berkeley's most exclusive neighborhoods, with large, beautiful homes and gardens and the spectacular Claremont Hotel. The Uplands neighborhood was designed by the firm of Frederick Law Olmsted to incorporate Harwood (Claremont) Creek and curving, tree-lined streets. There are some ups and downs but no long, steep climbs; options for shorter routes are provided.

Highlights:
- Classic homes by Julia Morgan and other top architects
- Creek running through Olmsted-designed neighborhood
- Historic Claremont Hotel

Distance: 2.4, 4.5, 6 miles
Time: 2–4 hours
Elevation gain: 100–560 feet

Start at the southwest corner of College and Shafter avenues in front of Market Hall, opposite the Rockridge BART station; the starting point is also accessible by several AC Transit buses. Parking is free in the BART lot on weekends, but strict limits apply at other times.

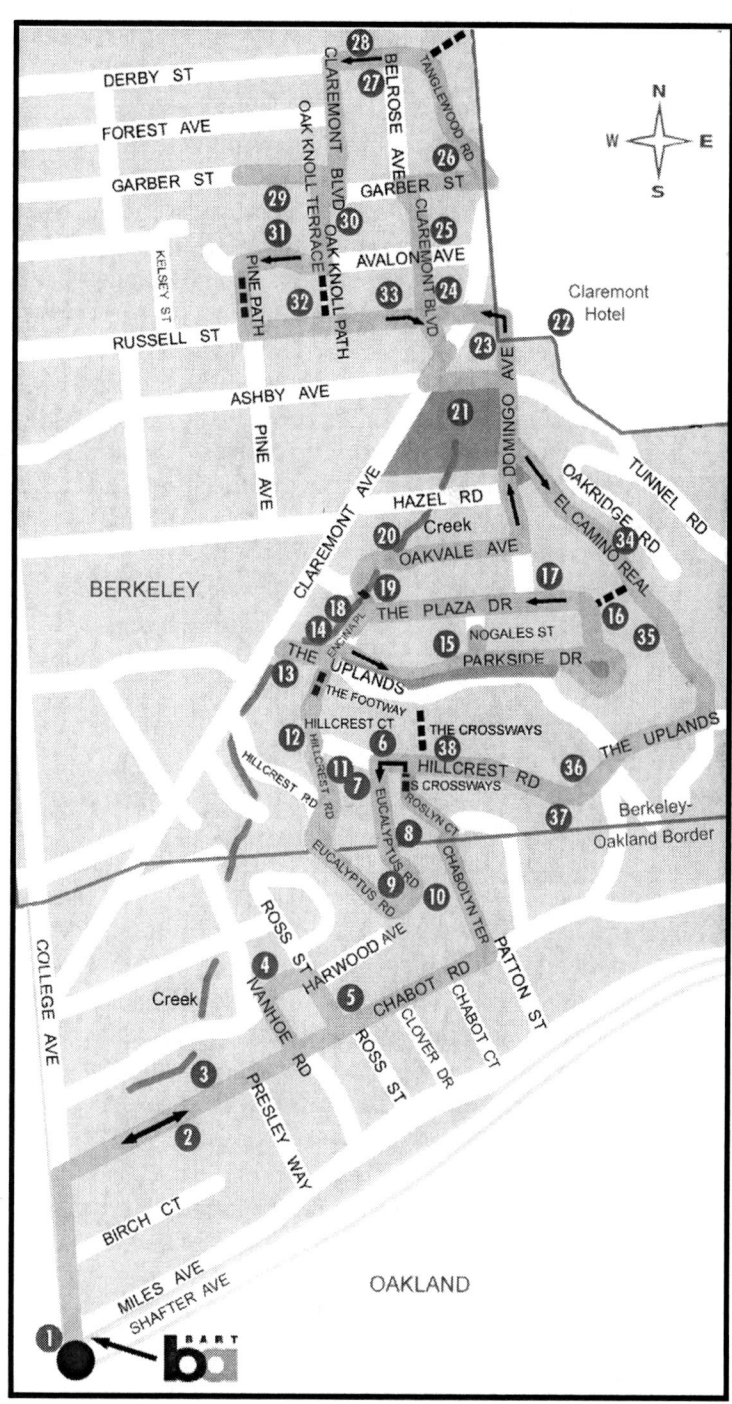

Notice the landscaping and large boulders forming a "rock ridge" in front of the BART station entrance.

You may want to visit Market Hall's food specialty shops for coffee or a snack before starting. Walk north on College, crossing Shafter and going under the freeway/BART overpass. The ❶ *Firestorm Community* **mural** under the overpass includes 2,000 handmade tiles commemorating lives affected by the devastating Oakland hills firestorm of October 20, 1991, which killed 25 people and destroyed nearly 3,500 homes.

At Miles Avenue, cross College, turn left, and continue on College to Birch Court. Retail and mixed-use buildings line most of College in typical main-street fashion, providing pedestrian ambience. Stores with large windows built up to the sidewalk, street trees, and parking provide a buffer between the street and sidewalks. In contrast, look across College to Trader Joe's: the parking lot fronting the street is not pedestrian-friendly.

Continue for a block on College and turn right on Chabot Road, a residential street. The houses are a mix of grand homes and modest bungalows, as well as new and older apartments and condominiums. 6100 Chabot is an attractive, older, four-unit apartment building; on the opposite side, 6101 Chabot is a newer multiunit development that lacks a good "face" to the street.

Notice the variety of street trees as you walk along Chabot. Chinese elms have peeling, varicolored bark; graceful curves; and small leaves. Tall, mature American elms—a classic street tree—abound, but they may not last much longer due to disease. In March/April, Japanese cherry trees become prominent as they bloom with delicate pink flowers.

At 6140 Chabot, look over the gate to the Japanese-style structures, garden, and pond. This is the ❷ **Oakland Zen Center**, a meditation compound headed by the Reverend Gengo Akiba, a leading figure in California Zen Buddhism. His wife Yoshie Akiba owns Yoshi's clubs in Oakland's Jack London Square and San Francisco.

Continue to a metal fence surrounding Gothic brick buildings. This is the chapel of St. Albert's Priory, founded in 1932 and currently housing about 40 Dominican friars. Its front entrance is at 5890 Birch Court, off of College.

Across the street, ❸ **6165 Chabot** is a large, wooden, Italianate house painted green with white trim and featuring elaborate woodwork over the curved-top windows; big brackets under the eaves; and a two-floor, polygonal turret. Built circa 1873, it is one of the oldest houses in an early subdivision called the White Tract (recorded in 1873). Harwood (Claremont) Creek flows behind the house, and a giant Canary Island palm is in the front yard. A pair of strange-looking giant yuccas is farther along in front of 6221 Chabot.

The diverse materials of Grimmon House.

Continue on Chabot, then turn left on Ivanhoe Road and walk one block to Harwood Avenue. On the triangular corner with Rockwell Street, 6172 Harwood is unique; cross and walk around it to get a good look. This 1911 Craftsman residence, called ❹ **Grimmon House**, combines dark and light brick, patterned concrete blocks, stone, diagonal wooden beams, a river-rock chimney, large arches over the porch, varied windows, unusual wall shingles, and fascinating gables. Although it looks imposing, this house is only 1,740 square feet. H. C. Brougher, an Oakland miner, built it with contractor and architect Layton Tibbals.

Catty-corner across the street, 6145 Harwood has unusual skylights along the roof ridgelines. Walk toward the hills (east) on Harwood to Ross Street, cross, and return right to Chabot. Turn left at the corner, passing along the concrete retaining wall and metal fence of a large house set back from Chabot (the address is ❺ **5920 Ross**) with a sizable garden in front that includes a bamboo grove.

Continue along Chabot. Next door at 6425 Chabot, there is a large brown-shingle house and extensive garden with brick and stone paving and features. Just before the stop sign, turn left onto Chabolyn Terrace. Along the street are a couple of podocarpuses, coniferous trees from the South Pacific with leaves in bunches, which look rather like a poodle's cut, as well as jacaranda, with ferny leaves and summer blooms of brilliant, violet-blue, trumpet-shaped flowers.

At the top of Chabolyn as it begins to curve to the right, take a left onto Roslyn Court, at which point you enter Berkeley. At the end of this short cul-de-sac, ascend South Crossways path. At the top, turn left on Hillcrest Road. At Eucalyptus Road, look across to **6 125 Hillcrest** on the right. Joseph Esherick, former dean of the UC Berkeley School of Architecture, designed this home in 1958 as one of the area's few modern houses. His philosophy was not to impose a style, but rather to design homes appropriate for clients' needs and for the environment. This house has an open corridor of sonotube concrete columns leading to the entry and a tennis court to the right.

Turn left on Eucalyptus Road for a pleasant loop that takes you briefly back across the invisible Oakland border. 1 Eucalyptus is an imposing **7 red-brick 1919 house by Julia Morgan**. This faithful Georgian Revival is not typical of her usual eclectic work.

Continuing on Eucalyptus, the **8 quaint English Tudor** at 28 Eucalyptus has a hipped roof and sculpted wrought-iron doors. At 36 Eucalyptus, the 1914 shingled house with storybook gables has classical columns supporting a porch pergola. At 40 Eucalyptus, the 1910 Craftsman house has two wings and lots of stonework.

Across the street at **9 41 Eucalyptus** is a grand house that Douglas Stone designed in 1929. Up on a rise, this house is in the style of England's Cotswolds area, with Hansel and Gretel brickwork on the chimney. Look carefully for the large rock outcropping in the front left garden, mostly covered by ivy. This is chert, a sedimentary rock with lots of silica, which often has embedded fossils. Chert is one of the rocks in the East Bay hills that are from the Cretaceous and Jurassic periods (think dinosaurs).

An impressive English Tudor from 1910 by Ratcliff stands at **10 44 Eucalyptus**, with a projecting room over the porch and a small bay window. Walk around to the right and turn right at the fork uphill onto Hillcrest Road. At **11 98 Hillcrest**, a 1907 Julia Morgan design in brown shingles is nicely sited on top of a steep slope (best seen from across the street). This is more typical of Morgan's Berkeley style than the earlier Georgian Revival. Holding forth on the rounded corner at 120 Hillcrest is an imposing white house with columned entryway, flagpole, and tall Canary Island palm.

Turn left on Hillcrest Court. At the corner, **⑫ 2 Hillcrest Court** is a large house from 1912 by John Hudson Thomas, another notable Berkeley architect. The house has a complex roofline, varied window treatments, half-timbering, an inset entrance, and a terrace in the rear. Typical of Thomas, it has Tudor elements but also incorporates other styles, such as Craftsman.

Hillcrest Court has a trove of homes designed by major East Bay architects from the early 20th century. 10 Hillcrest Court is also by Thomas, with elements of both Vienna Secession and Prairie School style; it has Thomas's signature of four squares together and vertical lines (look for it on other homes that he designed). 6 Hillcrest Court (to the left) was once a virtual twin, but subsequent remodeling left it with a very different facade.

Morgan designed 9 Hillcrest Court in 1921 in American Colonial style, while 12 Hillcrest Court is a 1913 house by Thomas with storybook elements and an unusual dormer. Next to it, at 16 Hillcrest Court, is another storybook house with an intricate roofline, by Walter Ratcliff, Jr., and dating to 1910. Because of the dense hedge, this house is best seen by looking back at an angle from in front of

44 Eucalyptus, in English Tudor style.

12 Hillcrest Court. Ratcliff also designed 15 Hillcrest Court in 1910; it has numerous semidormers.

Berkeley and parts of nearby Oakland boast a web of public paths and stairs; these were mainly laid out in the hills, where streets were designed to follow the contours of the hills. The paths provided easy access to streetcars and buses as well as escape routes in case of emergency. The Berkeley Path Wanderers Association is a nonprofit organization that advocates for the maintenance of paths and devotes volunteer labor to building paths in existing rights-of-way. (Its excellent map of Berkeley paths is available in local stores and at www.berkeleypaths.org.)

One of these paths is The Footway, between 18 and 15 Hillcrest Court. Descend on it to a street called The Uplands and turn left at the bottom. John Galen Howard, UC Berkeley's campus architect for many years, designed the **⓭ 1905 gateway columns** at Claremont. Made from local chert, the columns are topped by large lanterns with small pavilions on each side.

Across Claremont, the English Tudor–style central building in the commercial strip was built to serve the Uplands and Claremont areas. It includes a grocery, a cafe, Dark Carnival Bookstore, and a Judaica shop. (If you'd like to end the walk here, turn left on Claremont to walk back to College Avenue, then left again to return to the starting point.)

The landscaping firm of Frederick Law Olmsted, which designed New York City's Central Park and many other large-scale landscape areas, laid out this neighborhood, called The Uplands. The Mason-McDuffie real estate company was the developer; it also built Northbrae in North Berkeley. Duncan McDuffie

The gateway column at Claremont and The Uplands.

was not only a savvy real estate developer but also a renowned environmentalist. A friend of John Muir, he was twice president of the Sierra Club and helped found the East Bay Regional Park District and the state park system. The Uplands may be Berkeley's most elegant neighborhood, with the greatest number of houses by premier architects.

This area has several famous residents. Pulitzer Prize–winning novelist Michael Chabon—known for novels such as *Wonder Boys*, *The Amazing Adventures of Kavalier & Clay*, and *Telegraph Avenue*—lives nearby with his wife, Ayelet Waldman, also a writer. Also nearby is the home of John Adams, who composed the opera *Nixon in China* and many other works.

The landscape design of this development incorporates a creek into residential lots. Cross The Uplands to the right at the corner and walk back along The Uplands. A couple of square holes in the wooden fence allow you to peek through and see **⑭ Harwood (Claremont) Creek** running through a garden at 9 The Uplands; farther along in the front of the house are two rustic bridges and a grape arbor.

Cross Encina Place to the right and then cross from the median, angling to the left. Walk to the right along Parkside Drive, with a large 1910 English Tudor house on the corner at 35 Parkside. (Alternatively, walk up the path in the tree-lined median.) The street has sweetgum trees (seen on many streets on this walk) with maple-like, star-shaped leaves that turn brilliant colors in late autumn. Among the many attractive houses along the way, of particular note are 77 and 81 Parkside, intriguing **⑮ Craftsmans from 1907** by Leola Hall. Not formally trained in architecture, Hall designed, developed, built, and sold a number of highly regarded Craftsman houses in Berkeley from 1907 to 1912. She was also a painter and outspoken suffragist. At 77 Parkside, the porch's redwood columns retain their bark; 81 has a glassed-in entry porch along the right side.

At Nogales Street, turn left and walk to 6 Nogales, with a big stone porch and handsome wood siding. Walter Ratcliff, Jr., designed the well-kept 1910 Craftsman.

Return to Parkside and continue to the left. When the road forks, either cross the street to the right and make the little loop left around the median, or turn left at the next corner onto The Plaza Drive, crossing to the other (south) side of The Plaza before turning left. The median is full of tall pines and Canary island palms.

Thomas designed **⑯ 101, 99, and 95 The Plaza**, two of which flank The Cutoff path like sentries. These Thomas homes all have attractive window designs.

As The Plaza curves to turn north, 84 The Plaza on the left is a cottage designed by Walter Ratcliff, Jr.—an unusual house that seems to be all roof. Crossing Domingo Avenue on the right, notice the **⑰ 1913 Italian Renaissance–style house** on the corner at 77 Domingo, with an impressive entryway. The street ahead is lined with large London plane (sycamore) trees, and there are several classic Berkeley brown-shingle homes.

At Encina Place, cross the street and walk to the left a short distance to see a red-brick gate and bridge, the shared pedestrian entry for **⑱ 6 and 10 Encina**. Ernest Coxhead designed both homes in 1906. Born and trained in England, Coxhead initially designed churches when he came to California; later, he turned his attention to residences, combining Craftsman style with elements of traditional English rural homes. Although originally virtually the same, 6 and 10 Encina underwent alterations that made them very different. The creek is nicely incorporated into the front gardens, which are enhanced by native and nonnative trees and shrubs.

Return the way you came on Encina. Just before taking the path called **⑲ Encina Walk** to the left, note the impressive brown-shingle house to the right with a lovely garden in front (1 The Plaza); the house has been renovated and augmented in recent years.

Along Encina Walk, a bridge crosses over Harwood (Claremont) Creek where the creek passes under a large carriage house/garage; it looks like a log cabin and belongs to the big house back at 1 The Plaza. Turn right on Oakvale Avenue; just beyond the carriage house, 18 Oakvale is another large brick and brown-shingle house. Directly across the street, rocks in the front yard of 25 Oakvale form a garden grotto—a popular landscaping feature in the Victorian era. The grotto is made from locally quarried chert.

Continue on Oakvale, where the creek is on the right and then the left side of the street (the sidewalk comes and goes). Stop to view the creek and garden at **⑳ 33 Oakvale**, which has a big front yard. The creek is best seen through the hedge where the wall gets lower after the small stone bridge. The 1923 house is modeled after a British hunting cottage, according to the Berkeley Architectural Heritage Association (BAHA). 35 Oakvale, with a steep roof, can be viewed from the entryway. Next door, tall hedges obscure the view of 39 Oakvale, but look through the brick-and-iron gate framed by two redwoods for a glimpse. Both are storybook-style houses by Thomas from 1914 and 1925, respectively. Farther along at the next gate, 41 Oakvale is yet another Thomas design, with wisteria growing high up in the steep gable. The creek actually passes in an arched tunnel under the house; dense landscaping usually obscures it.

At the end of the block, turn left on Domingo, and continue past Hazel Road. Either proceed straight on Domingo to Tunnel Road, or, if school is not in session, take Oakridge Path just before 38–36 Domingo. The path goes down, then right and left; Harwood (Claremont) Creek is on the left in front of Tudor-style **㉑ John Muir Elementary School**, the smallest public school in Berkeley. It was designed in 1914 by James Plachek, who also did the main Berkeley Public Library. Walk past the playground, exit on Claremont, turn right, and then turn right again on Ashby/Tunnel Road and proceed to the signal at Domingo. This is a good spot from which to view the historic **㉒ Claremont Hotel**, set against the Berkeley hills and visible from across the bay.

Located just over the Oakland border, the Claremont Hotel was built mostly in 1906 by entrepreneur Frank C. Havens, although it was not finished until 1915 due to a shortage of materials and a financial crisis. The hotel was intended to be part of a grand real estate development. The Key System's Line E streetcar stopped between the tennis courts; it was initially supposed to extend all the way into the hotel lobby, but that never happened. The 1991 Oakland hills firestorm came dangerously close to destroying the hotel, but a change in the weather allowed firefighters to bring the fire under control. The hotel filed for bankruptcy in 2011 and was acquired

The historic Claremont Hotel.

by new owners in 2014. Listed on the National Register of Historic Places, it has 279 guest rooms, a 20,000-square-foot spa, 10 tennis courts, swimming pools, a conference center, a restaurant, and 22 acres of landscaped gardens. Berkeley Tennis Club, a separate entity established in 1906, is on the corner.

Cross at the signal and walk by the **㉓ shops on Domingo**. This charming mixed-use development has apartments and offices above the shops. The streetcar to the Claremont Hotel ran through the little plaza between Rick & Ann's and Peet's Coffee.

Optional: If you want to look around the Claremont, cross Domingo at Russell Street and walk through the hotel parking lot and up the hill to enter the hotel.

The walk can be shortened here by turning around, walking back down Domingo, crossing Tunnel Road, crossing over to the other side of Domingo, and then skipping to Site ㉞.

To continue, walk east on Domingo, which becomes Russell as it turns left. At the stop sign, cross Claremont Avenue, turn right to cross over Russell, turn left and then make the next right onto Claremont Boulevard at the stately brick and iron entry gates, which were designed by John Galen Howard in 1906. On the right is **㉔ St. Clement's Episcopal Church**, a simple yet elegant Arts and Crafts design by Willis Polk from 1909. Walter Ratcliff, Jr., designed the 1927 Palache Hall, behind the church, in Tudor brick. A contrasting ornate mansion is across Claremont Boulevard from the church.

Continue on Claremont Boulevard. Julia Morgan designed the 1928 **㉕ Italian Renaissance** villa on the northeast corner, 2821 Claremont Boulevard. It has lovely ornamental details, including Venetian Gothic tracery on the side windows (look through the gate from the corner), a front-doorway fresco, and wrought iron on the balcony.

Next door at 2815 Claremont Boulevard, brickwork was used to make fine patterns on this 1910 home. This is a rare example of Jacobean Revival manor house style in the East Bay. ("Jacobean" refers to the reign of James I of England, who succeeded Elizabeth I, the last Tudor monarch.) Turn right at Garber Street, which has sweetgum trees and large redwoods. At quiet Tanglewood Road, go around the corner to the left. Ernest Coxhead designed the house on the northwest corner at **㉖ 28 Tanglewood** in Spanish Colonial Revival style.

The entry of 2121 Claremont, by Julia Morgan.

Continue along Tanglewood past an austere modern house on the right at 25 Tanglewood. 18 Tanglewood has an elegant facade, but its most impressive feature is the large, sculpted, wrought-iron gate. As Tanglewood curves to the left, notice Tanglewood Path on the right. The path leads up to Claremont Canyon Regional Preserve, a park with a steep climb to expansive views of the bay and beyond.

Cross Tanglewood to walk down Derby Street on the right side. Catty-corner at the southwest corner of Derby and Belrose Avenue, **㉗ houses with steeply pitched roofs** have been combined into a single-family residence. They were originally a school with linked pavilions, designed by Bernard Maybeck in 1909.

Head west on Derby past UC's **㉘ Clark Kerr Campus**. The original location of the California School for the Deaf and Blind opened here in 1867, fully supported by the state. When the school moved to Fremont in 1980, most of the site became part of UC after considerable political haggling. The present complex consists of mostly Mediterranean-style stucco buildings with tile roofs dating from the 1920s and designed by Alfred Eichler and George B. McDougall, as well as modern buildings from the 1950s.

At the signal, cross left and proceed down Claremont Boulevard. Houses of note include a Tudor/Craftsman at 2731 Claremont Boulevard and a Tudor at 2737 Claremont Boulevard by Benjamin McDougall from 1911. Cross to the right before the minipark and ascend the hill on Garber. The narrow street is lined with tall plane trees, which form a complete canopy. Henry Gutterson designed four residences on the hill at **㉙ 2922, 2916, 2910, and 2904 Garber** (on the left starting after the corner house) between 1924 and 1936. Each is unique, but together they are harmonious. The stairway for 2910 Garber is actually at 2904; a path leads across to its entry higher up the hill. Gutterson's own residence was at 2922 Garber. From the crest, look down the other side to note that Garber here is a mini version of San Francisco's twisty Lombard Street.

Return downhill on Garber the way you came (toward the mini-park) and turn right at the first street, Oak Knoll Terrace. Across the street on the southeast corner at ㉚ **2801 Oak Knoll**, the 1914 Tudor house has a unique and appealing window design with many windows bringing lots of light into the house.

Continue to Avalon Avenue and bear right past the rose bushes, staying on Avalon. A large forest of diverse trees was planted years ago at ㉛ **2919 Avalon**. Just past 2922, descend left on Pine Path to Russell Street and turn left.

The 6,300-square-foot mansion on the left at 2911 Russell with large grounds behind a brick wall was built in 1907 and formerly housed the Magnes Museum (now in downtown Berkeley). A brown-shingle on the left at ㉜ **2925 Russell** was the home of J. Troplong Ward, a pioneer in television animation who helped create Crusader Rabbit and, with Bill Scott, launched the *Rocky and Bullwinkle* show, which included bits of Berkeley counterculture. On the right, at 2924 Russell, is the family home of Ann Yonemura, writer and museum curator of Asian art, who graduated from Berkeley High in 1965. Farther along, uphill on the left, the impressive 1914 neoclassical mansion at 2959 Russell is now part of the ㉝ **Yun Lin Temple of Black Sect Tantric Buddhism** (with a headquarters on Euclid), which integrates Buddhism and Chinese philosophies.

A statue at Greyhaven, a.k.a. 90 El Camino.

At Claremont Boulevard, turn right and then right again straight onto Claremont Avenue. Cross Ashby at the signal, then cross Claremont Avenue to the left and continue up the sidewalk on Tunnel to Domingo. Cross at the signal and turn right on Domingo.

Go straight on Domingo, cross El Camino Real, and angle left up this street past small Oak Park, which has lots of native plants. You might prefer to walk on the right sidewalk. Uphill on the left at **㉞ 55 El Camino Real**, a 1958 house is linked by a glass-walled and vine-covered passageway to a music pavilion on the right (as you face it). The modern redwood house includes elements of Japanese design such as sliding shoji window screens.

At 62 El Camino Real, just before a path, the 1922 house by Ratcliff has elements of Swiss chalet and other styles. At 90 El Camino, the house called **㉟ Greyhaven** has mythical creatures on the garage; over the years, the house has served as a collective for writers, including fantasy writer Marion Zimmer Bradley. At 98 El Camino, a brick bridge connects the street and sidewalk to the 1908 house. Comedian, actor, and writer Andy Samberg grew up in this neighborhood.

Turn right on The Uplands. After one block, at a complex inter-section, cross straight ahead and then bear left, crossing Hillcrest and turning right (southwest). The house at 226 Hillcrest was remodeled in 1988 with Arabian elements, particularly the central entry turret, with its dome and pointed arches.

Across the street, the brown-shingle at 217 Hillcrest was the **㊱ home of Richard Diebenkorn** from 1961 to 1966. Diebenkorn was an early abstract expressionist and part of the Bay Area Figura-tive Movement. His most famous paintings—particularly the Ocean Park series—bridge these artistic styles. He moved to Southern California in 1966 but returned to Berkeley's Elmwood neighbor-hood later in life.

214 Hillcrest is the **㊲ Claremont Assembly Hall**, a 1911 Arts and Crafts–style private clubhouse for the neighborhood that blends well into the row of single-family homes. Farther along on the right, **㊳ 159 Hillcrest** is a fine, wood-shingled Craftsman from 1910 designed by the owner (a builder) that is reminiscent of homes by Greene and Greene—masters of the style.

To return to the starting point, turn left onto South Crossways path, on the left just past 152 Hillcrest. Return to Roslyn Court, turn right on Chabolyn Terrace, and then right again on Chabot Road. Walk back to College and turn left toward the Rockridge BART station.

✳ ✳ ✳

WALK 14

ASHBY BART STATION AND THE LORIN DISTRICT

Overview: Covering mainly level terrain, this walk explores areas settled on the steam train line between Oakland and Berkeley, near what is now the Ashby BART station. The walk includes a wealth of Victorian, Colonial Revival, Craftsman, and California bungalow homes; diverse ecclesiastical architecture; and fascinating culture and arts. It may be done as one long walk or two shorter loops.

Highlights:

- Early train-oriented development
- Varied architecture, tree-lined streets
- Historic churches, Buddhist temples, disability rights center

Distance: 2.9–5.1 miles
Time: 2–3.5 hours
Elevation gain: 110–210 feet

Begin at the west entrance to the Ashby BART station, close to the corner of Martin Luther King, Jr., (MLK) Way and Ashby Avenue. The Ashby BART station is accessible by AC Transit. Pay attention to parking signs in the area.

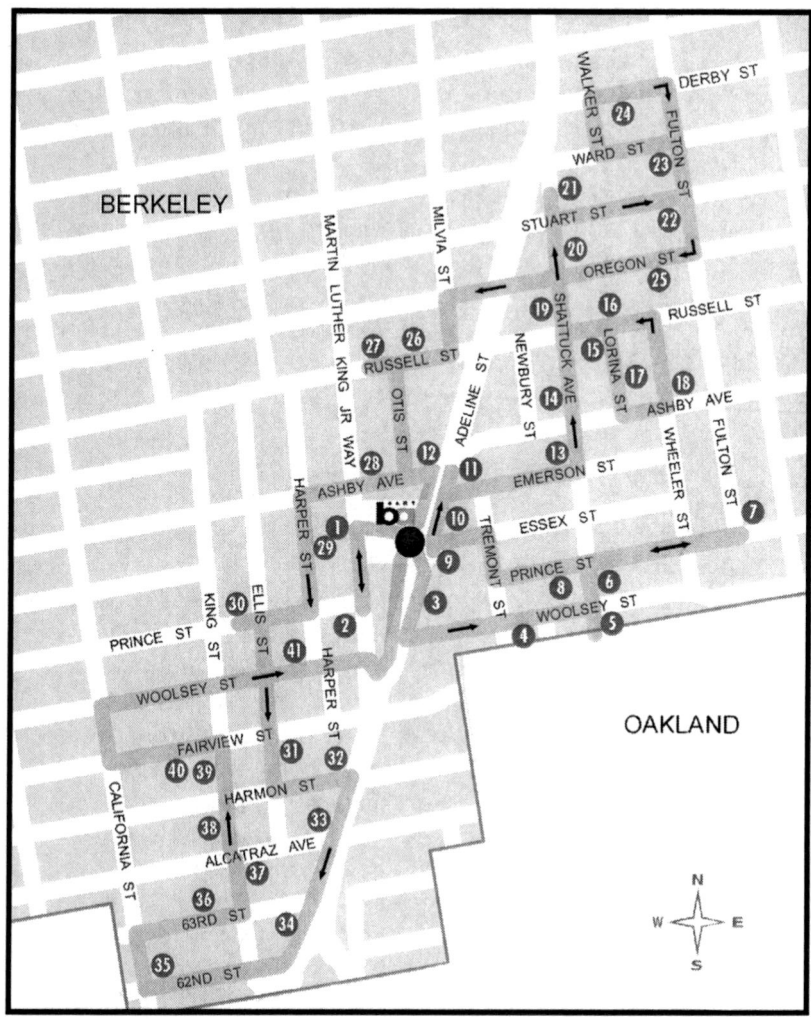

The Berkeley Flea Market, held in the BART parking lot every Saturday and Sunday from 7 a.m. to 7 p.m., features international collectibles and art, books, music, crafts and jewelry, clothing, household goods, and food. The flea market is operated as a nonprofit that supports local groups, including the Berkeley Free Clinic, East Bay Food Not Bombs, and the People's Park Project.

From the BART station exit (Ashby/parking lot side), walk right until you reach the stop sign, turn left to cross the drop-off lane, and walk straight ahead (on the sidewalk), away from the BART station to MLK Way. Across the street is a row of **❶ Colonial Revival houses**, as well as several Berkeley brown-shingle homes. The Colonial Revival style has simpler lines and less ornamentation than the Victorian style and includes two main forms—one squarish and one with a high-peaked roof with the gable facing the street, both of which are seen on MLK Way. The light-blue house directly across the street (3028 MLK Way) has some charming details; others have quaint features such as double gables over dormer windows on the upper south sides. Go left (south) on MLK Way; on the far (southwest) corner with Prince Street, **❷ 3102 MLK Way** is a fine house with Palladian windows. When the BART station and its parking lots were built in the 1970s, several historic blocks such as this were demolished.

Return to the BART station and cross through the ground-level station area to the other (east) side. Take the ramp or stairs up to enter the lower-level elevator lobby of **❸ Ed Roberts Campus**; take the elevator up to the main lobby on level 1. If the building is closed, take the stairs from the BART station to the right (to Adeline Street) and peek in the front windows. For handicap access, an elevator in the BART station goes up in front of the campus. Built on a former BART parking lot and designed to be universally accessible, the 80,000-square-foot building is named for Edward V. Roberts, an early leader in the independent living movement of persons with disabilities. Completed in 2011, Ed Roberts Campus is a nonprofit organization formed by various disability organizations; the building incorporates exhibition space, community meeting rooms, a child development center, a fitness center, offices for nonprofit organizations, and vocational training facilities. The lobby has a unique spiral ramp and atrium skylight.

Facing Adeline Street outside, walk to the left and turn left on Woolsey Street. An attractive fence demarking the campus along the left (north) side of the street incorporates Japanese elements such as wooden panels and trained spruce, but its height eliminates any view of the kids' play area.

This neighborhood includes numerous Colonial Revival, Victorian, and brown-shingle homes. The steam train that connected Oakland and Berkeley in the late 19th century included the Newbury station (at Ashby and Adeline) and the Lorin station (at Alcatraz and Adeline); this chapter features the historic districts that surrounded those stations. Major growth in these areas was spurred by installation of the Key Route streetcar line in 1903, connecting the steam train to transbay ferries, and the exodus of San Francisco residents to the East Bay after the 1906 earthquake.

Walk past Tremont Street to see examples of the ❹ **high-peaked Colonial Revival style** at 2000, 2004, and 2014 Woolsey. Builder John C. Rogers constructed 2000 and 2014 on spec in 1900 (he likely did 2004 as well); however, each home features different materials and design elements.

A local chapter of the ❺ **Self-Realization Fellowship** is located on the southeast corner of Woolsey and Shattuck Avenue at 3201 Shattuck. The yogi Paramahansa Yogananda founded this meditation and religious organization, headquartered in Los Angeles, after he came to the United States from India in 1920.

Turn left and walk north on Shattuck; a Tudor-style office building is at 3104 Shattuck. Next to it at 3102 Shattuck, the Victorian house has rough stucco in the gable and Palladian window framing with a glass window only in the center section. Across the street, ❻ **La Peña Cultural Center** opened its doors in 1975 to pursue the cultural, social, and political aspirations of Latino Americans; it was founded as a response to the 1973 military coup that overthrew the socialist government of Salvador Allende in Chile. The badly deteriorated but much-beloved *Song of Unity*

The Song of Unity mural at La Peña on Shattuck.

mural was restored in 2014, including 3-D relief. The center offers a cafe, classes, and several hundred events annually. Next door, the Starry Plough Irish pub has served food and ales and presented live music and poetry in an intimate setting since 1973. Murals are on both sides of the corner building, and it is particularly lively on St. Patrick's Day.

Fans of fantasy novels might want to turn right on Prince Street and walk a couple of blocks to 2221 Prince, the raised Victorian cottage just past Fulton Street that was the home of **7 Marion Zimmer Bradley** during the 1970s and 1980s. She wrote *The Mists of Avalon* and the *Darkover* series. Turn around and walk back on Prince toward Shattuck; on the west side of Fulton, at 2215 Prince, is the Chochmat HaLev Center for Jewish Spirituality.

If you made the detour, walk back (west) on Prince; otherwise, from Shattuck, turn left to go west onto Prince, another street with mainly Victorians and Colonial Revivals. Two of the most attractive are at **8 2028 and 2026 Prince**—high-peaked houses that are also shingled with large side dormers. At 2024, the house has been raised up (like many around here), with a bay/turret and an unusual roof. Like other blocks on this walk, the street is lined with tall, graceful ash trees with small leaves.

Turn right at Tremont, then left on Essex Street. At Adeline, note the **9 Swedenborgian Church of the New Jerusalem** on the left; it is now St. John the Baptist Russian Orthodox Church. Notice the striking blue Russian onion dome (best seen from around the front), which was an addition.

Facing the church, walk left (north) on Adeline, crossing

A storybook fantasy at 3049–51 Adeline.

Essex to see an amazing **🔟 storybook-style building** at 3049–51 Adeline, which, from 1976 to 2012, housed Marmot Mountain Works, a retail outdoor-goods store. Originally built as the Hull & Durgin funeral home in 1923, with additions in 1928, the complex includes the Little Chapel of the Flowers, which was used not only as a funeral parlor but also as a popular wedding chapel. Walking past the building, notice the rounded roof eaves; stonework near the foundation; half-timbering and stained glass on the side; wrought-iron work; a round window above the chapel entry; and a spire with an unusual roof cap, all of which contribute to the fairy-tale appearance.

Continue up Adeline and cross Emerson Street. The area surrounding the large intersection, called Ashby Adeline Antiques District, has featured an eclectic group of independent antique stores since the 1930s, when it was the Newbury stop on the F line trains. At the corner of Emerson, **🔟 3027 Adeline** is a landmarked Colonial Revival from 1905 with a rounded upper bay; it is currently a liquor store. The entrance may have originally been at the corner. 3023–25 Adeline is a wooden commercial building from about 1902; the second floor swells out like a huge bay, with smaller window bays angling out and a third-floor dormer. 3021 Adeline dates to 1901; its unique second floor has four sharp outward angles, and its first floor has pilasters (not true columns but slightly raised from the wall). Look across Ashby at the imposing Mission Revival–style **🔟 Webb Block**, built in 1905 and designed by Charles W. McCall, a prolific and versatile Oakland architect. It offers a sweeping curve from Ashby to Adeline and striking red walls. Apparently, it once housed the pharmacy of a man named Caldecott, who went on to become a county supervisor and for whom the Highway 24 tunnel to Orinda is named. To the right of the Webb Block—with more antique shops—is another building from 1905.

Backtrack on Adeline and turn left on Emerson, passing several Colonial Revival homes and a small cottage with a square turret across the street at 2064 Emerson that has a colorful glass panel in the porch. 2071 Emerson is a combination of Colonial Revival and brown-shingle, with a wall of bamboo facing the street. Turn left on Shattuck; on the corner at 3012–16 Shattuck is a large **🔟 Queen Anne Victorian** built in 1891, now housing a spa on the ground floor.

Cross Ashby at the signal and then cross Shattuck to the east side of the street. Continue north on Shattuck, noting the newer

A restored Victorian at 2919 Lorina.

commercial buildings opposite at ⑭ **2930 Shattuck**, with loft spaces over shops that are not fully successful in mimicking generic traditional design.

Turn right on Russell Street. At 2108 Russell, a 1908 church (originally Presbyterian) is now the ⑮ **Church by the Side of the Road** and boasts an Arts and Crafts design with great charm. It has a squat tower over the gabled entrance and arched windows, including one with stained glass and one with a gable above on the Lorina Street side.

Cross Lorina and look across the street at ⑯ **2123 Russell**, a well-kept, proper Victorian from 1894 with a pink and green color scheme. Raised up, it has a half-moon window in the lower gable and two stair-step windows in the upper gable. Turn right on Lorina, passing opposite the side of the church. Part of an earlier church can be seen in the rear on Lorina, as can an adjoining Colonial Revival cottage that is now part of the church compound. 2907 Lorina is a handsome 1894 Victorian with a bench protruding from the porch.

The ⑰ **1891 Victorian** at 2919 Lorina is a Berkeley landmark that was beautifully restored after a 2012 fire. Originally part of the village of Newbury (later annexed by Berkeley), it was built by Josiah John Rose, a pioneer carpenter who built many San Francisco and Berkeley homes. Also built in 1891, 2928 Lorina has several unique features, including inset windows in the shingled front and side gables, an oval window, and an oval ornament over a row of four small windows.

Turn left on Ashby. At the northeast corner of Ashby and Wheeler Street, the large yellow house at ⑱ **2151 Ashby** has Colonial Revival and Victorian elements; it appears to have been extensively expanded and remodeled, and its grounds include lots of skinny Italian cypress trees. Turn left on Wheeler, which has a mélange of houses and newer and older apartments. The front yard at 2927–29 Wheeler is an example of a small garden that gracefully uses rocks and different colors and textures. A large weeping willow presides over 2915 Wheeler.

Cross Russell and turn left and then right on Shattuck. At Oregon Street, the ⑲ **Berkeley Bowl** is across the street. The bowl has an extensive produce department with many organic and unusual offerings, as well as fine bulk goods, cheese, meats and fish, prepared foods, and natural health and beauty products. A second location in West Berkeley opened in 2009, reducing the checkout lines and parking headaches at this site.

Continue on Shattuck, walking past the ⑳ **Buggy Bank** at 2821 Shattuck. Opened in 1976, the Buggy Bank allows sellers to display and potential buyers to test drive cars. Next door, 2807 Shattuck is a lovely Victorian tucked away on a busy commercial street. The ginkgo trees on this section of Shattuck brighten the street with their golden, fan-shaped leaves in the fall.

Past Stuart Street is the site of the original Berkeley Bowl, a ㉑ **Streamline Moderne building** with a tower; before it housed a market, this building was a bowling alley (hence the name). This area was the scene of a heated political battle in the early 1900s, when the Southern Pacific railroad wanted to move its freight yards here from downtown. In August 1903, Berkeley's trustees voted four to three to allow the removal of 32 houses in the area bounded by Shattuck, Adeline, and Russell streets to make way for the yards. South Berkeley residents brought a map to the meeting bearing the inscription, "Will you destroy the front door of Beautiful Berkeley?" The city did: demolition occurred a few years later.

Turn around and return to Stuart, turning left (east) and continuing to 2109–11 Stuart, a high-peaked, shingled Colonial Revival/brown-shingle from 1899; the roof's slope gets steeper on the way up and there is a double gable on the side. Spanish-style garden apartments are across the street at 2116 Stuart. This street is lined mainly with camphor trees, which have shiny green or red leaves that are fragrant when crushed. After passing more stucco bungalows, notice the handsome Colonial Revival at **㉒ 2158 Stuart**. Turn left on Fulton; at 2744 Fulton, the high-peaked Colonial Revival painted yellow has an arch over the porch and a sawtooth pattern at the bottom of the second floor that projects outward.

Turn left at Ward Street; 2156 Ward on the corner is one of Berkeley's most splendid **㉓ Queen Anne Victorians** (another is the Captain Boudrow house on Oxford Street—see Walk 5, Maybeck Country). This 1889 design by A. W. Pattiani features decorative carved balustrades, fish-scale shingles, rough stucco at the gable top, a two-story turret with extensive ornamentation, and diverse window designs.

Continue going west on Ward. Across the street is a row of six

Victorian cottages (2155 to 2139 Ward), also by Pattiani, from 1889; 2155 has a square turret, and 2147 has a round turret. The cottages have elements of different Victorian styles called Stick, Eastlake, and later Queen Anne. The lavish features are typical of the Queen Anne style.

The Victorian at 2140 Ward, from 1891, has bays, a highly ornamented porch, a turret, and unusual angles and massing; there are several more attractive houses as you continue down the block.

Detail of Victorian at 2156 Ward.

At 2124 Ward, cross Ward and take a narrow little street—almost an alley—called Walker Street. Turn right on Derby Street, passing 2130 Derby, a **24** **Craftsman-style bungalow** with stone porch and chimney. At Fulton, turn right. The next three blocks of Fulton going north from the intersection are some of the most attractive in the area; admire an assortment of Colonial Revival, two-story Berkeley brown-shingle homes, and Craftsman bungalows.

Continue on Fulton to Oregon and turn right. The left (south) side of the street has a number of **25** **stucco bungalows** from the 1920s, simple single-story houses with a variety of facades, often with a bit of false front sticking up. A Victorian-style duplex is at 2145–47 Oregon; a few houses farther on, 2135–37 Oregon is a Victorian with a highly ornamented first-floor facade. Many homes on this stretch of Oregon Street put up elaborate Halloween decorations, making it a popular destination on October 31. The western part of the block is lined with sycamores, characterized by scaly bark and big leaves, and Chinese elms, with scaly bark and tiny leaves.

Carefully cross Shattuck and pass between the Berkeley Bowl and Walgreens, then cross Adeline. Writer Dorothy Bryant, known for her mystical, feminist, and fantasy novels and plays including *The Kin of Ata Are Waiting for You,* lived in this neighborhood in the 1950s. Continue on Oregon a short distance, turn left on Milvia Street, and then right on Russell.

Between 1933 and 1929 Russell is the entrance to the **26** **Berkeley Zen Center**, founded in 1967 and at this site since 1979. It offers instruction in *zazen,* or seated meditation; retreats; and a variety of other programs. You may go through the gate on the paved path past the mailboxes to see the wooden building in the back, but be quiet and respectful, as people may be meditating.

Just down the street is another Buddhist institution, the **27** **Wat Mongkolratanaram**, a Thai Buddhist temple occupying two older residences, 1911 and 1913 Russell. A brightly colored and elaborately carved entryway in traditional Thai style is the remarkable feature of 1911 Russell. Many Thai-American Buddhists and Thai students at UC attend the temple, which offers a popular Sunday brunch that raises money for youth programs and charitable causes. Backtrack a bit on Russell to Otis Street, cross Russell, and proceed down Otis on the way back to the Ashby BART station, which you can reach by turning left to cross Ashby at the signal.

Lorin Loop

Add this loop to explore the Lorin neighborhood, which includes tree-lined streets with a mix of Victorians, historic homes, commercial buildings, and churches.

From Otis, turn right on Ashby. At the intersection, note the **28 Ashby Stage**, home of the Shotgun Players. Founded in 1992 and in this space since 2004, the theater is notable for its highly original musical productions and focus on new work. Cross MLK Way and then Ashby to the southwest corner; walk west on Ashby (away from the BART station), noting the Berkeley-related mural on the Ashby Super Market building. Walk one block to Harper Street; turn left, passing a tall Canary Island palm on the corner. Colonial Revival homes from the late 19th and early 20th centuries line this block, often in the simple American Foursquare layout of entry/stair hall on one side in front, living room on the other, and kitchen and dining room to the rear, with bedrooms and bath upstairs in a squarish floor plan.

The family **29 home of gospel singer Tramaine Hawkins**, who grew up in the Ephesian Church of God led by her grandfather, E. E. Cleveland, is at 3019 Harper. She graduated from Berkeley High in 1969. The street is lined with Chinese elms with graceful curving branches, tiny leaves, and peeling multicolored bark. Found-object sculptures, mostly depicting dogs, are in the front yard of 3026 Harper on the opposite side.

Turn right (west) on Prince; at the corner of Ellis Street, 1800 Prince is an elegant Colonial Revival house with a columned porch, rectangular bays, pilasters, and fine decorative friezes. Cross Ellis and walk a bit farther to **30 Malcolm X Elementary School** (originally Lincoln School), designed by Walter Ratcliff, Jr., in 1920 with some later additions. Return to Ellis and turn right (south); at 1801 Woolsey on the northeast corner, note the 1901 brown-shingle house, large for the neighborhood, with multiple bays and Palladian windows on the Ellis side. Woolsey has numerous ash trees, which, like the Chinese elm, have graceful upward-spreading branches and small leaves.

Continue on Ellis to the corner with Fairview Street to see the **31 South Berkeley Community Church**, a city landmark and a unique structure. This Mission Revival church from 1912 has a complex massing and an unusual corner bell-tower entranceway with arches and an open bell housing above. Designed by Oakland architect Hugo Storch, the church incorporates Craftsman elements in its innovative design. The interior includes moveable wall panels to expand the sanctuary space. The congregation was among the first to be open to all ethnicities and was politically active in the civil rights movement in the 1960s. Continue on Ellis, passing more of the church and an attractive block of homes, including a Victorian at 3216 Ellis and a 1908 Colonial Revival brown-shingle apartment building next to it on the corner at 3220 Ellis.

Turn left on Harmon Street and continue back to Adeline; in early to mid-March, several pink-flowering crabapple trees may be in bloom on Harmon. At Adeline is the Lorin commercial district, home to a steam train station from 1876 to 1958. On the left (northwest) corner, at Adeline and Harmon, the **32 Carlson Block** is a 1903 Victorian, three-story, mixed-use building with a round turret. Although somewhat altered, it is a Berkeley landmark by William Wharff, who designed several buildings downtown. On the south side of Harmon at Adeline is the India Block, with a rounded corner and an attractive storefront in a two-story, stucco and yellow-brick, landmarked building, designed by A. W. Smith and built in 1903.

Turn right (south) along Adeline and continue to the next corner. The former **33 South Berkeley Bank** is at 3286–90 Adeline,

The tower of South Berkeley Community Church.

a 1906 building with corner entrance; it is by John Galen Howard, the UC campus architect who designed Classical-style buildings and the California Memorial Stadium.

Continue on Adeline, crossing Alcatraz; a popular farmers market is here on Tuesday afternoons. Continue to 63rd Street, where the **34** **Sweet Adeline bakery** at 3350–62 Adeline serves a variety of pastries, cookies, and baked goods. The 1927 building has brick storefronts with pretty outlines in blue tile.

Farther along Adeline, turn right on 62nd Street, continuing past King Street and a number of Victorian and Colonial Revival homes. At 1634 62nd, on the opposite side behind the purple and green half-timbered house, is a remodeled Victorian in bright colors. There is a charming, highly ornamented Victorian at 1622 62nd. At the corner of California Street, **35** **1601 62nd** is a sweet, high-peaked 1902 Colonial Revival in yellow with ornamental trim. Turn right at California, noting the Victorian across the street on the corner at 3342 California and its neighbor at 3334, both with oodles of ornamentation, both built in 1895. Between the two houses are large Canary Island palms, and behind the trees is a three-story tower that has been turned into a home.

Ornate Victorian at 1622 62nd Street.

Turn right on 63rd Street, where the charming Victorian at 1609 63rd has a complex roof. Go past the 63rd Street Mini Park. In the side yard of 1629–33 63rd is a **36 dense grove of large Canary Island palms**, one of which soars high above the others. Turn left on King; London plane (sycamore) trees, with large, maple-like leaves and multicolored, peeling bark, line the street for several blocks. The 1947 **37 Progressive Missionary Baptist Church** on the corner with Alcatraz was built in Moderne style with unusual decorative elements.

Cross Alcatraz carefully in the crosswalk, passing the 1960s Ephesian Church of God in Christ's modern A-frame at 1709 Alcatraz. The **38 Italianate cottage** at 3226 King is a very early (circa 1878) Victorian with rounded window frames. Continue past Harmon to **39 3208 and 3206 King**, Craftsman houses with delightful curves and other attractive features such as the porch columns and unusual window in the gable of 3206. Edward Dana Harmon was the developer of this tract. In addition to selling lots, he built 50 varied Victorians. The Berkeley Architectural Heritage Association estimates that 20 to 25 of these are more or less recognizable as period Victorians.

Turn left on Fairview Street. Two angel's trumpet trees (related to datura) have numerous large, yellow flowers hanging down in spring and summer. The Harmon-built house at **40 1626–28 Fairview** is remarkable for its turret and prominent gables.

Turn right at California and right again on Woolsey. Stucco and wood-sided bungalows and apartments line the north side, while the south side has a fine collection of Harmon Victorians. Most have been added onto and renovated; many have been divided into apartments, but enough of the original design elements remain to give them charm. Like Ellis Street, several blocks of Woolsey are lined with ash trees.

Stay on Woolsey, crossing King and Ellis, and passing on the left **41 1817–19 Woolsey**—a brown-shingle house with a corner bay on the second floor. At MLK Way, turn right, cross MLK at the signal (notice the *Welcome to Lorin District* mural just past the light), go left through the triangular median and across another crosswalk, and go around the curve to the right to follow Adeline. After crossing the BART auto exit, turn immediately left and walk down a sidewalk that curves back to the BART station entrance.

✳ ✳ ✳

Part IV
West Berkeley

✽✽✽

WALK 15
THE MCGEE-SPAULDING DISTRICT

Overview: The McGee-Spaulding District—bordered by Martin Luther King, Jr., (MLK) Way, Sacramento Street, University Avenue, and Dwight Way—was a center of progressive movements in Berkeley during the 1960s. The area close to downtown includes early Victorian, Colonial Revival, and Craftsman homes, while stucco California bungalows predominate in the western area. This is a flat, easy walk on wide, pleasant, tree-lined streets. Because it loops back and forth, it can easily be shortened.

Highlights:
- Communes and collectives, a center for progressive movements in the 1960s
- Former homes of Mario Savio, Jack LaLanne, Anne Rice, and Phillip K. Dick
- Victorians, Craftsmans, workers' cottages

Distance: 3.6 miles

Time: 2–2.5 hours

Elevation gain: 70 feet

Start at the corner of Addison Street and MLK Way. From the Downtown Berkeley BART station, walk down Center Street (there is a farmers market here on Saturdays), cross MLK Way at the signal,

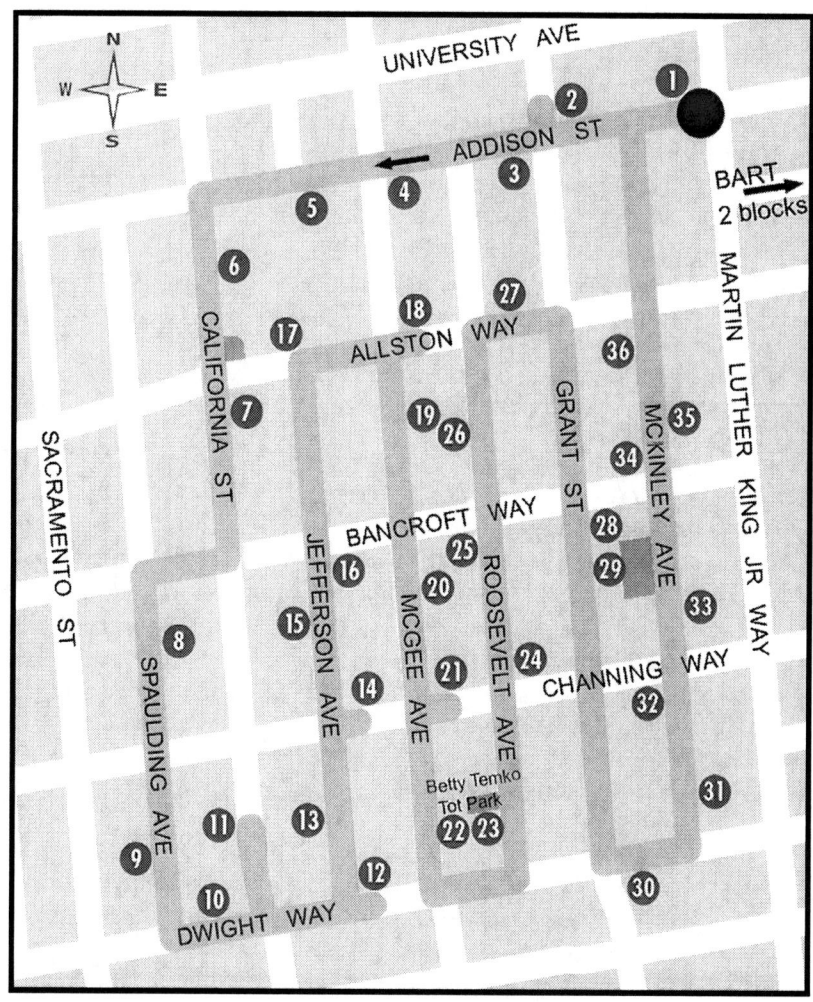

turn right, and walk one block to Addison. For street parking, check signs carefully.

Heading west (away from downtown) on Addison, walk down the north (right) side of the street; 1841 Addison is an ❶ **1885 Queen Anne Victorian cottage** with blue elephants painted on the upper wood trim. This was once the home of Jeffrey Moussaieff Masson, an American author who wrote several controversial books critical of psychoanalysis. He later became an animal-rights activist, writing *When Elephants Weep* (1994) and a number of other books on animal behavior; he added the elephant trim.

McGee's Farm

The Huchiun Indians thrived near Strawberry Creek—which flowed through this area—for 5,000 years, but their culture was destroyed with the arrival of Juan Bautista de Anza's expedition in 1776, followed by the establishment of missions and the spread of disease. In 1820, Don Luis María Peralta, who had come with his father on the de Anza expedition and served in the Spanish military for 40 years, was awarded a land grant of 44,800 acres stretching from San Leandro Creek to Albany Hill. In 1842, Peralta legally divided his grant among four sons, who had already been living there for some years. José Domingo received most of what is now modern-day Berkeley and Albany, although in 1853, he sold much of it to speculators for $82,000, including a large part of Berkeley.

In 1855, Irish immigrant James McGee bought a 115-acre farm stretching approximately from present-day Addison Street to Dwight Way, and from MLK Way to California Street. The land, good for crops and dairy, quickly increased in value, and McGee began selling off portions, which were initially developed as farming estates. McGee was a generous benefactor to the Catholic Church and became a local politician, serving on Berkeley's first five-member board of trustees (predecessor to the city council). In the early 20th century, the large gentleman farms were further subdivided as the space between the university town in the hills and Ocean View on the bay gradually filled in.

The build-out of this area was rapid after the 1906 earthquake, when many San Franciscans moved to Berkeley thinking it was safer (the disastrous 1868 earthquake on the Hayward Fault was by 1906 a distant memory); streetcar service was started by two different companies in 1911 and 1912 on Sacramento and California streets.

Residents of this area led the way in Berkeley's shift from conservative Republican to liberal in the 1960s, with communes and collectives, free speech and civil rights activists, anti-Vietnam war protesters, and Beat and hippie cultures animating the area. ✳✳

Next door, at 1837–39 Addison, is another Queen Anne from the late 1800s with attractive decorative features, well cared for and renovated. A self-described "Berkeley crackpot," Victor "Vito" Lab lived here until his death in 2013. He was a cofounder of Ohmega Salvage and designed beautiful stained glass windows.

Just past McKinley Avenue, 1814 Addison, on the left, is a house from around 1890 by John Paul Moran, an English ship's carpenter who designed and built several large, ornate Victorians in the city. Also on this block, notice examples of the concrete-block apartment buildings that sprang up willy-nilly in Berkeley's residential neighborhoods in the 1950s and 1960s. The Neighborhood Preservation Ordinance, passed by citizens in 1973, put a stop to this practice. Designed without any sense of their surroundings and often shoddily built, these buildings (sometimes called "dingbats") gave a bad name to the concept of infill development (building in already-developed areas). New buildings located on the city's main corridors in recent years provide better examples of infill.

A short diversion takes you around the corner to the right on Grant Street. The ❷ **three Craftsman-style homes** at 2021, 2017, and 2011 Grant from 1908 have similar shapes but different details. Returning toward Addison, on the northwest corner at 2022 Grant is an example of a fairly common type of building in this area, with a store on the first floor and residences above. The store is now an office, but other buildings in the neighborhood became entirely residential as the practice of shopping in small local shops died out with the rise of auto-oriented supermarkets and box stores.

Craftsman houses at Grant and Addison.

Cross Addison, turn right, and continue down the south side. The ❸ **cottages at 1746, 1744, 1742, and 1740 Addison** were built in 1906 as rental homes for workers; the small lots host compact structures with simple designs (1740 has been raised up and added on to). In the next block, 1720 to 1708 Addison is a row of typical stucco California bungalows from 1917. (The word "bungalow," from India, refers to a one- to one-and-a-half-story detached home with sloping roofs, usually with a veranda.)

An older four-unit residence at ❹ **1700–04 Addison** (southeast corner with McGee Avenue) represents a method for providing more affordable housing by placing several residences on a single lot. It may not be great architecture, but the Mediterranean-style residence has pleasing windows and fits into the neighborhood of single-family homes.

The American Foursquare at 1644 Addison was the home of Mario Savio, passionate speaker and leader of the Free Speech Movement. American Foursquare homes are two stories and fairly square with simple lines; usually they have entryways to one side in the front, where there are stairs, a wide opening to the living room, and a passageway to the kitchen. The architectural style can vary, but simple Colonial Revival elements are often included.

Next to 1644 Addison, ❺ **St. Joseph the Worker Church** is the site of Berkeley's first Catholic convent and school (Presentation Convent and Academy, which opened in 1878 on land donated by farmer James McGee). Sister Mary Teresa Comerford paid McGee a nominal $5 for the property, as she sought to expand her convents and schools and establish a place for nuns suffering from tuberculosis to recuperate. McGee's children attended the school, and he donated additional land to the church, which was built in 1886. The current Classical Revival church with two towers dates from 1907. If the door is unlocked, go inside to view the impressive interior. The church was well known for its advocacy of progressive social causes.

In 1988, the convent moved and the school downsized, leaving underutilized property. UC redeveloped the west side in 1994 as University Terrace, with 75 condominiums for faculty and staff housing. Turn left on California Street and walk to the garden at midblock, with ❻ **stone historic markers**. From the gate, you can see parts of the interior courtyard and the school building, reconfigured as condominiums.

Along the street on this side, the crabapple trees have pink flowers and lovely deep pink buds in late February and March. Walk on to the Presentation Mini-Park at Allston Way. Mature trees and the shared open space give it a gracious air. This is a much better example of infill development than many of the apartment buildings of the 1950s and 1960s. The city recently developed a swale to manage rain runoff using plant material (rather than concrete or metal pipes) at the corner of the garden.

Cross Allston. On the left, **❼ 2207 and 2209 California** are built very close together because the lots are unusually narrow. At 2221 California, a lovely Stick-style Victorian is somewhat altered but still intact. At the corner of Bancroft Way, turn right, walk one block, and turn left on Spaulding Avenue. The next two blocks are lined with sweetgum trees, colorful at their peak in late autumn through December, though some on the west side have been badly hacked to make way for utility lines. Most of the houses here are one-story bungalows with Craftsman features such as pronounced gables with extending eaves and brackets or California bungalows with Mediterranean features and flat roofs.

The **❽ 1898 Colonial Revival house** at 2315 Spaulding has a high-peaked roof—almost like an A-frame—and brown shingles, unusual for this type of home. In the next block on the right side, the apartment building at **❾ 2424 Spaulding** was the home of Ernest Landauer, cofounder of the Actors Ensemble of Berkeley and the Ecology Center.

Jack LaLanne moved to the California bungalow next door at 2430 Spaulding around 1929 with his parents and brother. The bodybuilder and physical fitness guru, who graduated from Berkeley High in 1934, swam and trained at the Downtown Berkeley YMCA and at nearby San Pablo Park. He founded the nation's first modern health club in Oakland in 1936 and became famous for his long-running TV show (from 1953 to 1985) advocating fitness and good diet. He lived to be 96.

Turn left on Dwight and walk a short distance to 1545 Dwight, the Stick-style **❿ Fish-Clark House** (named for its early owners) built in 1883 by A. H. Broad, who designed and built many of Berkeley's early schools. This grand Victorian is a survivor from the era when "gentleman farms"—hobby farms with big houses, orchards, and gardens on large lots—dominated this neighborhood, prior to subdivision in the early 1900s. The house, which reportedly has 17

The Fish-Clark House on Dwight.

bedrooms, was a commune run by former Free Speech Movement participants from the 1970s. Residents at various times included Lee Felsenstein, a computer engineer who played a central role in the development of the personal computer; a group that was an early promoter of alternative energy; a spiritual community called the Ark; and a substance-abuse recovery program called Steps. Financial and other difficulties forced Steps to sell the house in 2013, and it was then significantly renovated. The McGee-Spaulding-Hardy Historic Interest Group, which gathered much of the historical information on this interesting walk, prepared an application and advocated for the city to landmark this house in 2010.

Turn left on California and go just past midblock to **⓫ 2418 California**. This landmarked Victorian from 1894 has ornamentation and a Palladian window in the gable, design elements that anticipate the Colonial Revival style. The house was built by John Hunter, vice president of Parker Match Company, a West Berkeley company with a secret formula for match-head dip. The McGee-Spaulding-Hardy group was formed around 2000 to landmark and protect this property, which has since been restored and added on to, preserving a large lot that hints at the one-time minifarm here. On the opposite side, at 2417–19 California, is an attractive Colonial Revival, which was moved here in 1941 from the site where the Berkeley Community Theatre at Berkeley High would be built.

Return to Dwight, turn left, and cross California (walking toward the hills). A plaque in the median describes how the area was subdivided and the role that Southern Pacific railway played in the district. The landscaped area in the median was created by a joint community/city effort. Planted with natives, it is watered by members of the neighborhood group.

Continue on Dwight to Jefferson Avenue. When this neighborhood was laid out in 1892, it included St. Joseph Street (now Jefferson), named for the convent, and Catherine Street (now Roosevelt) and Mary Street (now McKinley), named for developer James McGee's daughters. Nearby, MLK Way was originally Sherman Street and then renamed Grove Street.

At the northeast corner of Jefferson, at **⓬ 1621 Dwight**, the fascinating 1906 house is a mixture of Craftsman and Victorian styles, but the wide veranda and the tropical trees are reminiscent of the South Pacific. In the 1970s, this was the home of Anne Rice, the best-selling author of Gothic fiction, Christian literature, and erotica. She wrote the short story "Interview with a Vampire" in this house; she later turned the story into a novel, which was made into a film. Her husband, Stan Rice, who passed away in 2002, was a well-known poet and painter; their Berkeley-born son Christopher Rice is also a best-selling novelist.

A few doors farther along, 1633 Dwight was the home of Feodor A. Postnikov, who changed his name to Fred A. Post when he emigrated from Russia in 1906 and settled here in 1911. He was an engineer who worked as a balloonist and an early promoter of the Esperanto language.

Return to Jefferson. Turn right and continue to 2437 Jefferson. This Craftsman sports pronounced gables, an unusual facade, and a heavy, projecting, stucco porch. On the west side and a few houses down, **⓭ 2428 Jefferson**, built in 1913, is set back from the street. Part of the house may have been transported across the bay from San Francisco after the 1906 earthquake. According to various sources, the large trees were originally potted specimens that rooted themselves when the Japanese-American gardener was sent to an internment camp during World War II. Note the elaborate tree house and tunnel slide among the large, coniferous trees. The Colonial Revival house at 2413 Jefferson has a rectangular window bay with stained glass over the garage.

Turn right on Channing Way and walk a short distance to 1626 and 1628–30 Channing, sizable houses that were moved here from Bancroft around 1920. Across the street, 1631 Channing was a 1960s and 1970s commune called ⑭ **Karl Marx's Magic Bus**, which was involved in the antiwar and Free Speech movements and ran an antiwar coffee house in Oakland. Several members were later prominent in Berkeley civic life.

Return to Jefferson and turn right. The ⑮ **row of California bungalows** on the opposite side, 2330–16 Jefferson, are prefabricated homes, ordered from a Sears & Roebuck catalog and assembled onsite. A charming Victorian at 2317 Jefferson has a small turret topped by a witch's-hat roof.

The northern part of the 2300 block and the entire 2200 block of Jefferson are lined with Australian *Melaleuca linariifolia* trees (also called paperbark or cajeputs). Their narrow leaves resemble those of coniferous trees, and they have spongy, papery, light-gray bark (touch it with your fingers). The trees flower between early May and early July; the spikes of bottlebrush-like white flowers are so dense that they resemble snow on the tree or broccoli dipped in sour cream. Blue-flowering jacaranda trees are also on this street, recognizable out of bloom by their feathery, fern-like leaves.

At the southeast corner of Bancroft and Jefferson, ⑯ **Congregation Beth Israel** is an Orthodox Jewish synagogue. The cornerstone was laid in 1924, a courageous move at a time of increasing anti-Semitism and discrimination in the United States. This was probably the first Jewish temple in the East Bay. The building underwent major renovation in 2004, but many of the original architectural elements of the front facade remain.

Continue on Jefferson to Allston. 1601 Allston, the low, brown building across the street, was once the ⑰ **Presentation Convent**. After Presentation High School closed in 1988, the Presentation sisters eventually moved out, and in 1992, the University Students' Cooperative Association (now known as the Berkeley Student Cooperative) converted the building into housing for UC graduate and re-entry students.

Turn right on Allston and walk to McGee Avenue. On the northeast corner at 1701 Allston is an ⑱ **1893 Queen Anne–style Victorian**.

A storefront was added on the Allston Way side, although it subsequently reverted to residential use and the shop windows were removed. A little farther up the block at 1711 Allston is the house where science fiction writer Philip K. Dick (the movies *Blade Runner* and *Total Recall* are based on his stories) lived with his mother while he was a Berkeley High School student in the mid-1940s.

Return to McGee and turn left. **⑲ 2217 McGee** was the home of Gus Newport, a progressive mayor from 1979 to 1986, who helped steer Berkeley politics to the left. On his watch, the city was the first in the nation to disinvest in apartheid South Africa.

On the next block, **⑳ 2315–17 McGee** is a large, two-story, brown-shingle house with Craftsman features such as the exterior construction and brackets supporting the extending eaves. Across the street, at 2316 McGee, a more modest Craftsman-style house has a peaked cap on the left entry. Next door at 2320 McGee, the curving, modern house is reminiscent of a long and narrow houseboat, with wood siding as well as cement and thin metal shingles. At 2338 McGee, a 1908 Craftsman has two gables, numerous brackets, and a large L-shaped front porch with hefty square columns grouped in twos and threes.

Turn left on Channing. The charming duplex at **㉑ 1705–07 Channing** has one side mirroring the other and extensive landscaping. The three-floor, multiunit building next door at 1709

2320 McGee, a contemporary home.

Channing has housed a private collective/co-op since 1973 called Razzlesnatch, one of the few surviving from the 1960s and 1970s. Out front is the Dona Spring Wishing Well, named for the Berkeley city council member who served this district for 16 years, overcoming significant disabilities; she died in 2008. Opposite at 1712 Channing was the home of radical activists Jerry Ruben and Michael Lerner in the 1960s (Ruben later became a multimillionaire businessman and Lerner became editor of *Tikkun* magazine and a Berkeley rabbi).

Return to McGee and turn left. At 2431 McGee was ㉒ **McGee's Farm**, one of the most active communes in the district and the home of a child-care center run by men in a 1970s attempt at gender role reversal. Although it took its name from the historic farmland in the area, this older, two-story house was not James McGee's original farmhouse.

At the northwest corner of Dwight and McGee, Helly Welly Lamps and Lighting sells unusual original lamps. Turn left on Dwight and walk to Roosevelt Avenue, then turn left. At ㉓ **2432 and 2428 Roosevelt**, the Colonial Revival houses were built together in 1907 but with different design elements.

Roosevelt Park—now called Becky Temko Tot Park—is next door at 2424 Roosevelt. In the 1950s, the city had upzoned most of the area to high-density residential, and citizens stopped yet another concrete-block apartment building from going up on this site. The Berkeley Flatlands Neighborhood Association, a coalition of progressive communes and collectives, created the park with the city's assistance in the late 1960s and early 1970s. The park was later renamed in memory of a local parks advocate.

At 2416 Roosevelt, a three-story apartment building is currently abandoned and crumbling, seemingly awaiting demolition or major renovation. Built in 1962, it is not nearly as old as the surrounding single-family homes, demonstrating the short life cycle of haphazard design. The Neighborhood Preservation Ordinance was the start of a move to downzone the area to single-family or duplex residential, which occurred in 1975, preserving much of the area's character. Notice the "traffic calming" measure at Channing; such barriers are common in Berkeley neighborhoods to slow down drivers and prevent certain streets from getting too busy.

Noteworthy houses on the next two blocks include:

* ㉔ **2343 Roosevelt**, a good example of a high-peaked Colonial Revival
* 2330 Roosevelt, a brown-shingle with a gambrel roof (the roof changes its slope, reminiscent of a traditional barn roof)
* 2307 Roosevelt, a simple worker's cottage
* ㉕ **2300–02 Roosevelt**, a ground-floor storefront, that has housed an art gallery and has murals on the Bancroft side
* 2231 Roosevelt, a shingled Colonial Revival/Craftsman with a very steep roof

At ㉖ **2224 Roosevelt**, Swedish immigrant Axel Larson established the Sanitary Bakery with brick ovens in the backyard in 1913; it operated here until the 1940s. Later, this was the home of Mike Myerson, a leader of radical causes from the 1960s onward, who helped organize sit-ins, set up a campus political party, and wrote a well-regarded personal account about the period. Later still, it was the home of Bettina Aptheker, lesbian activist, author, feminist, and UC Santa Cruz professor of feminist studies. Another resident was Michael Tigar, a human rights lawyer who defended controversial clients such as Angela Davis, Lynne Stewart, and Terry Nichols.

On the northwest corner of Allston and Roosevelt, the large, impressive house with a corner turret was built in 1905 with a mixture of Victorian, Colonial Revival, and Craftsman details. Turn right on Allston. The two-story Craftsman at 1728 Allston on the southeast corner was built in 1914. Across the street, ㉗ **1737 Allston** also has Craftsman elements; expanded and much altered, with a cheerful circular entryway, it is still full of character.

Turn right on Grant, noting the nicely restored Stick-style Victorian on the left side at 2223, built around 1894 but moved here from University Avenue in the 1970s. At ㉘ **2301 Grant** (southeast corner with Bancroft), the 1909 building was originally mixed-use, with flats upstairs and shops downstairs; now it is all residences. A commune and workers' collective called The Circus was here from the late 1960s to the early 1980s; members ran the successful mayoral campaign of Gus Newport in 1979. One of the founders was Robert Alan (Al) Haber, who in 1960 was elected first president of Students for a Democratic Society (SDS), a notable student activist movement. A substantial vegetable garden is behind the building along Grant.

Take note of the rather nondescript apartment building at 2304 Grant, built in 1964. By comparison, on the opposite side **㉙ 2315 and 2319 Grant** are older apartment buildings with decorative details that fit well into the neighborhood, while 2304 Grant reflects a 1960s-era lack of concern for how buildings look and relate to the surrounding neighborhoods. 2333 Grant is a large, shingled house with Colonial Revival details.

Continue on Grant past Channing and turn left at Dwight. The **㉚ Berkeley City Ballet** is on the southeast corner, with a concrete-grid form incorporating glass blocks. Turn left on McKinley, where the first two blocks are lined with tall sweetgum trees, especially attractive in October and November.

Noteworthy houses on the next two blocks include:

* ❊ **㉛ 2435 McKinley**, a latter-day brown-shingle with a turret
* ❊ 2433 McKinley, an older brown-shingle
* ❊ 2431 McKinley, with elements of American Southwest style, painted bright orange
* ❊ **㉜ 2400 McKinley**, with a diverse cactus garden
* ❊ **㉝ 2337 McKinley**, with a pointy cap over the entry and curving half-timbering

2231 (above) and 2233 (inset) McKinley were once part of the Dragon's Eye commune.

✻ Washington Elementary School, a Berkeley public school on the right

✻ 2304 McKinley, a former church now housing the Berkeley Buddhist Monastery, founded by Master Hsuan Hua for education and interfaith harmony

On the northwest corner of Bancroft and McKinley, **34 Berkwood Hedge School** is a progressive, independent K–5 school founded in 1946 that has been here since 1975. Known for its integrated curriculum, it was the first racially integrated school in Berkeley and was for many years run as a teacher collective.

The 2200 block evokes the rich heritage of late 19th- and early 20th-century homes in the McGee-Spaulding area. Two doors down from the school, 2240 McKinley is a charming Queen Anne from about 1893. On the opposite side, **35 2233 and 2231 McKinley** were home to the Dragon's Eye commune from 1965 to 1973. The oval shape of the entrance of 2331, a Craftsman, resembles a dragon's eye; 2233, a brown-shingle, has entertaining wall sculptures and decorations. Michael Rossman, a leader in the Free Speech Movement, was a founder and commune member. The group networked with other US communes and received grant money for some of its projects. It was active in the 1960s efforts to prevent development at People's Park and in planting Ohlone Park.

Opposite these, 2228 McKinley has an angled corner turret that looks toward its neighbor, while 2220 is a 1914 Craftsman with clinker brick on the porch columns.

In 1947, science fiction writer Philip K. Dick moved into a converted barn/warehouse at **36 2208 McKinley** that he shared with several writers and poets: Gerald Ackerman, an art historian at UC; the modernist poet Robert Duncan, an early writer about gay issues; and Jack Spicer, a poet, research-linguist, and cofounder of the West Coast Beat movement. The building was demolished in 1979 and replaced by a ranch house moved here from 4th Street.

Continue on to Addison and turn right to return to the starting point.

✻ ✻ ✻

THE OHLONE GREENWAY

Overview: This walk follows the Ohlone Greenway, a busy bicycling and pedestrian path built mostly on a former railroad right-of-way that connects Berkeley, Albany, and Richmond. When considering this walk, please note that it is not a loop. It is a pleasant and easy nonarchitectural walk on a level course from the Downtown Berkeley BART station to the El Cerrito BART station, with several options for shorter walks.

Highlights:

- Rails-to-trails pedestrian/bicycle path
- History of the bay mural
- Parks, community gardens, historical markers

Distance: 2.5–6.1 miles

Time: 1.5–3 hours

Elevation: 150-foot drop

This walk starts at the northwest corner of Milvia Street and Hearst Avenue. To get there from the Downtown Berkeley BART station (at the southwest corner of Shattuck Avenue and Center Street), cross Center and walk four blocks north on Shattuck to Hearst. Turn left on Hearst and walk west past Henry Street and one more block to Milvia. Cross catty-corner to the northwest corner of Milvia and Hearst. You can also park in the area, but be alert to parking restric-

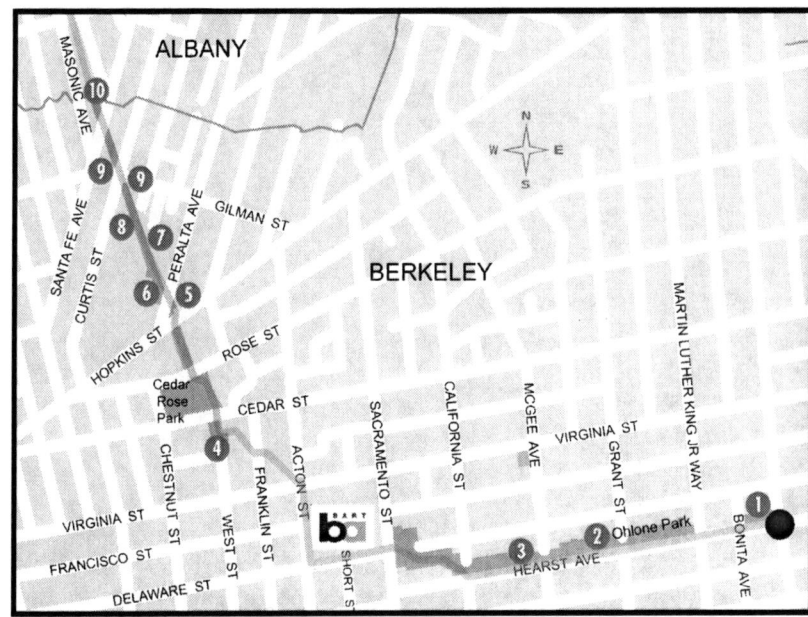

tions. Numerous AC Transit lines pass within a few blocks of the starting point.

Walk west on Hearst. The Ohlone Greenway begins here in Ohlone Park, which was built on top of BART's underground route. At the first section, just below Milvia, California Indian artist Jean LaMarr painted ❶ *The Ohlone Journey*, a 1995 mural on the BART venting structure. It depicts the Coyote creation story (east), a dance welcoming European entry to the Bay Area (north), prominent Native Americans from the 20th century (west), and retaining cultural identity (south). Continue walking past the North Berkeley Senior Center on the next block.

Cross Martin Luther King, Jr., (MLK) Way at the signal and continue west through Ohlone Park, walking on the sidewalk near Hearst or crossing the grassy lawns. Camphor trees partly line this block; their bright green or sometimes reddish leaves are fragrant when crushed. Next is a busy, fenced-in dog park. The city tried at one time to grow turf here, but eventually gave up and now simply mulches from time to time.

In the park segment beyond Grant Street, several ❷ **large climbing structures** were made from metal tubing and rope. The Ohlone Community Garden has more than 40 plots for neighbors

BART in Berkeley

The north side of Hearst Avenue originally had many houses that were torn down when the Bay Area Rapid Transit (BART) system was built in the 1960s; BART opened in 1973. BART's original cost-saving proposal was to follow the old Santa Fe Railroad right-of-way from Ashby Avenue to North Berkeley, with an elevated track that did not pass through downtown Berkeley. Berkeley citizens voted to pay extra to route BART underground and send it through downtown. BART has three underground stations in the city (Ashby, Downtown, and North Berkeley) and emerges from the tunnel near the Albany border. With nearby UC, downtown businesses, and cultural venues, the Downtown Berkeley BART station is one of the busiest stations in the East Bay.

From the south, BART passes under Adeline Street and Shattuck, which are wide streets. But in order to rejoin the Santa Fe right-of-way in North Berkeley, BART had to go under Hearst, which was not wide enough to accommodate it. As a result, the homes on the north side of the block were removed. BART wanted to build apartments above the underground train line, and there was also an early plan to place a community college here, but Berkeley citizens campaigned for a park and eventually BART turned the land over to the city, which developed Ohlone Park and the first section of the Ohlone Greenway. ❋❋

to grow fruits, vegetables, and flowers. Beyond McGee Avenue is another playground, picnic tables, ❸ **basketball and volleyball courts**, and portable toilets. A fence at the end of the grassy area near California Street stops soccer balls from escaping from this well-used field.

At California and Hearst, follow the curved path through the park toward the large rocks. At the fork before the rocks, take one or the other paved path heading west through the park—they join up near the fenced baseball/soccer field. On a clear day, you can see Mt. Tamalpais across the bay. After the field, cross Sacramento Street in the crosswalk at the signal, walking toward the North Berkeley BART station parking lot (you are now on Delaware Street).

Take the sidewalk along Delaware, skirting the southern edge of the BART lot, to Acton Street. Ginkgo trees with fan-shaped leaves that turn golden in late autumn line the south side of the station.

The Ohlone Journey, by Jean LaMarr.

Other trees along areas of the parking lot include plums that flower in January and February, crabapples that flower in February and March, sweetgums with bright autumn colors, and camphor trees.

Turn right on Acton, continue to Virginia, and cross catty-corner to the northwest to proceed along the Ohlone Greenway, which is situated here between a BART parking lot and a high hedge. Keep an eye out for bicyclists and walk on the right side. Cross unmarked Franklin Street and continue to the right of the final parking area, through the turnaround at the end of a small street, then to the right of a basketball court.

Notice ❹ **another path** that merges into the basketball court from the left. It is built on the right-of-way of the former Santa Fe Railroad, which ran passenger and freight trains from Oakland to the shipyards in Richmond. This spur of the Ohlone Greenway, completed in 2012, continues south to University Avenue and Strawberry Creek Park just beyond.

The Santa Fe Railroad service steadily lost customers after World War II but continued to run freight trains along West Street here and under the elevated BART tracks up until May 1979. When the line was abandoned, the rights-of-way were donated to cities along the route. The Ohlone Greenway was created not long afterward, one of the first rails-to-trails conversions in the country.

Follow the Ohlone Greenway as it curves right, toward Cedar Street. Cross Cedar carefully in the crosswalk, mindful that cars tend to speed here. Cedar-Rose Park was dedicated in 1980 with land from the Santa Fe right-of-way and land and improvements funded by a voter-approved bond measure. Walk north, away from Cedar, on the paved path to Rose Street, cross in the crosswalk, and follow the greenway as it continues to the left of three tennis courts.

Cross Hopkins Street in the crosswalk. The ❺ **Karl Linn Community Garden** is on the right side of Peralta. Just beyond it are explanatory plaques for EcoHouse (which faces Hopkins at 1305). Founded in 1999, EcoHouse has been a program of the Ecology Center since 2006. Located in a restored, formerly dilapidated home, it serves as a "living laboratory of practices and technologies"—a demonstration home and garden for ecological living with solar energy panels, solar water heating, rain catchment, water-conserving features, grey-water recycling, use of recycled and salvaged materials, and an organic garden with native plants. The garden shed on Peralta demonstrates sustainable local building materials such as straw bales, rammed earth, and recycled wood, as well as a living "green" roof.

Carefully cross Peralta (there is no crosswalk) to check out the ❻ **Peralta Community Garden**, which features plots to grow food and flowers as well as an attractive sculpted-metal gate depicting plants and animals. It took a long time for the garden founders, including Karl Linn, to convince BART to make the unused, weedy patch available for a garden. Linn was a landscape architect, psychologist, educator, and community activist, best known for inspiring the creation of "neighborhood commons" on inner-city vacant lots during 1960s through 1980s; he died in 2005. Feel free to explore the garden if it is open.

BART emerges from its tunnel here as the Ohlone Greenway heads toward Albany. Just beyond the garden gate, a cement, four-sided pillar tells the story of Spanish and Mexican colonization; the land-grant era from the late 18th century until after the Gold Rush, which included the huge Luís María Peralta grant in the East Bay; and how the gringos cheated the Californios of land that they had in turn taken from California natives. School children made the colorful tiles on the nearby bench.

The Peralta Community Garden.

As you continue on the Greenway, notice the many native shrubs and flowers that have been planted, including pink-flowering currant, fragrant sagebrush, coyote bush, blue-flowering ceanothus, coffeeberry, various salvias, toyon, lupine, California poppy, buttercup, red rock penstemon, gumplant, and checker-bloom; plenty of weeds such as oxalis and radish weed have also invaded.

Farther along on the right, where Northside Avenue angles off, a plaque describes farming in West Berkeley; the seating here is made from farm machinery, and there are metal ❼ **sculptures of cows**. On the right, where Nielson Street angles off, there is a mosaic; opposite on the left is a mural showing the bay's progression from Native American times to the modern day. Called ❽ *From Elk Tracks to BART Tracks*, it was completed by artist Alan Leon in collaboration with other local artists in 2002.

BART is elevated from here until the end of the line in Richmond. An extensive seismic retrofit was completed in 2012 that included greenway improvements.

At Gilman, look left and right to see shops in a ❾ **small commercial district**, built when the Santa Fe Railroad and Key Route streetcar line intersected here. Stop for a snack at the bagel store, bakery, or beer garden. Cross to the northwest corner at the four-way stop to continue on the Greenway on the other side of the BART tracks. A pocket park is on the left; when it is open, it is a lovely place for a picnic.

Just a bit farther, cross Santa Fe Avenue in the crosswalk and continue to the ❿ **tall railing** on the left where Codornices Creek emerges from a culvert heading toward the bay. Volunteers from Friends of Five Creeks, a local nonprofit organization, built this structure, which was completed in 2001, and restored the riparian habitat below. *Codornices* means "quail" in Spanish; hence the stylized sculptures at either end of the railing. Information plaques are at each end of the railing, and there are tall, native cottonwood trees near the stream. Codornices Creek is the least-culverted of Berkeley's creeks and is featured in another walk (Walk 7, Codornices Creek). The creek is the border between Berkeley and Albany.

At this point you can return on the Greenway to the starting point, return to the North Berkeley BART station and take BART, or continue the walk. Another option is to return on the Ohlone Greenway and take the greenway spur that runs from the basketball

BART tracks shading the Greenway.

court after Cedar Street; at Berkeley Way turn left and walk straight back to Milvia, where it is just one block, left, to the starting point.

If you plan to continue along the Greenway toward El Cerrito, note that the map ends here but the Greenway is easy to follow. In Albany and El Cerrito, the Ohlone Greenway was widened significantly in 2012–14. On most blocks from here onward, pedestrians can use either an older, narrow, paved path to the left or, on the right, a path with sections demarcated for bikes and pedestrians. (The path you choose may depend on the temperature and your preference for sun or shade.) In the first block of this section, to the west near the street, a line of sweetgum trees bursts into brilliant hues in autumn.

The elevated tracks mean that BART trains are quite noisy when they pass, but the structure creates welcome shade on warm afternoons. Cross Dartmouth Street and continue one long block to

Marin Avenue. The Albany Public Library and community center are on the northwest corner.

One very long block farther is Solano Avenue—another former streetcar route now lined with shops, restaurants, and other businesses—that extends from Albany to Berkeley. It is a pedestrian-friendly street, further enhanced by public sidewalk and crosswalk improvements in both cities. After crossing Solano, you can walk a short distance to the right to see a small veterans' memorial in the median of Key Route Boulevard.

It is a pleasant, easy walk from here on the Greenway to the El Cerrito Plaza BART station, albeit without major points of interest. Proceed to the BART station, or take AC Transit 18 going up Solano (to the east) back to downtown Berkeley.

Continuing on the Greenway, there are crabapple trees, with lovely pink blooms in March, and flowering plums, as well as more sweetgums beyond Portland Avenue. At Brighton Avenue, Albany Middle School and the town's athletic fields are on the right. From this point on there is only one path, without a demarcated side for pedestrians, so stay to the right. You will soon pass the El Cerrito Plaza shopping center. Developers denied citizens' calls to create a mixed-use town center and instead built a humdrum strip mall here that shows its age.

Continue on Ohlone Greenway and cross Fairmount Avenue to the El Cerrito Plaza BART station, about three miles from the starting point. From here, you can take BART to downtown Berkeley or North Berkeley, or you can walk back on the Greenway or another route of your choosing, such as Solano Avenue.

Alternatively, you can continue on the Greenway for another two miles to the El Cerrito Del Norte BART station. Just beyond that station, the path crosses Baxter Creek and turns west to become the Richmond Greenway. This trail extends another two miles and is lined with community-designed artwork, urban agriculture, and recreational spaces. After about a mile, you can detour a few blocks north through Richmond to the Richmond BART station.

✳ ✳ ✳

WALK 17
OCEAN VIEW

✳ ✳ ✳

Overview: Native Americans inhabited this fertile region by the bay for thousands of years. West Berkeley and Ocean View are a treasure trove of early structures and artifacts amid factories, residences, and modern buildings. This is an easy, flat walk.

Highlights:
- Earliest Ohlone and Anglo settlements in Berkeley
- Eclectic 4th Street shopping district
- Historic buildings, factories, modern condos, and offices

Distance: 1.2–2.4 miles

Time: 1.5–2 hours

Elevation gain: 50 feet

✳ ✳ ✳

Start at the northeast corner of Hearst Avenue and 4th Street. AC Transit buses 51 and 72 stop near the starting point; this corner is a 1.1-mile walk from the North Berkeley BART station. Parking can be difficult on weekends; pay attention to time limits and other signs.

Head north on 4th Street. The first floor of the historic 1877 building at ❶ **1809 4th Street** was converted from residential to retail space in 1992, so it may be somewhat altered from its original appearance. The style is Italianate (early Victorian period), with a balcony and shelf-like features over windows and doors.

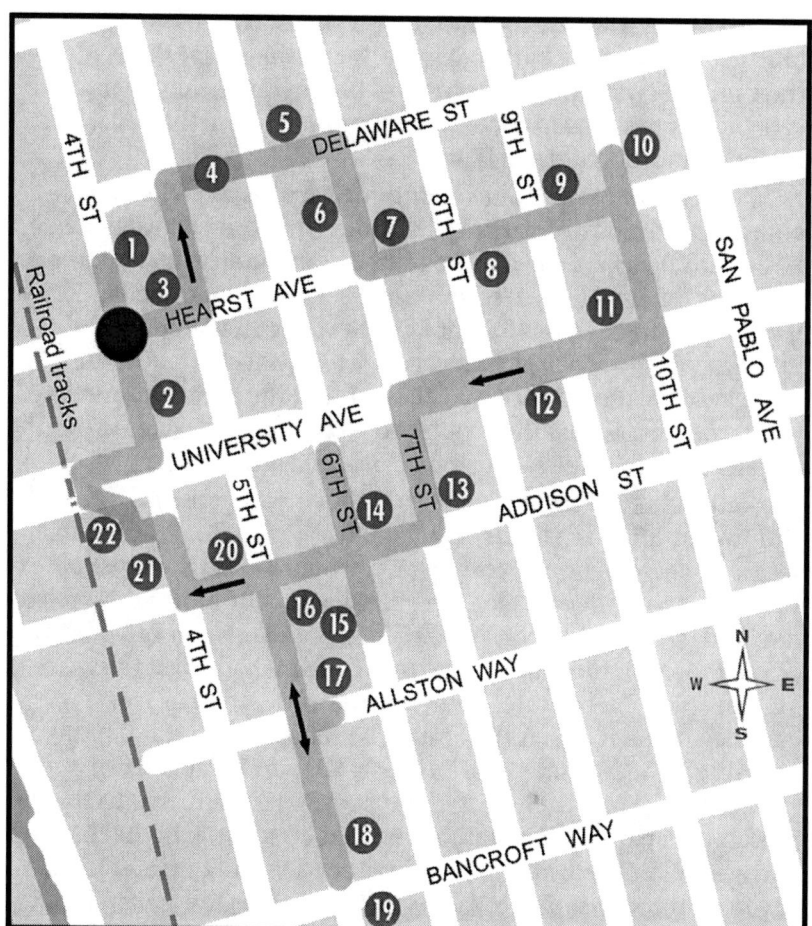

The commercial center of Ocean View was in decline in the 1970s when developer Denny Abrams saved some historic buildings from the wrecking ball with his vision of retail revitalization (see the Ocean View sidebar on page 236). It is now a destination shopping area specializing in home and garden products, gourmet food, and clothes. Builders Booksource, at 1817 4th, is devoted to books on architecture and design. Citizens have expressed concern about the balance of national chain stores and local independent stores, but the area maintains its uniqueness. In addition to a narrow street with slow traffic, tree-lined sidewalks, and shops, older buildings give the area its pedestrian-friendly ambience.

The street trees are mostly London planes (sycamores with multicolored peeling bark and large, maple-like leaves). Deciduous trees provide welcome shade in the summer and sunlight and intricate branch patterns in cooler winter months. Note the pedestrian-oriented traditional street lamps.

This area of Berkeley has a long culinary history. The French quarter, partly located to the north along 3rd Street between Cedar Street and Delaware (now railroad tracks and industrial buildings), was once home to French restaurants, bakeries, bars, and laundries. It was a popular destination for San Franciscans, including chefs, in the late 19th and early 20th centuries. However, in 1907, the Berkeley city council outlawed alcohol, and the French contingent moved to areas where they could wine and dine. Consider exploring 4th Street, perhaps stopping for a drink or a bite to eat.

Return to the starting point at the northeast corner of 4th and Hearst, cross 4th to the right, and walk left across Hearst and south on 4th, along the parking lot, for a view of ❷ **Spenger's Fish Grotto** on the east side. The middle structure with the gabled roof and large sign was originally a house and opened as a market around 1892; significant additions have been made over the years. Johann Spenger emigrated from Bavaria and settled in West Berkeley in the 1860s. A fisherman, he set up a clam stand in 1892 in that historic section of the building. His son Frank opened a full-service restaurant here in the 1930s; Frank's son, Frank "Buddy" Spenger, managed the restaurant from 1940 to 1998. In the 1950s, Spenger's claimed to sell 3,500 pounds of fish daily, greater than any restaurant west of the Mississippi. Although the ownership has changed hands out of the family, Spenger's continues to be a Berkeley institution, serving hearty dinners and selling fish from the shop.

Returning to Hearst, cross to the starting point and proceed up Hearst (away from the bay) to 5th Street. Turn left on 5th. On the corner, 1828–30 5th is a ❸ **Queen Anne Victorian cottage** from around 1890, with ornamentation on the protruding section with gable. Next door, 1824 5th is a worker's cottage, circa 1875–80, with a false front, brackets under the eaves, and shelves over the windows and door similar to the building at 1809 4th Street.

Just a little farther and across the street, at 1827 5th, is the East Bay Vivarium, which sells reptiles and invertebrates and offers an educational traveling menagerie of reptiles and other critters for

The water tower in the Delaware Street Historic District.

schools and parties. (Go in and look around if it is open.) Next door to the Vivarium, a residential development from 2015 utilizes part of an old brick industrial structure.

In the modern building at 1812 5th, on the left (west) side, TRAX gallery features prominent ceramic artists and sells to clientele around the world; it is open to the public. Next door at 1808 5th, the Charles Heywood House is an early Victorian built in 1878 in Italianate style, with rounded window tops; the house is fairly large for this district and well preserved. It houses the Golestan Center for Language Immersion and Cultural Education, for children learning Farsi and Iranian culture. Across the street, at 1801–03 5th, is another historic Victorian.

Cross 5th in the crosswalk at Delaware and walk through the ❹ **Delaware Street Historic District**. During the Gold Rush, Delaware connected the first local shipping wharf with Contra Costa Road (now San Pablo Avenue). The area was slated to be demolished, along with many other old structures, as part of a redevelopment scheme in the 1960s, and the buildings were boarded up as they became empty during a long battle over preservation. This area became a designated historic district under the Berkeley Landmarks Preservation Ordinance in 1979; some structures were preserved, while others were moved here from elsewhere, and some were reconstructed from old plans. So although it's not precisely historic in terms of the location and structure of all the buildings, the district re-creates the look of the pioneer period better than any other block in Berkeley (it even has wooden sidewalks).

On the right, the building with a store at 800 5th appears to be a reconstruction. 802 Delaware was built in 1878 and moved here from 5th Street. Just beyond 802 Delaware, the back of 1801 5th can be seen, as can a historic water tower that was moved here from 5th Street; it has the old tank on top, but a small condominium was built in the tower. The next building, 804–06 Delaware, is residential, as are a number of other buildings in the district, although some have ground-floor commercial space. Across the street, 805 and 807 Delaware are two of Berkeley's oldest structures—built in 1879—and they are at their original locations. 809 Delaware has a false front and was not originally at this location.

808–10 and 812–14 Delaware were moved here from nearby streets. Behind them (seen from the gate between the two houses), newer housing built in a simple, traditional style provides eight units of affordable housing. 816 Delaware was built before 1890,

835 Delaware, in Italianate style.

and 818 Delaware dates to 1878; both are quite simple. Toward the end of the block are two buildings in their original locations: 817–21 Delaware/1750 6th Street from the 1930s and 820–22 Delaware from 1908. In contrast to the bustle of 4th Street, this block has a quiet charm.

At the end of the block, cross 6th Street in the crosswalk and go east on the left side of Delaware to **5** **827–29 Delaware**. This high-peaked Colonial Revival—repaired and painted in 2014—has attractive porch decorations, first-floor fan windows, and second-floor walls that curve in to form a bay window. Above the third-floor window is a relief sculpture of a plant in a cup with handle; the shingles above form a wave pattern.

At 835 Delaware, a house from the 1880s has Italianate features such as rounded window tops. The structure was restored to show off fine ornamentation, including fish-scale shingles in the gable and carved wooden elements. The two-story building across the street at 834 Delaware was previously believed to be Bowen's Inn, established at Delaware and Contra Costa Road in 1854 by a Captain Bowen, which would have made it the oldest remaining structure in Berkeley. However, research by Berkeley Architectural Heritage Association (BAHA) member Jerry Sulliger revealed that the early inn was demolished and that Bowen did not come on the scene until later. However, it is firmly established that Captain J. Higgins had a grocery store in this circa 1875 pioneer building, which has been moved twice and is now a residence.

Cross Delaware to turn right on 7th Street. At 1814 7th, behind a high wooden fence, a **6** **large structure from 1887** has unusual gables due to the half-hipped (or Jerkinhead) roof design. Initially a school, it was designed by A. H. Broad, who designed and built many early Berkeley schools. In its original location, this is probably the oldest school building in the city, although it is now a residence.

On the northeast corner of Hearst, **7** **901 Hearst** was originally built as a house in 1878 but became an Italian greengrocers' shop around 1890; later it became a residence again, but it now houses Alembique Apothecary, which specializes in botanical and artisanal perfumes. Cross 7th and Hearst and go left on Hearst. On the right side, 906 Hearst has a fascinating wood and metal gateway made out of found objects, including old industrial parts. This block and the next feature several delightful historic houses, some quite

From Shellmounds to Fish Platters

Ten thousand years ago, the bay was just a river valley with the coastline at the Farallon Islands. As ocean levels rose at the end of the Ice Age, the bay gradually filled. Archaeologists believe the area near Hearst and 4th may have been the first native settlement on the shoreline of the "modern" San Francisco Bay. Ohlone Indians (Chochenyo group) lived here for about 4,500 years, and the Bay Area's largest shellmound stood where the Spenger's Fish Grotto parking lot is now. In addition to eating shellfish and acorns, native people competed with grizzly bears for the meat of whales that beached on the shore nearby.

Today, there are alternative theories on shellmounds: some people say they were trash heaps with human burials in them; others believe they were burial grounds at the center of rites to "feed" the deceased. Much has been lost since European settlers carted away most of the mounds for fertilizer, roadbeds, and artifact hunting, especially from the top—or more recent—layers. UC studies of the shellmounds have determined that oysters were a major food for Native Americans; clams replaced oysters as the bay naturally silted up, while mussels were a food all along. Researchers have found evidence of more than 90 human burials here, and in 2014, new archaeological digs were begun to more accurately locate the shellmound remains.

During the Gold Rush (around 1852), Anglos began settling in the area where Strawberry Creek entered the bay. Eventually, a wharf was built at the foot of nearby Delaware Street, and industries established themselves in the area known as Ocean View or Jacob's Landing. At Delaware and Contra Costa Road (now San Pablo Avenue), someone built an inn. The settlement grew gradually and merged with Berkeley in 1878.

Bath Beach extended from near this spot north to Fleming Point—the location of the Golden Gate Fields race track in Albany. It was a crescent beach with shallow, fairly warm water—unlike the water in San Francisco, where the bay is deeper and colder. The beach was lined with elegant bathhouses, but sewage became a problem and remained so until the 1950s, when treatment facilities were built, though wet-weather overflow problems persisted. Extensive landfill subsequently pushed the shoreline into the bay.

The Spenger's parking lot was also once part of a park called Willow Grove. Strawberry Creek came through it, with bridges joining its banks; it was a place for dancing, picnics, and drinking. As Ocean View became an industrial center—manufacturing starch and grist, soap, lumber, glass, and other goods—factory effluents fouled the creek and it eventually was put in a culvert. Today's 4th Street went right through the former park. ❋ ❋

old and simple, others more ornate—such as Italianate 914 Hearst, in bright colors with a long cupola along the roofline.

On the southeast corner of 8th Street, ❽ **926 Hearst** was once the First Presbyterian Church of West Berkeley, designed by Charles Geddes and built in 1879, making it the second-oldest church in Berkeley. This pleasant Gothic Revival wood building has an 80-foot corner steeple and pointed arches in the front and side windows. In 1914, a two-story clubhouse was added in the rear on 8th Street, designed by Walter Ratcliff, Jr. The Presbyterian congregation campaigned against nearby saloons in its early years; it stopped using the church in 1968. Lawrence Gerald Smith, a self-styled Catholic Orthodox priest (not associated with any official denomination), renamed it St. Procopius Latin Rite Church; he was a preacher there from 1972 to 1988, during which time he had an impressive mural painted on the back wall (now gone). From 1993 to 2005, the building housed an Ethiopian Orthodox Church. Now it appears to be a residence.

Two well-kept 1890 Victorians at 931 and 933 Hearst are attributed to C. W. Davis, a prominent carpenter. He also designed 935 Hearst, which has lost most of its Victorian features; 936 Hearst, by a different builder, is well preserved. Most of the raised-basement Victorians were raised even higher in later decades to accommodate a full floor underneath.

Continue to the ❾ **Church of the Good Shepherd** on the north-

The historic Church of the Good Shepherd.

west corner of 9th Street, at 1001 Hearst. Built in 1878, this is the oldest church in Berkeley and the oldest in the East Bay retaining its founding congregation. It is amazingly well preserved, with a unique and charming Carpenter Gothic design, which refers to North American Gothic Revival structures made of wood rather than medieval stone. The vertical board-and-batten siding—thin strips of wood over joints between wider boards—is distinguished by two different colors. A 1,000-pound Blymyer bell sits in the spire.

The left (north) side of the block features camphor trees, with bright green leaves that are fragrant when crushed. At 1014 Hearst, the high-peaked Colonial Revival from around 1905 has Ionian porch columns and a Palladian window above, and 1025 Hearst on the northwest corner with 10th Street is a Queen Anne Victorian that seems to retain its original garden wall and fence.

At 10th Street, turn left to see the large **⑩ Toveri Tupa Hall** at 1819 10th, built in 1908. This three-story building was originally the Finnish Hall, and the name means "friends' meeting place." It has distinctive blue trim and an intriguing hipped roof with a projection like the bow of a ship. In a 1934 night of Bay Area riots, rightist vigilantes who perceived the Finns as sympathetic to striking longshoremen vandalized the hall. According to a plaque, it is still a cultural and community center with several societies utilizing it.

Walk back to Hearst; if you are short on time, end the walk here by going back down Hearst to the starting point. Otherwise, cross Hearst and continue walking south to University Avenue. Turn right; at **⑪ 1007 University**, a concrete grid-form building features embedded glass blocks. The 1949 building was for many years home to Mobilized Women of Berkeley, formed during World War I to sponsor food drives, sell liberty bonds, support the Red Cross, and reclaim waste to recycle for the war effort. Later activities included providing assistance and educational programs to needy families, running a literacy school for immigrants, and offering youth recreation and camping; the group folded in 1969. The landmarked building is now a nicely renovated culinary arts school.

This section of University Avenue is a destination shopping district for people of Indian descent, with numerous stores selling saris, food, housewares, and other South Asian goods. Tall liriodendron, or tulip poplar, trees, with unusually shaped leaves, line the next several blocks. At 9th, cross University at the signal and continue down University to the right. In the next block on the left side, at ⑫ **982–84 University**, the commercial building built in 1878 remains largely unaltered. On the opposite side, housing units at 933–51 University, built in 1954, have a village-like feel.

After crossing 7th, notice the corner commercial building (Berkeley Indoor Garden) at 844 University, built in 1882, with latticed shop windows surprisingly unchanged from the original facade.

Turn left on 7th Street. On the right, 2016 7th, now part of Black Pine Circle School (a private K–8 school established in 1973) was an early town hall, built in 1879 and subsequently expanded. Near the corner on the left, ⑬ **2027 7th**, the former Berkeley Day Nursery #1 (now also part of Black Pine Circle) was designed in 1912 by leading Bay Area architect Ernest Coxhead. It has been significantly altered and expanded but retains some of the original features, including some attractive windows.

Turn right on Addison Street and right again at 6th Street to see ⑭ **Berkeley Day Nursery #2**, which takes up the southern half of the block at 2031 6th. Now a family medical practice, the 1927

Berkeley Day Nursery #2, a Tudor Revival by Ratcliff.

Tudor Revival design was by Ratcliff, who did a lot of ecclesiastical architecture; it features half-timbered stucco, wood carving on the front entrance, and a large window on the front bay. The nursery school, which also was housed in the building at 2027 7th Street, was founded in 1908 and was among the first child-care facilities for working parents in California. The 6th Street building is a city landmark; the clinic that resides there now worked with the Landmarks Preservation Commission to ensure that renovations and additions carried out between 2012 and 2014 would preserve important design elements while meeting current needs.

Next door, 2015 6th Street is a James Plachek–designed 1925 Colonial Revival–style building with classical columns on the entryway and numerous window shutters. It is now part of the Black Pine Circle School.

Walk to the corner and cross 6th at the signal. Turn left and walk back down the other side of 6th, with a wider view of the Ratcliff building. Both sides of 6th are lined with large London plane trees, generally older than those on 4th Street. After Addison, at 2100 6th (on the corner), a late Queen Anne Victorian has lots of detailing. Next door, 2102–04 6th was raised up in a recent redevelopment, but the Victorian details were restored on the upper floor.

A renovated Victorian at 2102–04 6th Street.

Carpenter Gothic at 2110 6th Street.

The house at 2106–08 6th was also raised up but was given a generic historic look.

Two houses built in 1888 are at 2110 and 2112 6th—these **⓯ Queen Anne Victorians** have lots of ornamentation (particularly 2110, which BAHA calls Carpenter Gothic style). Both have been raised to create a full lower floor. These houses are part of the Sisterna Tract Historic District. During the late 19th century, there was a major influx of immigrants from Ireland, Chile, and other countries; many of the new residents worked in West Berkeley factories. Concerned about preserving structures in the face of development pressures, more recent residents did extensive research and applied to the Landmarks Preservation Commission for historic district status, which was approved in 2004.

Next door at 2120 6th, a 1994 development includes 14 live-work condominiums in two to three floors. The design has a generic traditional look, with wood siding that blends in with the neighborhood and a pleasant courtyard. When the structure was built, neighbors felt it was too big and called it the gray whale, but it complements the historic neighborhood much better than some other modern buildings.

Go back to Addison and turn left; at 814 Addison, the historic district includes another ornate Queen Anne from about 1888 with a gable over a section that projects forward next to the steps. Turn left again at 5th Street; **⓰ 2105 and 2107 5th** are nearly matching, simple Victorian cottages, built about six years apart in the 1880s. The Velasca Kennedy House of 1878, next at 2109 5th, is an Italianate design with a less traditional facade. At 2129–33 5th, the backside of the live-work condos from 6th street can be seen.

Continue along 5th and turn left on Allston Way. At 805 Allston, the brightly colored Institute of Mosaic Art has exhibitions and classes; at 809A, **⓱ Kids 'n' Clay** is an innovative teaching studio founded by ceramic artist Kevin Nierman in 1988. Return to 5th and continue, crossing Allston Way carefully because traffic does not stop. At 2212 5th, the 1877 Italianate house has acquired pink asbestos siding but retains much of its original design. Modern units like the ones at 2209–11 5th have been popping up in the area. Farther along on the left side, at 2263 5th, the **⓲ Light Room photo studio** often displays works by local artists in its gallery, which is entered from the courtyard of Tomate Cafe, a popular neighborhood eatery. Several examples of the concrete grid form are on both sides of Bancroft Way. Two different local groups separately developed this construction method in the 1930s and 1940s; it includes diamond-shaped openings with glass blocks in lattice. Concrete grid form was used primarily in industrial buildings but also in others such as the Mobilized Women of Berkeley building on University. The greatest concentration is found in this area of West Berkeley.

At the southeast **⓳ corner of Bancroft and 5th**, an attractive newer office building is made of wood, concrete blocks, and metal with lots of windows, though the unpainted wood is deteriorating.

The Torpedo Room is at 2031 4th Street.

Turn around and head back two blocks on 5th Street to Addison and turn left, noting the well-maintained Victorian houses at **⑳ 743 and 741 Addison**, survivors amid newer buildings on this block. On the corner, 743 Addison is an Italianate design from the 1870s, with bracket and shelf design features, while 741 Addison is in the later Queen Anne style, built in 1890. Next door, the back of a recent mixed-use development has attractive windows facing the east courtyard.

At the corner of Addison and 4th is Takara Sake USA, which has a tasting room. Cross 4th Street and turn right. The apartment complex on the left side, **㉑ Fourth and U**, is mixed use, meaning that commercial space is on the ground level. The architecture of Fourth and U tries to adopt the industrial look of the neighborhood, with corrugated metal and other features, and mixes new and old design elements, but the result is only partially successful—a bit of a hodgepodge. Across the street, the mixed-use building (the back side was seen from Addison Street) is a far more sober and consistent design from the same recent period. On the first floor, Sierra Nevada's Torpedo Room at 2031 4th offers tastes of beer.

Turn left at Essex Way and walk to the plaza in front of the **㉒ former Southern Pacific Railway Station**, in Spanish Mission Revival style. A succession of restaurants has occupied the space, most recently Brennan's, a Berkeley pub and institution, which was in another building that was demolished to make way for Fourth and U. Unfortunately, because the station building is now a restaurant, there is no Amtrak station building—which many riders think is a shame—and some people would like at least part of the historic building to be used for that purpose again.

The pavement here has illustrations relating to Bay Area Native Americans and the area's natural history. Walk to the right through the plaza to see the Berkeley Amtrak platform, which features a mural of train passengers. Across the tracks, the commercial buildings replaced the four-story home of Standard Soap Works—at one time the largest soap supplier in the country—which was built on a small cliff above the historic bay shoreline (now Aquatic Park).

Crossing beneath the University Avenue overpass, look up to the right; a short poem is written on the large concrete beams. Walk up University on the other side and then turn left on 4th to return to the starting point.

✳ ✳ ✳

WALK 18

AQUATIC PARK AND THE MARINA

Overview: Rather than focusing on architecture, this walk features parks and water-oriented attractions along the San Francisco Bay, with great views and good birding. It is on mostly level terrain.

Highlights:
- Aquatic Park lagoon, Adventure Playground
- McLaughlin Eastshore State Park
- Bay views, kites, shorebirds, yacht marina

Distance: 4–6 miles
Time: 2–3 hours
Elevation gain: 70 feet

Start at the corner of Bolivar Drive and Addison Street in Berkeley's Aquatic Park. For AC Transit, take the 51B to 6th Street and University Avenue (for Marina-bound buses) or to the 4th Street terminal (for Amtrak-bound buses). From 6th, walk down University to 4th and turn left under University. Notice the songs and poems on both sides of the beams, as well as the Native American cutouts and murals of birds, wetlands, and native peoples on the apartment building wall to the south. Walk one block south to Addison and turn right. Cross the railroad tracks and continue to Bolivar.

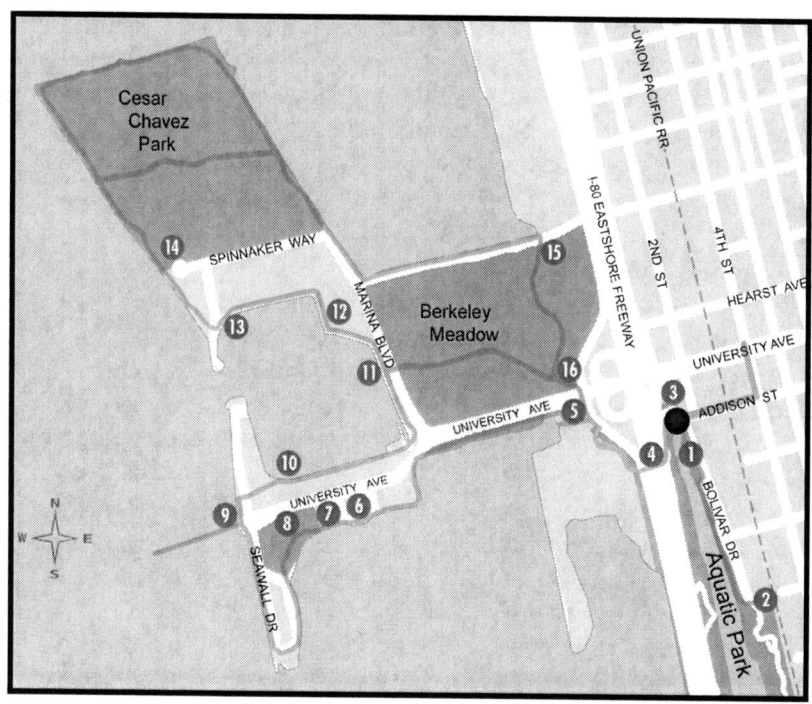

In the early-1930s, the Eastshore Highway (now I-80) was a causeway over nearby wetlands. Aquatic Park was constructed in 1935 and 1937 when a lagoon was created to make way for the freeway; this and the nearby Berkeley Marina were New Deal Works Progress Administration projects. Tide gates keep the water level fairly constant in the lagoon. Recreational activities include bird watching, boating, hiking, waterskiing, rowing, and picnicking. During some seasons, the lagoon is covered with a thick mat of algae; egrets, black-crowned night herons, ducks, and other birds frequent the park during migrating seasons and nest here.

Walk south along the lagoon path, passing the buildings of the Waterside Workshops, which offer vocational training for youth, weekend boat rentals, and Berkeley's only ❶ **waterfront cafe**. Stay on the path along the water. Mixed in with the weeds are native plants such as gumplant, with sticky buds and yellow, daisylike flowers.

The paved road ends at a playground, ❷ **Dreamland for Kids**. More than 2,000 volunteers built the playground in spring 2000 after hundreds of kids at Rosa Parks Elementary School shared design ideas with architect Robert Leather, known for his whimsical wooden play structures that incorporate input from kids. One critic said that the kids wanted natural places with creek beds, forest nooks, and mud holes, but parents pushed for "clean, safe, structured playgrounds"; the result includes some nontraditional features such as a spider-webbed climbing area, wooden walkways, railings, turrets, and tunnel-like slides.

Aquatic Park also offers picnic tables, a grassy bank, a playing field, and restrooms, as well as a mini-Frisbee golf course. It is possible to walk or bicycle all the way around the lagoon.

Return along the lagoon shoreline and follow the path as it curves to the left, passing on the right the ❸ **Dona Spring Municipal Animal Shelter**. Opened in 2013, this state-of-the-art facility is a huge improvement over the old shelter on 2nd Street.

Continue around the lagoon and walk over the ❹ **pedestrian/ bicycle bridge**, completed in 2002. It replaces an unpleasant and hazardous route to the marina that restricted access for people with disabilities. Lookouts on both sides of the bridge provide views of parks to the east and west and the speeding traffic below. The bridge has two bike lanes and a raised sidewalk and is wide enough for emergency vehicles. This elegant structure is also seismically sound.

The Berkeley pedestrian/bicycle bridge.

Saving Berkeley's Waterfront

A long crescent of sand near where Interstate 80 is now located was once called the Berkeley Bight. Wetlands were scarcer here than in other parts of the San Francisco Bay due to strong winds, but there was a willow marsh at the mouth of Strawberry Creek, the location of a Native American village. The remains of a shellmound are under and next to the Spenger's parking lot at University and 4th. The community of Ocean View developed in the late 1840s on firm land behind the beach, which became a working-class industrial area as sand was hauled off in the late 19th and early 20th centuries.

The waterfront began to be filled in after 1924, when garbage collection became a city responsibility. Much of this walk is on top of a historic garbage dump, now covered with soil and plants. The Santa Fe Railroad secretly bought up the tidelands and advanced plans for a huge commercial project for the marina area, and an international airport was proposed in the 1940s. In the 1950s, the city of Berkeley proposed doubling the city's size by further filling in the bay, but citizen groups succeeded in putting a halt to them.

In 1961, the *Oakland Tribune* reported that Berkeley planned to fill in another 2,000 acres of shoreline for development, including adding an airport. The story prompted Berkeleyans Sylvia McLaughlin, Kay Kerr, and Esther Gulick to call a meeting with local conservation groups and found the Save San Francisco Bay Association (now Save the Bay), one of the earliest and most successful regional environmental organizations. Another group from that era is the Greenbelt Alliance (originally People for Open Space), founded by Dorothy Erskine in 1958.

In 1982, conservationists were again galvanized when Catellus (a real estate spin-off of Southern Pacific Railroad, which merged with the Santa Fe Railroad) announced plans for a 3.8 million-square-foot commercial development. Save the Bay and numerous stakeholders rallied and lobbied for the creation of a park along the bay, and McLaughlin Eastshore State Park was established in 2002. It extends 8.5 miles along the East Bay shoreline from the Bay Bridge to Richmond and includes 1,854 acres of uplands and tidelands along the waterfronts of Oakland, Emeryville, Berkeley, Albany, and Richmond. The East Bay Regional Park District used funds from Measure AA (passed by Alameda and Contra Costa county residents in 1988) and state park bonds to acquire the property and clean up contaminated areas, at a cost of more than $33 million. ✳✳

Monumental sculptures were placed on each side of the bridge. Both by Scott Donahue, they symbolize the city, its people, and their activities—from protests to bird watching to disability rights. This being Berkeley, the sculptures have been fairly controversial. Some people like the lively portrayal of Berkeleyans while others object to the sculptures on cost, political, or aesthetic grounds. The bridge links to a portion of the Bay Trail, which will eventually circle San Francisco Bay. From here, segments stretch north to Richmond (with a gap at Golden Gate Fields) and south to Emeryville.

On the other side of the bridge, turn left when you intersect the Bay Trail and walk to **⑤ Sea Breeze Market and Deli**. A beach shack, this local institution serves beverages, sandwiches, and snacks. Behind the building on the west side of the parking lot (toward San Francisco), find one of many little paths and follow it to the shoreline. To the right, notice the culvert where Strawberry Creek emerges into the bay. This perennial stream begins in the Berkeley hills above UC and winds through and under the city until it emerges here. Depending on tide and season, you may see waterfowl and shorebirds. Volunteers have worked hard to remove exotic plants, and the number of native plants is increasing.

Return toward Sea Breeze Market, turn left (north) to University, and go left (west) on the pedestrian/bicycle path. You can take this path parallel to University Avenue, or use the small, old trail-of-use following the shoreline. There are lots of ground squirrels here, especially among the riprap (please do not feed these wild animals).

Continue along the path, following the shoreline as it angles left and then right, eventually coming to the **⑥ UC Aquatic Center (Cal Adventures) and the Cal Sailing Club**. The latter is a nonprofit run by volunteers that offers short-term memberships and lessons, equipment use, cruises, and other activities such as windsurfing.

Next you will find the **⑦ Adventure Playground**, run by the city of Berkeley. Opened in 1979, the playground encourages children to play and build creatively with hammers, saws, and paint. The idea started in postwar Europe, when a playground designer noticed that children had fun designing and building their own equipment and manipulating the environment. A zip line ends in a big pile of sand.

Continue along the trail. Beyond the traditional playground is Berkeley's **⑧ Shorebird Park Nature Center**, the first municipal straw-bale building in the United States. The structure utilizes solar and wind power, solar water heating, and rainwater harvesting. The adjacent visitor's center features green building materials and houses displays on native plants, birds, and sea mammals. Berkeley school children receive environmental education here, and it is open to the public during certain hours from Monday to Saturday.

From here, follow the path to the left along the shoreline. Bear right to pass in front of HS Lordships restaurant, and then right again to continue along the shoreline facing San Francisco to the ❾ **Berkeley Pier**.

In 1909, Berkeley built a municipal wharf at the foot of University for ferry traffic that never materialized, and the wharf was used instead for freight. In 1926, Southern Pacific built the current pier for ferries, extending about 3.5 miles into San Francisco Bay; due to shoreline infill, the pier now extends about 2.4 miles from the shore. Ferry service to San Francisco began in 1927, with Key Route streetcars taking passengers and cars to ferries that crossed the bay. The supports at the far end of the pier are still visible, indicating that the eastern side of the bay is quite shallow. Ferry service halted in 1939, two years after completion of the Bay Bridge. The first 3,000 feet of the pier are maintained for fishing and walking, while the rest is gradually disintegrating.

In summer 2015, the pier was closed to pedestrians for repairs. If it's open, walk out to enjoy the views. Returning from the pier, go left and then turn right at the crosswalk in front of Skates on the Bay restaurant, crossing the street and then the parking lot. At the far side of the parking area at the white post, pick up the path to walk counterclockwise around the ❿ **Berkeley Marina**. Originally constructed about 1935, the marina sits on 52 acres of water and can berth more than 1,000 boats. A wide range of facilities is available, from sailing schools to fuel docks, and the Berkeley Yacht Club schedules races and cruises. As you bear left around the east side of the marina, notice some large and unique houseboats.

From here, the walk continues to Berkeley's César Chávez Park. To cut the walk short and return to the starting point, turn right through the parking lot at ⓫ **piers G and F** and cross the street. Walk about 30 yards to the right and enter the gate into the Berkeley Meadow section of McLaughlin Eastshore State Park. This area may be brown and dry or green with wildflowers and ponds, depending on the season. Follow the fenced path until you come to a junction

The Berkeley Marina.

and continue to the exit. Turn right and walk briefly along the Bay Trail. Cross University at the crosswalk and pass the Sea Breeze Deli to the pedestrian/bike bridge and back to the starting point.

For a bit more exercise and some wonderful views, continue around the marina past the Hornblower boats on your left and the **⑫ hotel** on your right. Continue past the hotel as the path angles left, then right, then left again. Just past the end of the hotel is a small community garden. Continue heading west toward the bay with the marina on the left.

Pass some **⑬ boat ramps** as the path curves to the left and then pick up the curving paved path to the right along the shoreline heading northwest. Just past the buildings on the right at a circular parking area, enter **⑭ César Chávez Park**. This 90-acre open space was constructed on landfill that was a dump between 1953 and 1967. Essentially unregulated for 50 years while development plans were proposed and rejected, the area was in significant disrepair until it was sealed in 1991 and opened as a park soon after.

César Chávez Park is a world-class kite-flying venue and the site of the annual Berkeley Kite Festival on the last weekend in July. From semiprofessionals to kids, kite fliers are always busy in the park, and their maneuvers are great fun to watch. The park is also popular with dog walkers and picnickers. The winds are so reliable here that you may see people flying along the paths on skates, bicycles, and skateboards powered by sails.

Take the paved or dirt paths along the shoreline (about 1.25 miles around the shoreline periphery), with views of San Francisco, Richmond, Golden Gate Fields, and the Berkeley hills, or explore the dirt trails that cut over the top of the hill, with its mixture of native and nonnative plants, ground squirrels, and dogs. Adorable burrowing owls often overwinter on the east side of the park (facing the Berkeley hills); during the winter, this area is fenced off to protect them from dogs.

To the north, take note of the Albany Bulb, a small peninsula made from construction debris, which some day may be part of Eastshore State Park. A rocky sandstone outcrop similar to Albany Hill, still visible, was leveled to make way for Golden Gate Fields racetrack; a low, stone bluff remains as one of the few pieces of original shoreline. The racetrack area has long been the focus of commercial development plans, routinely opposed by Albany residents who would prefer a park.

When you get back to the road, continue along the shoreline parallel to the road and then turn left on the unpaved road, heading east, with the water still on your left.

Beyond the fence on the right is the 72-acre **⓯ Berkeley Meadow**, bounded by the marina, César Chávez Park, University Avenue, and the bay-front path. Formerly part of the landfill, a habitat restoration of seasonal wetlands, coastal prairie, and coastal scrub was undertaken in the 2000s. It is now a diverse and thriving habitat for plants and animals in an urban area. About one-third of a mile along the unpaved road, enter the gate on the right to the meadow. The wheelchair-accessible path, with interpretive signs, provides the opportunity to enjoy seasonal wildflowers, ponds, and birds.

At the intersection in the path, bear right to explore more of the meadow or turn left to exit to the **⓰ Bay Trail**. Turn right, cross University in the crosswalk, and follow the trail past the Sea Breeze Deli to the pedestrian/bike bridge to return to the starting point. On the way out, consider stopping at Takara Sake's tasting room (708 Addison), which offers samples of numerous varieties of Japanese-style rice wine produced here in Berkeley.

❅ ❅ ❅

BERKELEY ARCHITECTURAL STYLES

Victorian: Victorian architecture changed significantly during the latter half of the 19th century, from early Italianate (late 1840s to 1880s) to late Queen Anne (1870s–1890s). Italianate features lower-pitched roofs, overhanging eaves, decorative brackets, and narrow windows arched on top, while the later Stick and Queen Anne styles share elements such as steeply pitched roofs with numerous gables, porches, and wooden siding. Queen Anne is the most common Victorian style in Berkeley

An Italianate-style home at 835 Delaware.

and also the most flamboyant, with turrets, cut-away bay windows, fish-scale shingles, spindles, complex roof massing, and elaborate decorative materials in wood. Lathes and other new machine tools of the machine age made these elaborate ornaments possible.

The Captain Boudrow House, a Queen Anne villa.

A Craftsman bungalow at Grant and Addison.

Craftsman and Berkeley brown-shingle (late 1890s–1930s): Fairly common in Berkeley, these styles share many design elements. A reaction to Victorian style, the Craftsman style was influenced by the British Arts and Crafts movement. Homes are usually constructed of wood or wood and stucco, featuring moderately pitched roofs with extending eaves, prominent rafters and brackets, front porches, windows with the upper part divided into smaller lites, and simple wood ornamentation, sometimes with stone foundations. Berkeley brown-shingle houses—as the name implies—have walls covered with unpainted wooden shingles (influenced by a the New England shingle-style movement of the late 19th century) and include some Craftsman design elements, but generally are simpler with less ornamentation. Brown-shingle homes often have two full stories and more steeply pitched roofs, whereas Craftsman houses tend to be one to one-and-a-half stories.

A classic Berkeley brown shingle at 2797 Benvenue.

Colonial Revival (1890s–1910s): Colonial Revival does not precisely mimic homes from the American colonial period, but employs its various elements in a new style. There are two main versions: one with very steeply pitched gables on the front, and one with more rectangular massing. Both tend to use symmetry, classical columns, prominent entrances, fan-light windows, Palladian (Serlian) windows, and simpler ornamentation than is found in late-Victorian homes.

The McCreary-Greer House, with rectangular massing.

829 Delaware, with a high-pitched roof.

Swiss chalet (1900s–1920s): This style was influenced by rural Swiss homes, with elements of Craftsman style. It often has stucco or wood siding, balconies, and shutters, and was one of many period or exotic styles popular at the time.

A Swiss chalet–style home at 2700 Virginia.

An English Tudor house at 2325 Piedmont.

English Tudor (1910s and 1920s): Steeply pitched roofs and stucco with half-timbering are characteristic of the Tudor style, as well as brick and stone, bay windows, leaded-glass window panes (sometimes in diamond patterns), and large chimneys and gables. Tudor buildings are usually asymmetrical overall but individual sections may have symmetry.

Beaux-Arts/Neoclassical (late 19th/early 20th century): Both these styles emphasize the use of classical Greek and Roman design elements, including columns. Based on architecture promoted by the École des Beaux-Arts in Paris, the style usually has symmetry, flat roofs, and no gables; masonry wall surfaces; decorative garlands and shields; and numerous columns or pilasters. Neoclassical often features a columned portico with Greek-style gables, sloping roofs, and less ornamentation.

The Spring Mansion, in Beaux-Arts style.

Mission/Spanish Colonial Revival (late 19th/early 20th century): Launched at the California pavilion of the 1893 Worlds' Columbian Exposition in Chicago, Mission Revival style subsequently became popular in California, particularly for public buildings such as churches, railway stations, and libraries. Modeled after the early Spanish Mission church compounds, it usually features stucco walls, clay tile or red roofs, cupolas, arcades, curving gables, arches (including arched windows and doors), and some ornamentation. Other variants are highly ornamented Spanish Colonial Revival and simpler Spanish eclectic styles.

St. Mark's Church, in Mission Revival style.

Italian Renaissance (late 19th/early 20th century): One of several related styles adopted from southern Europe, Italian Renaissance emphasizes stucco walls and clay tile roofs, arches, window grills, balconies (in wood, wrought iron, stone, or cement), smaller upper-story windows, and varying levels of ornamentation.

An Italian Renaissance–style mansion at 2395 Piedmont.

Gothic Revival (19th and 20th centuries): Due to the popularity of medieval cathedrals, the Gothic Revival architectural style was widely adopted by American churches, though often simplified. Reflecting the prestige of Oxford and Cambridge universities, the style was popular in academic buildings and emphasizes pointed arches, stone or brick, small-paned or stained-glass windows, finials, and vestigial buttresses.

Gothic Revival Holbrook Hall at the Pacific School of Religion.

Storybook (early 20th century): Storybook style incorporates fanciful designs that call to mind fairy tale cottages. Based on premodern European rural or village architecture, it is characterized by asymmetry, with high-peaked roofs, wood or stone ornamentation, wall paintings, shingled roofs, and small-paned windows.

Normandy Village, a storybook-style development.

Art Deco/Streamline Moderne/zig-zag (1920s/1930s): In response to the period revival styles that prevailed in the early 20th century, these styles were an attempt to modernize architecture. Art Deco is an eclectic style with Arts and Crafts influences, employing modern machine-age materials, rich colors, and lots of ornamentation, with both geometric and nature-related designs. Zig-zag is a variant of Art Deco with zig-zag shapes, chevrons, and other geometric motifs. Streamline Moderne has simpler lines with curves and geometric shapes and much less ornamentation. Art Deco and Streamline Moderne are found primarily in commercial and public buildings, but sometimes in residences (particularly Streamline Moderne).

An Art Deco commercial building at Shattuck and Addison.

The Streamline Moderne Whittier School.

Modern institutional: The Tang Health Center at UC Berkeley.

Modern/contemporary: Modernist architecture refers to the clean break from traditional styles made between the world wars by leading architects such as Le Corbusier, Ludwig Mies van der Rohe, and the Bauhaus school, in parallel with developments in modern art such as cubism. Many different "modern" or "contemporary" schools and styles were defined post–World War II, including International, Brutalist, postmodern, and structuralist. Materials range from rough concrete (Brutalism) to glass used in curtain walls. Some buildings display a return to traditional style elements such as pitched roofs, gables, dormers, and earlier window treatments. Because Berkeley was mostly built out by World War II, contemporary or modernist architecture is not as prevalent here as in many other American cities, but it can be found on campus, downtown, and in residential areas, often when older buildings are replaced.

Modern residential: The Olsen House in the Berkeley hills.

❅ ❅ ❅

GLOSSARY OF ARCHITECTURAL TERMS

Balustrade: Low wall of short posts topped by long rail, placed at the side of a stair, balcony, or other architectural element.

Bargeboard: Board fastened to projecting gable of roof to strengthen the gable and hide ends of exposed timbers.

Bas relief: Raised (three-dimensional) wall sculpture.

Beam: Long, sturdy piece of timber or metal spanning an opening or part of building, usually to support the roof or floor above.

Board and batten: Thin strip of wood, metal, or other material placed over the space between vertical boards in siding.

Bracket: L-shaped decorative or weight-bearing unit, which forms a right angle with a wall and eave or overhang.

Buttress: Architectural element built against or projecting from a wall to help support it.

Casement: Window attached to its frame with one or more hinges at the side to open inward or outward.

Clapboard: Long, thin boards used to cover exterior walls.

Clerestory: High windows above eye level to bring light or air into the interior.

Clinker: Brick burned at high temperature that is denser and heavier than regular bricks, often misshapen.

Colonnade: Long sequence of columns joined at the top, either free-standing or part of a building.

Corbel: Supporting element on a wall, a kind of bracket that is solid and often decorated.

Cornice: Horizontal decorative molding that crowns a building element such as a door, window, or top of building wall.

Dentils: Small blocks used as a repeating ornament where a cornice or eave joins the wall.

Dormer: Structural element that protrudes upward from a sloping roof surface, usually to provide a window or add space for the area under the roof.

Double-hung window: Window with two parts that overlap slightly and slide up and down inside the window frame.

Eave: Lower edge of a roof that overhangs the wall.

Finial: Decorative element, typically carved, to emphasize the apex of a dome, tower, roof, gable, or other architectural element.

Fresco: Mural or wall painting in which the painting is done into fresh, wet plaster.

Frieze: Stretch of wall that is painted, sculpted, or otherwise decorated; usually placed above eye level.

Gable: Triangular portion of a wall between the edges of a sloping roof.

Gambrel: Symmetrical, two-sided roof with varied slope on each side, in which the upper slope is shallow and the lower slope is deeper in pitch.

Gothic arch: Two arch segments coming to a point; can reach higher with less outward thrust against the wall than a rounded arch.

Half-timbering: Exposed wood framing in a wall with spaces in-between filled with brick, stone, plaster, or stucco.

Hipped or hip roof: Roof with four sides sloping downward to the wall, usually with a fairly gentle slope and no gables; sides may meet in a central point (like a pyramid) or there may be a ridge along the top.

Lites: Individual panes of glass in a window.

Loggia: Exterior gallery or corridor at ground level, or higher floor open to the air on one side with columns or pierced openings.

Mansard roof: Hipped roof with slope that changes to a steeper angle on the lower side of each face, usually with dormers.

Massing: General shape and size of a building, which could, for example, be irregular, symmetrical, or complex.

Mullion: Vertical unit that forms a division between units of a window, door, or screen, including vertical framing between panes of glass; usually made of wood, metal, or stone.

Muntin (also glazing or sash bars): Strip of wood or metal holding panes of glass in a window.

Palladian (or Serlian) window: Three-part window with a large, central, arched section flanked by two narrower, shorter sections. Popularized by Italian architect Andrea Palladio in the 16th century, but described decades earlier by Sebastiano Serlio.

Parapet: Barrier that forms the top of a wall at the edge of a roof, fence, balcony, or other architectural element.

Pediment: In classical architectural styles, a gable (usually triangular) sitting on top of a structure that is often supported by columns; relief sculpture may be in the triangular area.

Pergola: Garden feature forming a shaded walkway or seating area with posts supporting an open framework for vines.

Pilaster: Ornamental element that gives the appearance of a supporting column; usually placed on the surface of a wall or along the sides of a door.

Porte cochere: Porch- or portico-like structure at a main or secondary building entrance, which provides covered entry access for a carriage or vehicle.

Portico: Porch leading to an entrance or extended as a colonnade, with a roof structure over a walkway and supported by columns.

Rafter: One of a series of sloped, structural, support elements that extend from the ridge or hip to the edge of the roof.

Rusticated: Built or faced with usually rough-surfaced masonry blocks having beveled edges and pronounced joints (generally in the foundation or first-floor wall).

Shingle: Covering element for a roof or wall; can be wood, slate (stone), metal, asphalt, or composite.

Spindle: Rounded pieces of wood used to hold up a porch rail or similar; often created on lathes in ornamental shapes.

Stucco: Material made of aggregate, binder, and water that is applied wet and hardens to a dense solid; used as an exterior wall covering or sculptural material.

Transom window: Window or row of windows above a door supported by a crosspiece.

Trellis: Open architectural structure of wood, metal, or other material often used to support plants such as wisteria, vines, or roses.

Turret: Small tower that projects vertically from the building wall; used in castles and later as decorative elements.

Veranda: Roofed open gallery or porch along one or more sides of a building; usually enclosed by a railing.

INDEX

CREDITS

All maps and photographs, including cover photos, are courtesy of Robert E. Johnson unless otherwise noted.

Page 92: Courtesy David Lance Goines.

Page 102: Copyright Dorothea Lange, 1957. Photo from PBS.org, *American Masters—Dorothea Lange: Grab a Hunk of Lightning*.

Page 187: Courtesy Claremontresort.com

Page 226: Courtesy Lynn Mundell.

Page 239: © John Sutton Photography 2014.

Page 242: From http://www.sierranevada.com/brewery/california/torpedoroom.

ACKNOWLEDGMENTS

Many of the walks in this book were initially developed for the Greenbelt Alliance outings program; from time to time, we have led similar walks for other local organizations.

Rusty Scalf created our customized Berkeley map based on publicly available data, allowing us to make individual walk maps. We are grateful to Lynn Mundell, Gary Parsons, and Steve Price, whose guidance was invaluable in developing this project. Thank you also to Judith Dunham, Beth Graubart, Robin Meadows, and Christopher Vaughan for their advice and support. Walkers who helped enormously by serving as beta testers and providing feedback include Elaine Byron, Chris Hamilton, Tatsuya Kasai, Cynthia Kintigh, Gary Parsons, Steve Price, Edith Reiner, Paul Takayanagi, Elsa Tranter, Lobsang Wangdu, and Kathleen Wong.

Sources of essential information and support for this project include Berkeley Architectural Heritage Association, Berkeley Historical Society, Berkeley Path Wanderers Association, Berkeley Public Library, Berkeleyside, and Oakland Cultural Heritage Survey.

Written sources that were especially helpful include *41 Berkeley Walking Tours: Architectural Walks through the University Town*, by the Berkeley Architectural Heritage Association (Susan Dinkelspiel Cerny et al., eds.); *Berkeley Landmarks: An Illustrated Guide to Berkeley, California's Architectural Heritage* by Susan Dinkelspiel Cerny et al.; *The Guide to Architecture in San Francisco and Northern California* by David Gebhard et al.; *Berkeley Bohemia: Artists and Visionaries of the Early 20th Century* by Ed Herny et al.; *The Campus Guide: University of California, Berkeley; An Architectural Tour and Photographs* by Harvey Helfand; *A Field Guide to American Houses* by Virginia and Lee McAlester; *East Bay Heritage: A Potpourri of Living History* by Mark Wilson; *Berkeley Rocks: Building with Nature* by Jonathan Chester; and newsletters of the Berkeley Historical Society. (A full bibliography is posted on www.berkeleywalks.com.)

Finally, we thank Deirdre Greene and Nigel Quinney of Roaring Forties Press for taking us on and for their dedication to helping us publish these walks for the world to enjoy.

About the Authors

A St. Louis native, **Robert (Bob) E. Johnson** has lived in Berkeley for 30-plus years, following 13 years spent in Japan. He has always been an avid walker and hiker. For the past 20 years, Bob has led group walking tours around the Bay Area, including many in Berkeley, for groups such as Greenbelt Alliance (of which he is a board member), Berkeley Path Wanderers Association, the Berkeley Historical Society, and *BayNature* magazine. He has retained a strong interest in architecture since his student days, when he took art history and a two-year architecture basic design studio. Johnson was a commissioner on the Berkeley Landmarks Preservation Commission from 2003 to 2011, and spent 15 months as its chair. Thanks to years of observation and classes with botanist Glenn Keator, Bob has learned a good deal about native and non-native plants. Since retiring from a career in financial analysis, he has worked part-time with Steve Price of Urban Advantage producing sophisticated photorealistic images envisioning better urban design for planning professionals around the country.

In addition to walking all around town, **Janet L. Byron** loves to run, hike, bike, swim, and watch birds. She has led hikes for Greenbelt Alliance, Berkeley Path Wanderers Association (BPWA), Girl Scouts, Congregation Beth El, and other local groups, and has served on the boards of Greenbelt Alliance, BPWA, Friends of Strawberry Creek, Willard Neighborhood Association, and Berkeley Partners for Parks. She attended the Graduate School of Journalism at the University of California, Berkeley, and works as a professional science writer and editor, currently with the Kaiser Permanente Division of Research. Her previous book, *The Country Music Lover's Guide to the U.S.A.*, was published by St. Martin's Press in 1996. A New York native and Berkeley citizen for nearly 25 years, Janet lives in her dream house in West Berkeley with her daughter.

CPSIA information can be obtained at www.ICGtesting.com
Printed in the USA
LVOW10s1922151215

466705LV00013B/57/P